"If you feel the need to be inspired to DO something rather than just talk about it, or simply to smile rather than frown, reading *The Marrow in Me* is the answer. Kevin Walsh's story of how he tried to save the life of a 16-year-old boy is a winding, whimsical tale of good luck, good works, and one good man's decision to face the pain of a bone marrow transplant in the hopes of ending the pain of someone he'd never met. It's a lesson that one person can do more than we may think and a reminder that we've really all been put on Earth to work together. When we do, miracles can happen. *The Marrow in Me* is one of them."

– RON BORGES,
Sports Columnist Boston Herald

"Kevin Walsh captures in words the essence of what people from our island State have believed for generations, and what underlies our Aloha spirit— that we are all linked together by a common welfare, and that every one of us is a member of a huge ohana consisting of all mankind."

– RANDAL K. WADA, M.D.
Medical Director, Hawaii Bone Marrow Donor Registry &
HI Cord Blood Bank Board of Directors, National Marrow Donor Program

"Kevin Walsh is really good on TV—and even better on the printed page. His story will touch a nerve—and a bone. He has given the gift of life, and now he's sharing it."

– MICHAEL BAMBERGER
Sports Illustrated

"Every now and then you need to read a profound book that gets you back in balance with what life's all about. Kevin Walsh's *The Marrow in Me* is one of those books."

– LENN ROBBINS
Writer, NY Post

"Golf often has a spiritual way of bringing people from all walks of life together. Kevin Walsh's *The Marrow in Me* is one of the coolest examples of that gift that golf gives."

– MARK CANNIZZARO
NY Post Golf Writer, Contributor ESPN and Golf Channel

"Kevin Walsh merges his journalistic skills into a personal narrative that brings a tear to the eye and a glow in the heart. His is a story of raw courage, of the people who need it the most as they walk the fine line between life and death."

– LARRY KANE
Retired Television News Anchor
Author of *Ticket to Ride* and *Lennon Revealed*

"As a long time entertainment reporter I've read and seen on the big screen some amazing stories based on real life experiences. Kevin Walsh's *The Marrow in Me* offers a glimpse at what real courage and compassion are all about. A read guaranteed to inspire and motivate you in ways you never imagined."

– SARA EDWARDS
Media Consultant

"*The Marrow in Me* is both an inspiration and a call to action. Kevin Walsh brilliantly illustrates there is living proof that the human spirit can go toe-to-toe with leukemia and be courageous in the fight, whatever the outcome."

– ROB ELLIS
Sports Talk Show Host, 610 WIP Philadelphia

"Kevin Walsh has always been a great story-teller through his work on television, but excels in sharing his personal journey of becoming a bone marrow donor in *The Marrow in Me*. It's a compelling and courageous profile of those who fight and win their battle against cancer, a loving tribute to those who don't, and an inspiration to all of us to help by becoming a donor like Kevin."

"This book is about the story of rebirth and a second chance at life. One person can make a difference. Kevin Walsh tells the wonderful story of the miracle of bone marrow matching and stem cell donation. A must read for anyone who would love to save a life."

"A golf ball is no bigger than a rock, filled with dimples and lost about as regularly as a rock thrown in the ocean. But one golf ball with two poignant words *"beat leukemia"* on it, served to inspire and change the life of Kevin Walsh. One golf ball meant becoming a bone marrow donor, it meant trying to save someone's life, it meant running a marathon to raise money for leukemia research. Most of all it meant exactly what the golf ball said, *"beat leukemia."* Kevin Walsh's story of fate, perseverance and even humility will inspire and hopefully energize people to follow the simple words on a golf ball."

"Kevin Walsh's *The Marrow in Me* is so refreshing. When was the last time you read a book that really made you wonder about the depth of your own courage and charity? After reading Kevin's account of going to transplant for a boy he'd never met, I think you'll look for something to do in your life to make the world around you a better place."

"What a wonderful story about living for something larger than ourselves and connecting with others in poignant life-altering ways. Kevin is a good golfer, but an even better guy. *The Marrow in Me* will inspire many others to follow his example. The results will mean countless more lives can be saved."

"I'll never forget the day I sat in a hospital room in Fresno, California and Jenny Eller witnessed to me, a Fresno Bee sportswriter. Jenny quoted to me Philippians 4:13: I can do everything through Christ who gives me strength. Jenny forever touched my life. Now, readers have an opportunity to learn about Jenny through Kevin Walsh's writings and his experience as a bone marrow donor. How wonderful."

THE MARROW IN ME

Kevin Walsh

Foreword by
Liz Scott

Kevin Walsh recreating Chris Pablo's amazing discovery of a special golf ball in his basket.

Digital Composition by Ilene Griff Design

Publisher
Sports Challenge Network
Philadelphia, PA 19102
267.847.9018
www.sportschallengenetwork.com
email: sales@sportschallengenetwork.com

DEDICATION

To the recipient of my bone marrow and his family. Thank you for your courage in fighting a most difficult disease, and for giving me the honor to join you on the front lines of a grueling and deeply personal battle.

To Chris Pablo, Alana Dung's family, and all those who encourage others to register as potential bone marrow donors. Everyone is a bone marrow match for someone somewhere in the world. It's just a matter of whether you are in a registry, and ready to go all the way when someone gets sick with leukemia or other cancers of the blood.

And to my loving wife Jean who's always believed there was more to me and my purpose in the world than simply taking up space.

FOREWORD

LIKE A GLASS OF COLD LEMONADE ON A HOT SUMMER DAY, stories about life's goodness are refreshing too. Sometimes though, we have to sample life's bitterness to appreciate the flavor of what we take in. In 2004 we lost our only daughter, eight-year-old Alexandra or "Alex", after a long, brave fight with neuroblastoma. She hardly knew what it was like to feel well as she was diagnosed with a form of childhood cancer shortly before her first birthday.

As parents we spent so much of our daily lives trying to make her feel better, to cure her illness. Alex had a different focus. She wasn't so much worried about herself, but more with the other kids who were also facing pediatric cancer. What a lesson in selflessness taught to us by a four-year-old. Take life's lemons and make lemonade. Alex got the concept before she'd ever heard the phrase spoken.

When Alex started her lemonade stand on the front lawn of our house with a dream to raise money for pediatric cancer research, never could we have imagined how big Alex's Lemonade Stand would become. Neither did we realize how the kindness of strangers and other stories of inspiration would touch our hearts and souls; giving us a lift when we needed it most.

The Marrow in Me is one of those uplifting stories that everyone should taste and savor. Kevin Walsh gave a part of himself because he wanted a 16-year-old cancer patient, a boy whom he'd never met before, to have a second chance at life. By donating his bone marrow, Kevin gave the boy and his family all anyone who's ever been down that dreaded pediatric cancer road could ask for, a chance. Had Alex been one of the many children who desperately need to find a marrow donor in order to be cured, we very well may have been looking for someone outside our family to give a part of themselves to Alex, much like Kevin did for his recipient.

I am in a bone marrow donor registry. So is my husband Jay. We don't know if we'll ever get the call to donate our bone marrow and stem cells to someone in need, but we would love to have the chance. Giving a part of yourself is really the greatest gift of all. We see it everyday with Alex's Lemonade Stand Foundation for Childhood Cancer. We are so blessed that so many people donate their time, money and spirit to honor our daughter and the other children who've benefited from the $25 million we've raised over the years.

In the end we hope to find a cure for all childhood cancers, giving the blessings of good health and happiness to every child and family touched by the disease. It's how we honor Alex's memory. We're honored to be a part of Kevin Walsh's journey and generous spirit which live on in the pages of *The Marrow in Me*.

– Liz Scott
Mother of Alex Scott, Creator of Alex's Lemonade Stand Foundation

ALEX'S STORY

ALEXANDRA "ALEX" SCOTT WAS BORN TO JAY AND LIZ SCOTT in Manchester, Connecticut on January 18, 1996, the second of four children. Shortly before her first birthday, Alex was diagnosed with neuroblastoma, a type of childhood cancer. On her first birthday, the doctors informed Alex's parents that if she beat her cancer it was doubtful that she would ever walk again. Just two weeks later, Alex slightly moved her leg at her parents' request to kick, the first indication of who she would turn out to be-a determined, courageous, confident and inspiring child with big dreams and big accomplishments.

By her second birthday, Alex was crawling and able to stand up with leg braces. She worked hard to gain strength and to learn how to walk. She appeared to be beating the odds, until the shattering discovery within the next year that her tumors had started growing again. In the year 2000, the day after her fourth birthday, Alex received a stem cell transplant and informed her mother, "When I get out of the hospital I want to have a lemonade stand."

She said she wanted to give the money to the doctors to help them find a cure. True to her word, she held her first lemonade stand later that year and raised an amazing $2000 for "her hospital." While bravely battling her own cancer, Alex continued to hold yearly lemonade stands in her front yard to benefit childhood cancer research. News spread of the remarkable sick child dedicated to helping other sick children. People from all over the world, moved by her story, held their own lemonade stands and donated the proceeds to Alex's Lemonade Stand Foundation.

In August of 2004, Alex passed away at the age of 8, knowing that, with the help of others, she had raised over $1 million to help find a cure for the disease that took her life. Alex's legend and legacy have only gotten bigger since her passing. Her Lemonade Stand Foundation has now raised over $25 million. Alex's family-including brothers Patrick, Eddie, and Joey and supporters are committed to continuing her inspiring legacy through Alex's Lemonade Stand Foundation.

You can make additional donations to Alex's Lemonade Stand Foundation by visiting **www.alexslemonade.org.**

x

INTRODUCTION

EVERY ONE OF US WHO HAS STEPPED ON TO A COLLEGE basketball court as a player or coach appreciates the passion that surrounds us. At Villanova, we feel that energy from the Nova Nation each time we take the court at the Pavilion and Wachovia Center.

But away from the spotlight, there is an element that we never overlook in our program. As coaches, we have been entrusted with developing young men, not just as athletes, but as students and representatives of our university. It's something we talk about every day within our basketball family.

One of the themes we stress is understanding that life isn't just about you or this game we are fortunate enough to be a part of. It's about giving of yourself and being a part of a community.

When I returned to Villanova in 2001 as head coach I saw firsthand the commitment my Philadelphia Big Five colleagues had made to Coaches vs. Cancer. In the eight years since we have followed the lead of Temple's Fran Dunphy and Saint Joseph's Phil Martelli in raising funds to fight this disease that touches every family. In the course of that time, I have frequently been struck by the generosity of spirit of the caregivers and volunteers. These people share their time, effort, money and kindness quietly with no expectation of recognition.

In our program, we like to call that attitude. It's our way of saying that, while you can't always control what happens to you, you do have the ability to respond in a positive way.

Kevin Walsh's *The Marrow in Me* is a testament to what it means to have a great attitude. Kevin donated his bone marrow to give a young man with cancer of the blood a second chance at life. The two had never met. At a time when it would have been easy to cite his career or family obligations, Kevin stepped forward with the kind of unselfish act we can all admire.

Here at Villanova, we are especially aware of how critical the need for bone marrow registration is. Our head football coach Andy Talley has been a leader in the National Bone Marrow Donor Program and his efforts have resulted in over 11,500 donors being successfully tested and entered into the registry since 1993. It's a great cause and one that you'll have a better understanding of when you're finished reading *The Marrow in Me*. My sense is the book will affect you in a meaningful way and you'll be left with a profound feeling of satisfaction that reaches deep into your bones, where the marrow lives. And it's my hope you'll consider registering as a potential bone marrow donor at www.bethematch.org. You never know when the call for help might come.

> – Enthusiastically,
> Jay Wright
> *Head Men's Basketball Coach, Villanova University*

FROM THE AUTHOR

AS MUCH AS WE TRY TO MAKE OUR WAY IN THE WORLD, SO much of the good stuff that is eventually bestowed upon us is not from our doing. It simply finds us. I think I knew that, and a conversation with a wise man at the neighborhood Jewish Community Center not long ago convinced me of it.

Richard was doing 100 pound bench presses. I was doing 90 pound leg curls. Between reps we had a good talk. I told him I was putting the finishing touches on my book about being the only bone marrow match in the world for a 16-year-old leukemia patient I had never met. He asked how I became a donor. I told him the background which is detailed in the pages to come, but more than anything else; I told him it all just sort of found me.

"Ah," he said. "It's kind of like love."

And he's right. So much of what I've wanted to happen in life didn't happen because I tried too hard to *make* it happen. Sometimes it's best to just let things evolve.

I went to work one day at KGMB TV in Honolulu, Hawaii and my life changed forever. I didn't do anything special, I just sort of showed up. I was told to cover the story of Chris Pablo, a man with leukemia who found a golf ball in his basket at the driving range with the words *beat leukemia* stamped on the side. I still get the chills thinking about it.

After meeting with Chris and hearing his story, I was convinced his great discovery was more a matter of the ball finding him than the other way around. And the fact that a bone marrow match was found for him in a man who lost his legs in a Good Samaritan accident years earlier, I mean really; where do you find this stuff?

By telling Chris Pablo's story, other compelling characters came into the picture, including Renee Adaniya. Renee was a cute island girl of Japanese descent who was a very rare, but very perfect bone marrow match for a white military man in Tennessee. As you'll come to see later race and ethnicity really matter when it comes to matching.

There was also Alana Dung, a two-year-old girl with an aggressive form of leukemia who inspired more than 30-thousand people to give a sample of blood in the hopes of being the bone marrow match that could ultimately save her life. The chance of any one person matching someone outside of their family and going to transplant is about one in 200. Of those who turned out at Alana's drives, none matched her. But 86 people went the distance for someone else.

I am one of the 86. Along with my wife Jean, I quietly registered at one of Alana's bone marrow drives to honor her and my friend Chris Pablo. Four years later, and at a time when I was going through a very rough career patch, I got a phone call from the Hawaii Bone Marrow Donor Registry that I had matched a 16-year-old boy who was very sick with leukemia. The woman on the line asked if I would go to transplant to give someone a second chance at life. We were strangers at the beginning of the conversation, but toward the end I think we both suspected perhaps we had met before. We did. On TV. The caller was Renee Adaniya. That's when I knew something special was going on.

I didn't do anything special, I just made myself available. By trusting in faith and fate so many things that had to happen did happen. And I did little else other than let it fall into my lap. The donor experience found me, and I would love for it to find you.

At the back of the book I added a page that tells you how to become a potential bone marrow donor. It's actually much easier today to register than it was when I did it. Much of the tissue typing is done now with a simple cheek swab. There are links to the National Marrow Donor Program's www.bethematch.org website where you can start the registration process. It is a wealth of information and has stories from bone marrow donors and recipients. It is my goal that after reading *The Marrow in Me* you will strongly consider joining a bone marrow registry. Giving someone a second chance at life is a gift that comes back to you too. Trust me when I tell you there's no richer feeling than to be a part of something that is bigger than you. You are a bone marrow match for someone somewhere in the world. It's just a matter of will that person ever get sick?

ACKNOWLEDGMENTS

I BELIEVE THE BEST DISCOVERIES ARE THE ONES WHICH FIND you. Chris Pablo reaching into his basket at the driving range and finding a ball with the words *beat leukemia* stamped on the side was the find of a lifetime. But I can't help but think that ball found him.

I've dug up a lot of good stories in my day as a journalist, but I didn't discover Chris's great find. He found me through other people who thought, because I was an avid golfer, I might have a better appreciation for how special his golf ball hook really was to the bigger issue of bone marrow donation.

In telling Chris Pablo's story of hope, courage and the spirit of giving, more people—especially Alana Dung and Renee Adaniya found their way into the pictures I put forth on the television set and later in the written word. With new players and compelling details falling out of the sky and into my lap I couldn't help but find myself wondering if I was somehow being sucked into something bigger and more important than anything else I had ever known. With reflection and spiritual guidance from those I love and trust I found an answer. "God is working through you Kevin," Sue Reilly told me after I shared with her the details of my bone marrow journey in its earliest stages. "He wants you to tell this story."

What amazes me is how amazingly simple the premise of bone marrow donation is on the giving end. Anyone can save a life by simply being themselves-getting into a registry and answering the call to action when it comes. Be yourself, all of yourself. I did some lifting, but others did far more than me. I'm just the witness, the glue that holds it all together as their voice and storyteller.

A book like *The Marrow in Me* doesn't come together without a lot of people coming together and inviting you into their most personal of worlds. God bless you Chris Pablo. Not only did you *beat leukemia*, you had the vision to realize how your unique golf ball story could help far more people than you alone. What a legacy you've left behind. But it wouldn't have happened unless you made yourself and your family visual and vulnerable. Letting the outside world see the suffering you and your family went through inspired a collective people to not let you go it alone. Spending quality time with you, Sandy, Nate and Zack are memories I'll cherish forever.

Renee Adaniya-Chung. Your being one of the first unrelated bone marrow donors to come out of Hawaii is truly a blessing to us all. And what a face for the cause. Not only did you give your marrow to Butch Lane, you kept giving by your tireless efforts at the Hawaii Bone Marrow Donor Registry. Your story of donation was a huge part of me eventually rolling up my sleeve to register as a potential donor. And the fact that it was you who called me with the news that I turned up as a potential match years later-well I still get chicken skin just thinking about it.

To the family of Alana Dung. Now that I'm a father of young girls, I can only imagine the depth of your loss. Chris Pablo and others may have started the process of educating the public about what blood cancers are and how they can be cured with bone marrow transplants, but your daughter Alana is without question the person who pushed potential donors out the door. How do we explain more than 30,000 people showing up to give a sample of blood and the dozens of bone marrow matches that resulted from her registration drives? God worked through Alana, making her an angel on earth if only for a brief time.

Like the story of Alana's illness at a young age, I see a part of my life through the eyes of Jennifer Eller. When I look at Jennifer's picture now, I'm struck by how my eyes are drawn to hers. They're striking. The relationship she had with her father Dean is the type of relationship I hope to strike with my girls Samantha and Amanda when they grow into their teen years. Dean you may not know this, but our conversations before I had my kids really taught me how to love a girl.

To the people at the Sacramento Medical Foundation Blood Center. You shepherded me through a maze of medical tests and procedures. I know in the end what was most important was to get my marrow, but you completely understood the emotional investment from a donor's perspective. I will never forget the phone call that I was indeed the preferred match to go to transplant and then the word that my bone marrow recipient had died. Sharon Redding got me pumped up early on and Lupe Valdez let me down with a strong but compassionate tone when the end result wasn't what we all had hoped for.

To Molly McMillen, my friend and former news anchor. You told the story on TV of my donor journey with the perfect balance of information and inspiration. After seeing your reports on TV I can't imagine anyone not at least thinking about registering to become a potential bone marrow donor. I've had plenty of people tell me it was your reports that sent them to register.

To Sue Reilly, Claudia Smolda and Luz Bergstrom. Your thoughtful prayers and spiritual guidance reinforced my faith. Mrs. Reilly you really convinced me that I had a book to write. Claudia, you reminded me that prayer isn't always specific-His Will be done. What we want and what we think is right isn't always so. So it's best to leave it to God and trust that he will do what's best, even if we don't agree with it at the time. I remind myself of that time and time again. And Luz, I just love your love for Christ. Anyone who has that many portraits of Jesus in their home has to have pull with the guy. Thank you for your prayers and please keep them coming. I need all the help I can get.

To my parents Bob Walsh and my late mother Carole. Your love and encouragement were the foundation to my personal, spiritual and intellectual growth. It's not easy being Catholic. Your decision to not force the faith on us as children eventually let us discover it ourselves.

To my friends at the Leukemia and Lymphoma Society's Team in Training. For a guy who hates to run, you convinced me that the daunting challenge of completing a marathon was within reach. By striving for a goal one stride at a time, and combining it with friendship, inspiration and a solid training program; it is truly amazing to see the sea of purple tank tops and singlets pounding the pavement in marathons around the world. And the fact that hundreds of millions of dollars is raised for blood cancer research and treatment puts TNT among the most noble of charities.

The Spirit of Aloha lives in me long after leaving the most beautiful place on earth. It's one thing to see and visit the islands, but something much more meaningful to live there. To Don and Sandra Edwards and their daughter Jennifer Allen. You always made me feel at home in Hawaii. To the people of Hawaii who know Live Aloha is not just a snazzy slogan, it's a way of life. And Auntie Iwalani. Will you some day teach my daughters the Hula?

To my in-laws on the South Side of Chicago, Dr. John Gnap and Jeannine Gnap. Above all else thank you for letting me marry your daughter, and for supporting our dreams throughout the years. It's wonderful to be welcomed into such a large and loving family. To Paul and Jennifer Gnap for making family visits and vacations a blast. And to Dick and Ellen Smith for your love, career advice, and of course letting us come over to your house to swim in your pool, eat your food, drink your beer and letting us rock out in Dick's Love Dart Lounge in the basement. I love that place.

To Eli Kowalski and the Sports Challenge Network. Thanks for taking chance on a rookie author.

And to my lovely wife Jean who has followed me around the world as I've chased my broadcast dreams. Someday I'm going to fulfill all this potential you think I have. Life is a journey and I couldn't think of a better traveler to have with me. And now that we have two little girls along for the ride too, a great ride is even better.

TABLE OF CONTENTS

CHAPTER ONE

An Odd Golf Ball

TO ANY OTHER GOLFER ON THE RANGE OF KO'OLAU GOLF
Club that one odd golf ball in a basket of identicals would have been kicked aside.
It was old-maybe 20 or 30 years old. It was discolored, scuffed up and had a different dimple pattern. But *something* about that ball that called out to Chris Pablo. He
didn't know why but he couldn't bring himself to hit it.

The view surrounding the golf course was stunning. On the mauka side the
majestic and mossy green Koolaus rose into the sky. The mountains caught the
clouds which drifted across the sky with the help of the trade winds. With nowhere
to go the clouds dumped rain, which bounced off the mountains as mist. Sprinkle
the mist with brilliant Hawaiian sunshine and you had the most gorgeous rainbows
you'd ever want to see.

On the makai side, the Pacific Ocean had its collage of colors too. For about as
far as Tiger Woods could hit a drive, the water off the windward side of Oahu
looked white. It was the function of the sun shining through the clear shallow water
and reflecting off the white sand below. Farther out where the jet skiers and surfers
romped, the water turned aqua green. Past that the water got deeper and bluer.
The deeper it got, the bluer it became. It was better than a postcard.

Who could have known paradise like this was the backdrop of a living hell for
a 45-year old married father of three children? Chris Pablo looked the part of someone living the good life. He was six feet tall, slender, with brown hair, chocolate
eyes and a decent smattering of freckles on his handsome face. His age didn't
mirror his body. He ate right and was probably in better shape than most 25-year
olds, putting in impressive gym workouts that included serious weight lifting and
cardio.

Chris worked as a lobbyist for Kaiser Permanente, a major medical provider in Honolulu. He put in long hours at the office, successfully persuading island senators and house members to look kindly on the medical industry with legislation and funding. Even with a crazy schedule like his, Chris always had time for his beautiful wife, Sandy; and two good looking sons, six-year-old Nate and three-year-old Zack. When he wasn't at work, or at home, Chris spent time with friends strolling the Bermuda grass fairways of Oahu's golf courses.

To anyone else Chris's schedule and lifestyle would have been exhausting. He got by because he had a zest for life and an abundant well of energy-obvious byproducts of his physical fitness. Not that anyone else would have noticed, but Chris hadn't felt well for weeks. The energy he could always count on was in steady decline. So he went to the doctor looking for reassurance that he had some kind of minor ailment that would eventually be cleared up with rest and medicine. He went in with hope and came out with cancer.

Three weeks after being diagnosed with Chronic Myelogenous Leukemia, Chris went to the driving range, if for nothing else, to get away from the chronic worry that came with such a thing. All types of leukemia can kill, and CML is about the worst you can have. Cancer cells develop in the bone marrow and can travel in the blood to the spleen and other organs. At the very least Chris was looking at serious chemotherapy and a bone marrow transplant. Whatever the case, it was going to be a long, tough road ahead. And even with all the right treatment there was no guarantee he would live.

Hitting golf balls was good therapy. It was physical without being physically taxing, and it took a certain amount of mental focus, which was good for Chris because it took his mind off his health problems. He was about halfway through the basket when he saw that odd one in the mix. Something about it compelled him to take a closer look. He bent down, plucked it out and turned it on its side. Printed on the side of the ball was an inspirational message. When he saw the words *beat leukemia* looking back at him he got the chills. That's really saying something because it's never cold in Hawaii.

Chris Pablo, leukemia survivor and founder of beat leukemia golf ball.

Almost immediately Chris's lips quivered, his eyes watered and his heart screamed out in joy. For him it was clear. The *beat leukemia* golf ball was a sign that he would be cured. He would see his young boys become men and he would grow old and walk with his wife on the beautiful beaches of Hawaii. He felt that sense of goodness, that spirit of hope all the way down to his bones-where the marrow lives. Few people and certainly not the other golfers on the range could have known what finding that ball meant to Chris Pablo. In someone else's basket the ball and words would have meant nothing. In Chris's basket it meant *every-thing*. How it got there, God only knows. He put the ball in his pocket and went home.

The diagnosis of CML

Chris Pablo's beat leukemia golf ball. It's hard to read in this picture, but the words beat leukemia are spelled out in the center of the ball. Chris found the ball in a basket at the driving range.

was bad luck for sure. Even with his lucky discovery, a golf ball wasn't going to cure his leukemia. Chris had a lot of work to do and he would probably need more miracles in addition to the one in his pocket. His best hope for survival was a bone marrow transplant. No luck finding a match within his family, so he would have to find a match from someone on the outside. That would take a lot of luck too.

Chris was Filipino and minorities are vastly underrepresented in bone marrow registries. Unlike a simple blood transfusion, a bone marrow transplant involves a much more specific match of tissue markers that falls almost exclusively along racial and ethnic lines. If you get sick, the chance of you finding a match outside your racial and ethnic identity is not nearly as good as finding it within. But there have been exceptions. Later I would meet a pretty lady who was the exception and, as luck would have it, was a friend of Chris Pablo. Something else; in a place like Hawaii so many people are of mixed race and ethnicity. It wasn't uncommon to have someone who was a quarter Japanese, a quarter Filipino, a quarter Chinese and a quarter white. Now imagine they got sick and needed a bone marrow transplant. There are not a lot of potential donors registered who are of that same racial medley. The same thing happened to baseball Hall of Famer Rod Carew's daughter.

The first place to look for a bone marrow match is within your family and usually from a sibling. Even then there's only a 25 percent chance you'll find it. If there's no match in the family you look on the outside. To this point international registries showed no match for Chris Pablo anywhere in the world. But considering his lucky find with the golf ball, he thought luck would strike again. First he would need a partner who had access to a lot of people, a media friend perhaps, who could get the word out that Chris needed help. Despite the odds the concept was simple. Somewhere in the world there might be a match for Chris. He needed a lot people to sign up at registration drives and hopefully one in the bunch would match him. Applying the concept wasn't so easy.

Culturally speaking, a haole boy from Meadowbrook, Pennsylvania hardly seemed like a likely media partner for an islander like Chris. He was brown, I was white. I was Catholic, he was Episcopalian. He was thin, and don't we wish we all were? Chris was kamaaina-of the land. I was raised in the white-bread Philadelphia suburbs. But even if our lives were worlds apart, geography and culture wouldn't get in our way. It would just take a little time for the course of my life and livelihood to unfold before Chris and I hooked up.

Before TV there was radio. I'd only been out of college for ten months and I was reading crop reports on the radio for a small AM radio station in Frankfort, Indiana. Being something of a big city kid I knew absolutely *nothing* about farming. But with a little help from those in the "agricultural know" I learned how to read the Associated Press wire copy in the farmer's language. "Corn futures up a penny and-a-half, soybeans..." On and on it went.

When I wasn't delivering the ag report, we did small town news at WILO Country. Frankfort is an hour north of Indianapolis and an hour southeast of my alma mater, Purdue University in West Lafayette. The people in Frankfort are very nice, solid Midwesterners. But there's not much to do there. Teenagers pile into cars and cruise. They drive a loop from the courthouse, to the strip, past Stock's Laundromat and turn around in the Marsh grocery store parking lot. They do it for hours, honking their horns and occasionally stopping to talk.

The only cruising I did was back and forth to the radio station. I buried myself in my work. Other than talking on the radio I didn't have anyone else to talk to. The hours were long, the pay sucked and the early morning hours were murder. It was a start. Nobody would hire me on TV.

For fun I did overnight ride-a-longs with the Frankfort Police Department. Part of my reporting duties included going to the police department every morning to read the arrest reports. The reports were typed on four by six cards. I noticed the stack was a lot thicker on Monday mornings. I asked the clerk if I could talk to the chief about that.

Seconds later a large man walked out of an office. "Can I help you?" Jim Skinner asked.

"Are you the chief?" I asked hardly believing someone who looked so young could have such an important position.

"Yeah," Chief Skinner shrugged, acknowledging that most people couldn't believe it either.

"How old are you?" I asked.

"Thirty."

Jim Skinner took over when the previous chief, Harold Woodruff, retired and became Mayor of Frankfort. Even if Chief Skinner looked 20 years too young to be the top cop, he still looked like a cop. He was a big boy with a standard police officer's mustache, about 6'3", 6'4" and somewhere in the neighborhood of 240 pounds.

"Chief I come in here on Mondays and I just can't believe how thick the stack of arrests is. I don't get it. The town seems very quiet to me, but then again I go to bed early. What's going on?"

"Oh it gets a little crazy when the sun goes down and the alcohol starts kicking in. You should come along and see it for yourself sometime," he told me.

So that's when I started rolling overnights with the cops. I rode with the mayor's son, Gary, a few times. Gary Woodruff was about 30 years old and he was a cop's cop. We would drive down the street and he'd see potential trouble before it happened.

"Okay watch this Kevin. See that guy walking? He saw us and that's why he turned down that street. He's going to loop back around as soon as he sees us turn the corner. What he doesn't know is I'm gonna make another right turn, drive back along a parallel street and make my way back to where we first saw him."

Sure enough Officer Woodruff was right. The guy seemed annoyed that were on to him. Woodruff concluded if the young man was really up to no good he would have ran. So we simply drove by slowly giving him "the look", a subtle message that tonight was not the night to be a troublemaker. And we did the same thing with others, occasionally stopping, but usually moving on.

We went on calls, which were sometimes intense, and other times hilarious.

Dispatcher: "Frankfort units, a report of a naked man standing outside of an apartment complex making threats to his girlfriend."

"Oh I just gotta see this," Gary said when the call came across the police radio.

It was a cold winter morning just after midnight and temperatures were in the single digits. We could only imagine what awaited us. Gary floored the Ford Crown Victoria. We hit triple digits on the speedometer in no time and within a minute and-a-half we were out of town and in the countryside. Still we were late. By the time we got there the naked guy was inside.

Gary knocked on the door with his flashlight.

"Tommy, c'mon out, we want to talk to you," he said loudly.

"Oh no you don't. I'm not coming out. I'm not *stupid.* If I come out you mother f....rs will arrest me just like you always do," Tommy responded.

"No we won't," Officer Woodruff said. "Not if you didn't do anything wrong. C'mon out Tommy."

"Nope not doin' it. You guys do it to me every time. You tell me to come out for a talk and then you arrest me and take me to jail. I'm not fallin' for it," Tommy said wickedly.

"Well at least come to the window so I can see that you're okay," Officer Woodruff said.

To that Tommy was agreeable. We heard his feet shuffle away from the door and over toward the window. He pulled the curtain back and sure enough he was in the buff like the dispatcher said he would be, and he wasn't happy about having an audience.

"Who the f..k is that co.. sucker?" he screamed pointing at me.

By now backup had arrived and the other cops were doubled over in laughter. As the reporter tagalong I had turned into a joke. I thought it was funny too, but I wasn't sure if it was appropriate for me to laugh. Tommy wouldn't let up.

"Who the f..k is that co.. sucker?!" he demanded to know.

"He's just a friend," Gary Woodruff told him. "Calm down Tommy. He's not going to bother you."

"He is bothering me! Tell that co.. sucker to get the f..k out of here!"

Eventually I walked around the corner and the boys went in and got him. Later that night we stopped by the Clinton County jail to take care of some paperwork. As I walked by the steel door of a holding cell I heard a loud BANG on the reinforced glass window. Reflexively I ducked. Someone in the lockup banged his fist on the window and gave me the most chilling look I've seen since Jack Nicholson in *The Shining.* It was Tommy and he scared me. *I almost pissed my pants.* The jailors loved it!

Take my word for it when I say the early stages of a media career are not glamorous. There's plenty of heartbreak and rejection to go along with all the riff raff. I sent out close to 100 audition tapes to small media markets hoping to break into television. I got one phone call. I drove eight hours to the interview in tiny Alpena, Michigan on the shores of Lake Huron in northeastern part of the state. The drive was so far out in the sticks I was wondering if people hunted for sustenance. Then out of nowhere the little town of 11,000 appeared. From what I could tell it was a hardworking, old mill town with brutally, cold winters.

Small markets are proving grounds. If you're good you'll move up. If you're talking market sizes north of 200, you're probably not going to see many people with the natural ability to make it to the network level. Alpena is market 208 out of 210 television markets in America. I thought the job was mine. I couldn't miss. Well... I missed. The news director called and said I didn't get the job.

I was *crushed.* If I couldn't get a job in a place like Alpena, Michigan I wasn't sure I could work in television anywhere. I *thought* I had potential and a good future ahead of me, but I was beginning to wonder if all this rejection was telling me something I didn't want to hear. Maybe I just wasn't cut out for this line of work. I was depressed. So like any good Catholic, I prayed.

You don't find a lot of Catholics in media, at least not practicing ones. And even then, you might not know who they are because most Catholics don't advertise. I never did because I knew what I had and that was good enough for me. Plus there's always been a fair amount of Catholic bashing inside newsrooms and, well, who needs the headache?

When Catholics are really desperate they pray to St. Jude. He's the patron saint of hopeless causes; the miracle worker, the first cousin and best friend of Jesus. Obviously he has pull. I pull out my miniature ceramic statue of St. Jude and pray novenas when my life gets tough. He, as you will come to see, would play a recurrent role throughout my personal life and career.

Although we revere St. Jude at our home, my children are rough on him. My little girls lump him in with their Barbie Doll play and Jude takes his fair share of lumps. When his limbs break off I

Walsh family 1989. L to R, Chris, Michael, Carole and Kevin Walsh

glue them back on. He's even lost his head a few times.

My relationship with St. Jude started just a few years earlier at the suggestion of a hospice worker who cared for my mother. My mom, Carole Walsh, had a malignant brain tumor. I took a semester off from college to help care for her. In her final two years she had two cranial surgeries, chemotherapy and radiation. The cancer really beat her up physically, emotionally and to some extent spiritually.

The second surgery left her semi-paralyzed on her right side. Her right arm just hung there, sometimes getting tangled up in the hospital bed we had for her at home. The right side of her face and mouth drooped, making eating tough and her once perfect speech slurred. One of my most painful memories was our last family dinner together. We had seafood. The bay scallops kept falling out of her mouth and the brown sauce smeared on her cheeks. My mom was always one of the neatest and well-mannered eaters I'd ever seen. The messiness robbed her of her dignity, so I kept wiping her face clean. Finally she'd had enough and broke down in tears, *"What are you so embarrassed you can't stand to see the sight of me being messy?"* she asked.

Her question killed me because part of it was true. I was embarrassed, but I didn't want her to be embarrassed too. That's why I took a napkin to her face. Prior to our last supper my mom never would have allowed herself to continue eating with food on her face. That's when I *knew*.

If there's anything tougher than watching your mom wither away I don't know what it is. Mom is the one who carried you, gave birth to you and the one who comforted you. When you're sick you don't want your dad, you want your *mom*. Losing her was a loss on so many levels. All along I prayed to St. Jude; if not for cure, then for peace and strength. We didn't get a cure, but I got plenty of peace and strength and I know mom did too.

Before she died I had a lot of talks with my Mom about family and God.

"Do you think Dad will remarry after I die?" she asked.

"I don't know Mom. I haven't asked him and I don't think he's gone there in his head yet," I told her.

"Do you think I'll go to heaven?"

"Definitely, don't you?"

"I don't know. I haven't been perfect."

"Nobody's perfect Mom. I don't think you have to be perfect to get in."

"Sometimes I have doubts about God and whether there is a heaven. Doesn't that mean I won't go to heaven?" she asked.

"I don't think so. I think we all have doubts about God and heaven from time to time. I do. I think if you want to believe it and try to believe it in your heart of hearts, that's good enough for God. So even if you have some doubts, your *desire* to believe is what makes the difference in his eyes," I told her.

"Are you guys gonna be alright without me? What about Michael?" she asked.

My younger brother Michael was just 14 at the time. He never had the chance to experience my mother like my older brother Chris and I did. Even before my mother was diagnosed two years earlier, we believe she'd been sick long before and just wasn't herself for some time. Soon she'd be gone and Mike wouldn't have someone to help him get ready for the prom, cook him chicken soup when he was sick, and to love him as only a mother could.

"He'll be fine. He's a good kid, very mature for his age. He'll grow up and make us all proud," I told her.

"And Chris?" she asked.

"He's an adult. He can handle it."

"What about you?"

"Mom I'm 21. I'm an adult. I'll be alright."

"Are you going to miss me?"

"Of course I'll miss you Mom."

And with that she cried with intensity that I've never seen before and hope never to see again. It was a full body cry, her head and upper torso stuck in a rocking motion back and forth. She was so spent from the release that she didn't have the strength to wipe herself, even with her good hand. I would lose my mom to cancer just a couple of weeks later at the age of 51, one day after my parent's wedding anniversary.

Life was bad during my mom's illness, but I didn't realize how bad it was until I really put some time and distance between it. Getting through it took more strength than I had on my own. The extra help came from faith and prayer. I believe the biggest lift came from St. Jude.

There was another living saint in my life, my future wife Jean Gnap. She consoled me when I lost my mom and was always just a phone call away when I would whine about the slow progress in my career and being stuck in radio. She assured me that I was a good broadcaster and that my time to shine on TV would come. Even if my career didn't take off she said she'd love me just the same.

Then one day the break I had been waiting so long for appeared to present itself. "Hey Kev, are you still looking for a job in TV?" asked Jeff Marchesseault, my radio pal at Y-lo Country in Frankfort.

"Yeah, why?" I asked him.

"Well I think I got a job in Guam, and the news director says they need one more. Want me to tell him about you?"

"*Where* is Guam?" I asked.

"It's out in the Western Pacific near the Philippines," Jeff said.

I was still getting over my Alpena, Michigan rejection when I took out a globe. I kept turning it and turning it looking for a land mass. I couldn't find it. Eventually I found a dot with the text **Guam** next to it. The dot told me it was small. The endless turning of the globe told me it was at the edge of the earth. And there was something else about Guam that made it even more unnerving-*snakes!*

From the limited number of articles I could find on Guam, all of them talked about an abundance of brown tree snakes that bordered on the apocalyptic. Snakes weren't falling out of the sky, but they were slithering down power lines and coming up through toilets! *Lovely.* And I thought I was out of my element in the cornfields of Indiana.

After a couple of days Jeff needed an answer.

"Uh, why not? Tell 'em I'm interested," I told Jeff, not knowing this really was the lucky break I needed and never imagining what would later become of my life.

I got the job. Before setting off on the cross-world journey my future in-laws in suburban Chicago threw a sendoff party for Jean and me. Jean came from a large, close-knit family. Nobody in her family ever moved away. The Gnaps liked me, but they didn't like the fact that I would be taking their girl so far away. Nobody in the family knew a thing about Guam. And, as fate would have it, on the day of our party the front page of The Chicago Tribune had a headline that read: **Guam: The Land of Ten Million Tree Snakes.** I saw the words when I fetched the paper from the end of the driveway early in the morning. I knew it would be trouble when visiting family arrived later in the day.

"Ooooh my Gaaad!" successive aunts said in their vowel challenged Chi-caw'-goh accents. "Did you see the paper today about Guam? Jean's going to a place where there are all these snakes! Ooooh my Gaaad!"

It wasn't the encouragement we were hoping for, but we were going just the same. Because Guam Cable TV was paying my fare, I had to fly its route. Jean flew on her own dime and a few hours behind me. I had my suitcase, my golf clubs and a sense of adventure. I started in Chicago with stops in Minneapolis and Honolulu. The layover in Hawaii was brief, but long enough to climb to the top of the parking garage where I had a good look at downtown Honolulu. It was my first time in Hawaii and something inside told me it wouldn't be my last. What I couldn't possibly know at the time was the Hawaiian Islands would later make a home for me. But the path to Hawaii and future acts of charity went through the Marianas Islands and Guam.

The last leg of the long journey to Guam was an eight-hour flight from Honolulu to Agana. The first thing I noticed about the people getting on board the flight was their clothes. It was truly island wear with flowered prints, untucked aloha shirts and muumuu dresses. Then I noticed color. Not the color of their clothes, the color of their skin. Aside from the flight crew I was the only white person on board. That was a first. I'd never been the lone minority anywhere. I didn't just see the difference, I could *feel* it.

Until then, the only culture I'd ever known was what I learned in school and read about in books and magazines. It's one thing to read about culture, another thing to live it. I was nervous, but excited about the possibilities. Then I looked down at the passenger footwear. I had just left the Midwest in the dead of winter so my feet were covered up. Most everyone had on sandals. Some didn't wear shoes at all. And it wasn't because they took them off-*they didn't own shoes.*

The long flight over the Pacific gave me plenty of time to think. As darkness fell some of my thoughts turned as dark as the night sky. About six, or seven hours into it, it really hit me that I couldn't undo this even if I wanted to. I was locked in a plane 35,000 feet above the Pacific Ocean, seven thousand miles away from home. I didn't have enough money to buy a return ticket if the place turned out to be a dive. I was stuck. I had to make it work. Most of my life I lived with the comfort of knowing I could always go home to my parents if things got bad. This time that option was out.

The engines on the Northwest DC-10 slowed and the plane started to descend from the dark sky. People in the cabin started to stir. Flight attendants came through to pick up drink cups and the captain came on the intercom with word that we would be landing soon. I looked out the window and saw nothing for a good 15 minutes of the descent. I thought I might see the lights of a ship at sea, but there was nothing, absolutely nothing. I wasn't sure there was land this far out in the ocean to land on. Then on final approach I saw lights flickering between the cloud cover. As we got closer the lights became colorful. It would be Christmas in a couple of days and I had almost forgotten it was the holiday season. I wasn't sure what Christmas would like in such a faraway land, but from the sky it looked almost like it did back home. That was comforting.

We landed at A.B. Won Pat Airport, which shared runway space with Naval Air Station Guam. I could tell it was a warm, humid night by feeling the temperature rise in the cabin as dew formed on the windows. I was really looking forward to some warm weather after what had been a cold start to the winter in the Midwest. But whatever warm thoughts I had about the weather and good feelings about a fresh start in a faraway land all but disappeared as soon as I set foot in the terminal.

The airport was dimly lit and smelled of mold. I thought there would be families waiting for loved ones with smiles and flowers-just like Hawaii. There was hardly anybody. My fellow passengers got off the plane and trekked through the terminal like they knew what they were doing and where they were going. Me? I was lost, sad and really hungry.

I thought I might be able to get something to eat at the food court. No food court here. There wasn't a restaurant or a vending machine to be found. As my stomach growled my heart and spirits sank. I thought Guam was supposed to be semi-modern, but it all seemed third world to me. And I couldn't imagine what Jean would think when she landed. Over and over I kept thinking what have I done? What have I done?

John Ryan, the assignment editor and investigative reporter for Guam Cable TV was waiting for me and picked me out of the crowd. That was pretty easy to do, one white guy finding another in a sea of brown people. We loaded my luggage into the back of his pickup truck and then it rained on my stuff. It was not a good start.

We went to the TV station to pick up a compact station vehicle that would be mine to drive for the week. The driver's side seat had a Glad trash bag draped over it. Once I started driving through the driving island rain I understood why the bag was there. The window leaked and the dripping water soaked my pants. It pissed me off. I was wet and it looked like I pissed my pants.

My hotel for the week wasn't much better than the car. There were dozens of lizards crawling on the stucco wall outside the hotel entrance and there was a cockroach the size of a Hot Wheels car zipping around inside my room. Jean was

L to R, Jeff Marchesseault and Kevin Walsh. U.S. Territory of Guam, 1994

connecting through Narita, Japan and would be arriving in Guam within the hour, so I quickly unpacked and started making my way back to the airport. Aside from cursing the car's leaking window on the drive over, I rehearsed a speech in my head that I would deliver once I picked Jean up. She was all smiles when I saw her make it through customs. But when she saw me, her happy face turned to concern.

"What's wrong?" she asked.

"Oh honey. I don't know about this. This may be rougher than we thought it would be," I told her.

"What do you mean?" she asked.

"Well let's put it this way. There are lizards everywhere. There's a huge roach in the hotel room. And there's a leak in the window of the car," I told her.

She took it a lot better than I thought she would, assuring me that she would stay as long as I did. And despite the early roach race and gecko gatherings the hotel, we eventually found more permanent digs with a nice little condo on East Agana Bay. It had a wonderful view of surf and sand. No roaches here, just the occasional gecko. Geckos we later learned were good luck.

Overall my luck was good in Guam. I learned TV from the ground up, advancing from the reporting ranks to the anchor desk within six months. Television aside we had a ball swimming and scuba diving with some of the most colorful fish in the world. The nightlife? You couldn't beat it. We went out and danced like we did when we were back in college. Everyone dances in Guam and they dance well. What's more, everyone knows how to dance with a partner. When was the last time you saw a 20-something guy who really knew how to dance with a girl?

I learned island culture the Chamorro way, going to festivals in the villages, loading up on tasty pork, chicken kelaguen, pancit, barbecue chicken and plenty of red rice. I even picked up a little of the Chamorro language which is about 80-percent Spanish and what's left of the original island tongue. We were strangers in a strange land, but after a few months the people of Guam began to accept us and treat us like family.

Going to church was especially comforting because 99.9 percent of Guam is Roman Catholic. Jean and I definitely stood out because we were the only white people at Mass. But Catholic Mass is pretty much the same wherever you go in the world provided that land's primary language is yours. And in Guam, English makes the world go round.

Guam wasn't forever. I mailed audition tapes out and had been in contact with news executives in Honolulu in early 1995. I was planning a trip back to the mainland and hoped to set up getting-to-know-you interviews during a long layover in Hawaii. Then, unexpectedly I got a phone call from Don Rockwell, the news director at KGMB TV in Honolulu. Apparently a reporter called a producer a sperm receptacle. It was certainly not a nice thing to say to a young woman, and considering that sexual harassment was the *big* politically incorrect taboo at the time-a comment like that couldn't go unpunished.

"We had an unfortunate incident here and had to let someone go. I was wondering do you still want to come here?" Don Rockwell asked me.

"Sure I'll be there for the interview during my travels in a couple of weeks. I'm looking forward to meeting you," I told him.

"No you don't understand. We want you to *join* us," he said.

"What do you mean? Are you hiring me without an interview?"

"Yes. We liked your tape and you obviously know TV. What do you say?" Don asked.

I cupped my hand over the phone, whispered the good news to my wife Jean and asked her if she wanted to move to Hawaii. She said yes.

"Yeah sure Don I'll come," I told him.

It really wasn't much more than that. Don and I worked out a few details and within a couple of weeks I was on a plane for Honolulu.

My first assignment as a reporter at KGMB-9, the CBS affiliate, could have been a precursor to what good would come my way in Hawaii. It was a slow news day and the assignment desk sent me to a crafts show at Ala Moana Park with instructions to make something newsy out of it. I met a beautiful 40-something woman named Iwalani Tseu. Iwalani had the standard long, black island hair with a slight curl and skin lighter than most other local women. She was stunning. Her looks and her dancing ability made her one of the original hula dance girls in Waikiki entertainment shows. Twenty some years later, she still looked like she could perform if she wanted to. But she was a working mom now with a crafts business. She

L to R, Rod Antone and Kevin Walsh outside KGMB TV. Honolulu, Hawaii

made kukui nut leis. Not only did she make them, she told interesting stories about them. According to Iwalani kukui nuts had special healing powers and were good luck.

"You're new to the islands, yaah?" she asked in her island accent.

"Well new to these islands. I lived on an island before, Guam; so I'm familiar with island lifestyle," I told her.

"Be good to the islands the islands will be good to you," she told me while placing one of her expensive leis around my neck. "I'm gonna take care of you and be your hanai auntie now that you're here. So you make sure you keep in touch with your Auntie Iwalani okay Kevin?"

A Hanai auntie or uncle is like your mom or dad's best friend. They're family without a blood connection. I don't know what it was, but I felt a strange connection with Iwalani, almost like we'd met before. Of course we hadn't. Aside from an airport layover more than a year ago I'd never been to Hawaii. And I was pretty sure Iwalani hadn't spent much time on the east coast. But later that night after my story with her hit the air, I got a call at the TV station.

"Kevin! It's Auntie Iwalani. You didn't tell me your last name was Walsh," she said with a sense of astonishment.

"I didn't? Well, it is. Why does it matter?" I asked.

"I'm a Walsh too!" she screamed.

"What?" I said incredulously.

"My father was an Australian sailor who came through the islands and met my mother. I'm hapa," she explained.

Hapa is short for hapa haole. In island parlance that's someone of mixed race. Iwalani's goodwill filled me with the Aloha Spirit. And once you have the Aloha Spirit in you, you are to share it with others. In true Hawaiian translation, *Aloha* means sharing the breath of life. I just needed some luck to find the right opportunity to share some Aloha of my own.

The alarm went off at 6:30 on a May morning in my tiny fourth floor apartment in a Nuuanu high rise. I reached over my wife on the spring day to turn the alarm off before slipping into the kitchen to make coffee. As the smell of the Lion Kona Coffee filled our place, I gazed out of our bay window. Straight ahead about a mile away was the Honolulu skyline. To the west, 747's from long trips across the Pacific Ocean made their final approach over Honolulu Harbor and into Honolulu International Airport. The rising sun lit up the lush green Waianae Mountains and the morning trade winds gave the branches of palm trees a lift. It was a beautiful morning. In Hawaii most mornings are.

I love watching planes. How aeronautical engineers can get something that big to take flight, stay in the air and land gracefully is a constant source of wonder for me. And it's not just that. I wonder who's on the plane? What do they look like? And where are they coming from? Were they senior citizens who saved their whole lives for a trip to the most beautiful place on earth? Were they young lovers starting a long life together? Were they families who wanted to see the usual Hawaiiana stuff-luaus, volcanoes, leis and Da kine? I'm a people-watcher. I love to see people's passion for what usually is their trip of a lifetime.

Not on this day, but every now and then during my morning routine the phone would ring, and Brenda Salgado, the assignment editor at KGMB TV 9 News would tell me to get to the airport as fast as I could and get on one of those island-hopping smaller jets flown by Hawaiian, or Aloha Airlines. I'd be going to the outer islands to cover a news story. I had a booklet of tickets for both airlines that I could hand-write in the information and go straight to the gate. Seems hard to imagine with today's strict security, but back then that's the way we did it. When we got to the outer islands we'd rent a car, shoot our story, fly back and have our story on the air that night. I just loved Hawaiian mornings because they were always exciting to wake up to.

On that May morning over a bowl of Rice Krispies, with coffee and orange juice on the side, I listened to the most popular radio show in all of Hawaii to see if I could get an idea of what happened overnight and what might be the news of the day. If it mattered, Michael W. Perry and Da Coach, Larry Price, would be talking about it on KSSK, 92.3 FM. It didn't seem like they had much to say, so I wasn't really sure what my reporting assignment would be when I got to KGMB TV.

I took a last swig of coffee, brushed my teeth, kissed Jean goodbye and headed out the door. Waiting for me on the other side was the Honolulu Advertiser. I grabbed the newspaper and marched up the hill on Nuuanu Avenue, and plunked myself down on a bench next to the old Chinese cemeteries. Soon *The Bus* would turn off the Pali Highway and make its way down the hill. It wasn't just any bus, it was *The Bus,* part of America's best public bus system. Everyone took *The Bus*- the distinguished and the degenerates. The Number 21 cruised through Chinatown passing by the hookers and hobos still out after a long night. It made a left on South King Street, snaked through the Capital, past Honolulu Hale and the sea of strip clubs and hostess bars on Kapiolani Boulevard, before dropping me off at Piikoi Street, about a block away from work. During the 30-minute ride I read the news- paper, which on this morning didn't have much more to add than what my friends Michael W. Perry and Larry Price talked about on the radio, so I wasn't exactly sure what my story for the day might be.

Most reporters at Channel 9 brought at least two or three story ideas to the morning editorial meeting. You made your pitch, got your assignment and off you went with a cameraman. If you didn't bring an idea with you, you were chastised and you got what was left. As an anchor I was given a little more slack. If I didn't have my story all set up and ready to go on my own, I'd be given one that was pretty easy to turn before I anchored the 5:00 news. On that spring day the assign- ment editors thought I would best handle the story of Chris Pablo, mostly because of my background as a lifelong golfer. I liked what little I knew about it. The *beat leukemia* stamping on the side of the golf ball was certainly attractive, but what I couldn't possibly know at the time was how covering Chris's story would give me a chance to share the Aloha Spirit and be witness and participant to life-changing and life-saving opportunities. And like the golf ball finding Chris, it was as if my own special finds somehow found me.

First though I had to find Chris. It wasn't all that hard because he was fairly well known in the media long before he was sick. He worked as a lobbyist for Kaiser Permanente, a major health provider. Whenever there was a medical story that needed news coverage, Chris was the go-to guy to find a doctor, or some other expert to talk about the subject. He knew how the media worked and he knew we loved stories with a hook. The *beat leukemia* golf ball was a helluva hook. It had all the elements you needed for a good TV news story-heartbreak, hope for a cure, in- spiration and a family willing to give all access.

Chris had an agenda and wasn't shy about it. He needed publicity about his plight and plugs for the bone marrow registration drives he organized. Sure he had a lucky golf ball that he lugged around in his pocket to give him a lift, but the ball wasn't going to cure his cancer. If he didn't find a bone marrow match in a limited pool fairly quickly, he was going to die. I didn't want that to happen. So I picked up the phone and gave Chris a call.

It was the end of the school year and Chris was busier than even a healthy man should have been. He was putting in full days at the office, working several more hours when he got home arranging and promoting his bone marrow registration drives and he was raising a young family. We agreed to meet on the last day of class at the

Pablo Family 1999. L to R, Nate, Sandy, Zack and Chris

prestigious Punahou School-the same place where Barack Obama and golfing great Michelle Wie went to school. I met Chris outside the pickup line where we waited for his six-year-old son Nate. I knew Chris by reputation, but I had never met him in person. When he climbed out of his car Chris looked tired, but he put a good face on it just the same. He needed to. He understood. He knew a lot of people would be seeing him for the first time and maybe the only time on TV, and he wanted them to believe he was well enough to make it through the grueling bone marrow transplant if he was lucky enough to find his match.

Nate Pablo came out and shared a warm embrace with his dad. He looked just like his dad in facial features and fatigue. The other kids seemed full of joy, clearly stoked about not having to come back to school for a couple of months. Nate looked tired, like he had heavy thoughts on his mind, which of course he did. He was not exactly pleased that he would have to share time with a TV crew, but he was polite, the product of parents who cared about manners and made sure their kids did too.

Later Sandy Pablo and their younger son Zack, who had some of the curliest boy hair I've ever seen, joined us on the infield of the school's track. It was the same track that hosted the old Superstars program on ABC's Wide World of Sports back in the 70's. We sat on the grass and chatted about hopes and fears for the future. I almost expected Sandy to be more of a cheerleader. Her candor and concern really brought home the gravity of what the Pablos faced as a family. She clearly saw the possibility of having to raise her children alone.

As I talked with Sandy I also kept an eye on Chris. He was intently focused on his sons, enjoying watching them play together with a newly purchased action figure. Nate took the lead as the eldest, twisting the action figure into different shapes and contortions before handing it over to Zack. Zack would do his own moldings and show it to his big brother for approval. Back and forth it went and there was never a tug-of-war. Chris had a look of satisfaction on his face that I guess was a reflection of how much he loved them and how proud he was that they got along so nicely.

As a future parent I wondered whether I would watch my children with a similar joy. Would I have boys, girls, or a combination? The Pablos play session made me reflect on my own youth and relationships with my brothers. I loved my brothers Chris and Mike, but we *never* played with such peace. There would've been a war between us over that action figure. We would have twisted each other into some of the same positions Nate and Zack did with the toy. A part of me was jealous.

I knew at some point I would have to talk to the boys about their dad's illness. I wanted to choose my words carefully so I would get a mature response. As I often do I rehearsed a few lines in my head, trying to imagine how they would take it and how they would respond. I plunked myself down the grass so I would be on their level. I started with Nate. I asked him if he understood what his dad's illness was. He did, and he put it in a child's terms.

"He's not all better and needs his rest. He needs a bone marrow donor," Nate said.

I asked three-year-old Zack the same thing. I'm not sure he understood the question. He was much more interested in his play than he was in me. So then I asked, "Zack why do you love your Dad?"

His face lit up and his tongue wiggled out of his mouth. Then he said with a cute lisp, "Because we play together, spend time together and have fun together."

That's what it all came down to-togetherness-and a family trying to keep itself together as illness tried to pull their foundation apart.

When we were done talking, Chris and the boys tried to fly a kite. Hawaii may be the easiest place in the world to fly a kite because there's almost always a steady breeze. But the trade winds weren't active that day and the kite hardly flew. I wondered if that was a bad omen. After an hour or so we were done with the Pablos and off to cover the other elements of Chris's story with someone who had a similar story to tell.

The whole ride over to Ala Moana Park I couldn't stop thinking about how lucky Chris would have to be to find a person to match him, and how lucky that person might be to become a part of Chris's life. Secretly I wished it would be me. I also knew whomever it was that matched would have to have a lot of guts. They would have their pelvis drilled with the thickest of needles and then have the marrow sucked out. It kind of freaked me out.

Chris was smart enough to know that others and I would have queasy feelings about bone marrow donation. So in a brilliant PR attempt to get his story out for potential donors and to alleviate fears like mine, he put another face on leukemia. And what a pretty face it was. Chris set us up with Renee Adaniya, a charming

Renee Adaniya, perfect bone marrow match for white military man in Tennessee.

twenty-something island girl. Renee was kamaaina, a petite girl with a cute, toothy smile. She looked local and talked local with a hint of Pidgin English. Renee worked at the Hawaii Bone Marrow Donor Registry as an administrator. It was more than just a job for her. Renee was one of Hawaii's first non-related bone marrow donors and was happy to tell anyone who would listen about her good luck to match a man named Butch from Tennessee. What made the story even better was the contrast. She was Asian and hip. Butch was a white military man from Tennessee.

We used Renee as a sidebar, interweaving her story with Chris's. We wanted the viewers to see the big picture. Be like Renee-register at your local blood center, or at the next bone marrow registration drive and who knows? You could be the one to save a life. It worked, viewers responded. Chris started being recognized at the grocery store, the gas station and well-wishers would tell him they were praying for him. He told them he appreciated it, but if they really wanted to help they'd come to his bone marrow registration drives. They did, by the hundreds.

I felt lucky and blessed to cover Chris's story because, selfishly, it came when I needed it most. Being a street reporter is not unlike being a cop, or a firefighter. Much of what you see is heartbreaking and there isn't much you can do about it. It carves at you. A lot of my colleagues were numb to it and were able to separate their own emotions from the mess. I couldn't. Sure I got to go home to a happy and loving wife each night, but it didn't change the fact that I'd probably cover a bleed-it-leads news story again tomorrow. Chris's story gave me a break from the negative news cycle. I prayed for him, especially to St. Jude.

The difference with Chris's story was there was something that could be done about his misfortune. He didn't have his health, but he had hope of recovery. He had a loving family and friends. And the community couldn't help but fall in love with him because he was a proud man who made himself vulnerable. Not a lot of guys can get in front of camera with tears in their eyes and tell a bunch of strangers they're hurting and need help. Chris could, and he let me be a witness to it.

Chris also let me address a personal question I think a lot of us harbor within. Am I really making a difference? Before Chris's story I wasn't so sure. His story gave me internal validation. My work was worthy. There was more to me than just a talking head on the tube. I don't know if anyone else saw a difference, but I certainly *felt* it. I felt that feeling of satisfaction deep in my bones, where the marrow lived. And later I would find my marrow wasn't just for me.

CHAPTER TWO

An Island Princess
with an Ugly Disease

AS MUCH AS CHRIS PUT A FACE ON LEUKEMIA, IT WAS SOME one else who sold it. Chris Pablo became a household name, but a little girl who was not yet two, came waddling forward and became a rock star. Alana Dung was cuter than a button. Her baby teeth looked like little Chiclet gum pieces. She was the happy child of a prominent Honolulu family with deep ties to the medical and insurance communities. But something wasn't right, and even if Alana wasn't quite old enough to put it into words, pointing at her tummy and making ouchy faces said plenty to her mother.

"She was about a year and-a-half old and was just beginning to talk. We thought it was stomach pains," Adelia Dung said. "She would point to her stomach and we could see her body tighten and she would cry."

They went to the doctor. He thought it was constipation. Adelia Dung took her daughter home. Over the next two and-a-half weeks mother's intuition and observation told Adelia Dung her daughter's condition was more than just a pooping problem. "She would scream out in pain," Adelia Dung remembers.

With her daughter's conditioning worsening, Adelia took Alana to Kapiolani Medical Center for Women and Children. After a battery of tests, the Dungs sat in the waiting area awaiting the results. When they saw Alana's pediatrician and an oncologist walking down the hall toward them they knew it was trouble. The doctors' body language gave off a bad vibe. Two days before Easter on *Good Friday*, doctors diagnosed Alana with Acute Myeloid, Type Seven Leukemia.

Acute myeloid leukemia is a very aggressive bone marrow cancer that can easily spread from inside the bones to the bloodstream, to the liver, spleen and central nervous system. The average age of a person diagnosed with AML is 67. Most are men and few are under 40. It very rarely targets children. It is among the worst leukemias one could have.

Alana's story was a tough one for me because through her I saw my own future. I knew it wouldn't be long before Jean and I started a family of our own. When I saw other parents with young children I wondered how my future family might look. Would the kids look more like me, or more like Jean? When I saw toddlers tumbling and splashing at the beach with their moms and dads, I saw myself doing the same thing in the not-too-distant future. Seeing Alana with her parents, Adelia and Steve, made me wonder how I might feel as a parent if I had sick child. It really scared me.

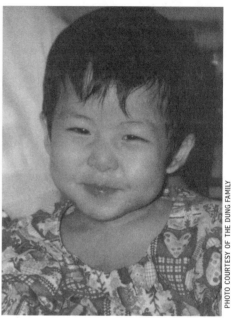

PHOTO COURTESY OF THE DUNG FAMILY

Alana Dung, leukemia patient who inspired more than 30,000 registrants and ultimately dozens of bone marrow matches which went to transplant.

Alana's best hope for cure was a bone marrow transplant. Like Chris Pablo she faced the same issue involving minority donors. The Dungs had an extended family in Hawaii and abroad. Everyone chipped in to help. Relatives and friends in California, Oregon, Washington, New York, New Jersey and Vancouver, British Columbia, Canada organized bone marrow registration drives where they lived. But home base and the focal point of the Alana's plight was Honolulu.

What Chris Pablo got in terms of publicity, Alana got all that and *much* more. There's just something about a small child. Without a bone marrow match and donor she wouldn't live a fraction of the life that Chris did. Alana's story quickly became *the* story in Hawaii. She was one of those rare people whom everyone knew on a first name basis. Where Chris's bone marrow registration drives drew hundreds of people, Alana's drew *thousands*. The turnouts were so big they outgrew the early venues. Eventually Honolulu's Blaisdell Arena had to be put to use, hosting 30-thousand people over six weekends!

Alana's drive wiped out Honolulu's supply of surgical gloves so they flew in more supplies from the outer islands. And when there was no spare pair of surgical gloves to be found anywhere in the state, family members flew to Los Angeles and bought out Costco's supply. Then there was something else-someone had to draw all that blood. When the local blood centers ran out of manpower, doctors, nurses and dentists donated their time. There was even talk that some people who maybe weren't fully certified to draw blood did so anyway, poking alongside the pros. I don't think anyone who came to register would have cared. I didn't.

What made Alana's story so special is how it galvanized a community. Hawaii is a lovely place with a lot of fun things to do. But there's a price to pay for that. With all those distractions, it's usually hard to get people to come together. Not in this case. Many people flew in from the outer islands in the hopes that they could be the one to save a little girl's life.

I was swept up in it, all too happy to report on Alana and to encourage more people to come to her drives. I probably got a little too preachy on the air, a semi-violation of journalistic objectivity. I couldn't help myself. It just felt right. But there was a sad side to it too. Practically lost in the Alana coverage was the man who really got the leukemia awareness thing in Hawaii rolling-Chris Pablo.

I've always believed the best stories on TV and in print are the stories *behind* the stories. Chris Pablo was a big story again for unfortunate reasons. While one couldn't deny that Alana's publicity was good thing for good many people, one couldn't help but wonder if Chris Pablo felt left out. Bringing it up ran the risk of making Chris look jealous. Jealousy rarely plays well in the public eye. My station decided it was a fair question because we figured we weren't the only ones thinking about it. The question was how to pose that question to Chris.

I called Chris and told him I needed to speak to him. We agreed to meet outside Blaisdell Arena at one of Alana Dung's weekend bone marrow registration drives. On the ride over to the arena I rehearsed in my head what I would say to Chris when I saw him. I probably did it a half-dozen times before settling on what I thought were the right words. Of course when it came time to ask the question for real, what came out of my mouth wasn't as good as what was in my head.

"Uh Chris, knowing that you did so much to educate people about bone marrow transplants and having hundreds of people come out to your drives, but then seeing *thousands* of people and so much media attention for Alana Dung; is it hard not to feel a bit jealous?" I asked.

Chris let out a deep sigh and just looked at me for a few moments. I think the question made him sad. Then he looked away at nothing in particular as if to ponder a response. He turned back, looked me in the eye and softly said, "It's only human nature to feel a little jealous, but it's okay. At the same time I'm praying that Alana will find her match here, I'm praying that I'll find my match. The same people that are coming for her are the same people who could match for me (same ethnicity)."

Chris made it easy on me. I think he sensed how awkward I felt asking the question, but he had to know it was coming, if not from me, then from someone else. And he was right about possibly finding his match at Alana's events. Even though the people were coming there for her, their genetic information would be entered into a computer database which would compare their data with all other transplant candidates, wherever they were in the world.

Inside the Blaisdell Arena, Alana's drives were enormously successful and many were entertaining. One of her drives featured Hawaii's most famous musician of the time-Israel Kamakawiwo'ole. The fact that Iz could make it there, let alone perform really said something about his desire to help out a little girl whom he had fallen in love with. Iz was morbidly obese and weighed somewhere in the neighborhood of 800 pounds. He was on oxygen and was the only living brother of what was once a large family in number and size. He could hardly walk, so they brought in a forklift to lift him on stage.

Many people came to Alana's drive that day for the sole purpose of seeing Iz play. He played with passion and purpose, constantly needling people who came to see him to get off their okoles and go over to a testing site. Iz strummed his ukulele, which looked miniature in his massive hands, and his melodious voice carried across the arena soothing the hearts of those anxiously waiting their turn to get pricked with a needle. As a reporter sometimes you just know when you're on the scene of something special, something *bigger* than the event itself, something lasting, something life changing. You feel it in your gut. I didn't just feel it in my gut; I felt it in my bones-where the marrow lives.

I got back to the station, typed my story into the computer, printed out copies for the editor and me and voiced it. It was an hour before the six o'clock news; plenty of time for the editor to put together a nice piece, and time for me to bang out the anchor lead and tag. It doesn't matter how good the reporter's piece is if it isn't set up with a well-written and delivered anchor lead. I wasn't worried about the delivery part. If any two people could empathize with a family's struggle with cancer it was Sandra Sagisi and Dave Carlin.

Sandra had a young daughter not much older than Alana Dung. When parents of healthy children see sick kids, I don't think there's anyone who doesn't envision a role reversal. Sandra was also just a couple of years removed from her own very public and traumatic battle with breast cancer. Dave, and this isn't nearly as well known, was more than a TV partner to Sandra. He was a great friend and a source of strength for her. On days when she was too sick to drive herself to doctors' appointments, Dave took her. So I knew those two could more than add some emotion and credibility to my story that night.

I watched the news from my desk, and everything I thought Dave and Sandra could do they did. Glen Foley edited the piece, doing a fine job piecing together the right pictures with the right sound and emotion. I got emotional watching it on air. And then something else happened. What felt so good in my bones just a couple of hours earlier felt miserable in my heart. I felt good about the reporting effort, but I didn't feel good about myself. I didn't understand. Why should I feel bad about myself for doing such good for so many others? So I prayed on it. I prayed to St. Jude.

When the newscast was over Dave and Sandra came through the newsroom with congratulations.

"Great story Kev. Really nice," they said.

"Ah thanks. You guys did a good job too," I told them.

But I still didn't feel much better and I couldn't figure out why. I had given what I thought was a huge part of myself to a noble process. I did several heartfelt and meaningful reports on Alana Dung and Chris Pablo and became something of a crusader. But a part of me felt empty. I had done a lot, but not enough. And there was only one way to feel better. I picked up the phone and I called my wife Jean.

"Honey after you pick me up we're going to go over to Blaisdell Arena to register in Alana's bone marrow registration drive," I told her.

"We are?" she asked curiously.

"Yes. I can't live with myself expecting others to register and not do it myself. And I want you to do it too."

Jean wasn't exactly thrilled because of her past experiences with blood donation. Her skinny arms and tiny veins didn't exactly make her an easy stick. A few weeks earlier we'd bumped up the life insurance and a nurse came by the apartment to draw blood and take our vitals. She poked Jean four times and had no blood in the vial to show for it. So memories of that day stuck with Jean on this one.

We parked our car in the garage next to TGI Friday's and walked across Ward Avenue to Blaisdell Arena hand-in-hand. Just before we walked in I told Jean that it was very unlikely we'd match either Alana Dung, or Chris Pablo because of the different ethnicities. But I told her *"I will be a match for somebody."*

The numbers certainly didn't support my bravado. The chance of being a bone marrow match for an unrelated person at the time was about one in 200. But I felt confident that my number would come up and I'd have a chance to save a life. It wasn't just hope. *I felt it*-in my heart, my soul and in my bones.

Dozens of chair-desk combinations that looked like they could've been borrowed from the local Baskin Robbins ice cream parlor littered the arena floor. They were filled with people giving two tablespoons of blood. After a couple of pages of paperwork, I plunked myself down, a technician plunged a cold needle into my arm and I promptly passed out, falling through the illegal side of the desk.

Fortunately it was a short way down, but it wasn't a clean fall. The back of my head and shoulders were on the floor and my legs were mostly tangled up in the crooked metal arm that attaches the desktop to the chair. My wife and others managed to untangle me and eventually I was completely on the floor, flat on my back. My body wasn't moving but my world was spinning and my stomach was queasy. Then a very big Hawaiian man came into focus.

"Whoa! That haole boy looks *white!*"

It wasn't big Iz, but even with my blurry vision I'm guessing the guy went about 350. He was nice though and fetched me a cold rag for my forehead. Someone else put a towel under my head to act as a pillow. I actually got comfortable on the cool concrete floor. Pretty soon I started to feel a lot better and the medical staff moved me to one of the cushier chairs on the arena risers. A couple snacks and a few bottles of water later, I felt like myself again. Actually I felt better than when I came. The blood draw was rough, but it was done and I finally felt like I went all the way. And Jean? She did great. No drama at all.

After we left the arena we went to Sunday evening Mass at The Cathedral of Our Lady of Peace on Bishop Street in downtown Honolulu. The Cathedral was old and had loads of architectural character. It was wedged in between tall buildings so you almost couldn't get a good enough look at it to see it for all its majesty. It was also right on the edge of Chinatown. Chinatown was the seediest part of Honolulu, so you were never quite sure what you might see from a sociological standpoint.

Inside the Cathedral it was gorgeous. There was an abundance of marble and the pews were darkly stained solid wood. There were enough pillars to hold up the roofs of two Cathedrals, let alone one. It was long and skinny. From the back, it must have been a good pitching wedge to the front. Not all of the pews faced forward toward the altar. About half were along the side walls facing in. Instead of looking at the back of peoples' heads, you saw a lot more faces. It also gave the priest a chance to take a stroll to the center of the Cathedral to give his homily.

I spent most of the Mass sitting next my wife quietly reflecting on my day at Alana's drive. I looked down at my left arm and saw a couple of drops of blood on a sterile gauze pad being held in place with a clear strip of surgical tape. I thought about Alana and Chris. I thought about Israel and the thousands of people who donated their blood, time, money and hearts. And I felt good about myself becoming a generous soul, giving until it hurts they say.

Between the Profession of Faith and the Our Father I prayed quietly on my own to St. Jude, asking that he would give strength, peace of heart, and of course bone marrow matches to the families of Alana Dung and Chris Pablo. I prayed for me, that I would someday turn up as a bone marrow match and have the courage to go through with the surgical extraction. I felt good about myself as a person and as a Christian, secure in my faith, feeling generous of heart.

My quiet reflection didn't last long and my generosity was tested in a most usual way. Out of the right corner of my eye I saw someone walking through the pews as the entire congregation sat. It was a man in tattered clothes, with a couple weeks growth on his face. It had probably been about as long since he'd taken a bath. I recognized the face, but not the place. Within seconds it started coming back to me. Most days on the ride home from work The Bus would drop me off in Chinatown, where I would wait for the transfer. Between buses I'd spend the time people watching. I saw the same folks and the same patterns. There was the old haole guy who would feed the pigeons his fast food scraps and let them drink water out of his Styrofoam food box. There was the 40-something drug addicted American Indian Princess in the buckskin vest who challenged anyone and everyone to a fight. And then there was a guy who always seemed to have his head in a trashcan. It was this very same trash diver who was about to invade my personal space in the pew.

Most people work their way through church pews by sliding their feet side to side. Not the trash guy. He was walking straight ahead, one foot in front of the other. He looked drunk, or high, and I wasn't sure what he wanted because I couldn't make out what he was saying to fellow parishioners. But it was obvious he was making people very uncomfortable. When he got to me he presented a small basket and asked, "You got any money?"

"What for?" I asked.

"For *me*," he said, as if I was an idiot for asking such a stupid question.

If there ever was a man who could've used God in his life, this may have been the guy. As Christians we're taught God loves the poor and we are to share with those less fortunate. Everyone else in my pew turned him down. I was the last one in the row and I didn't know what to do. I felt conflicted. I was just an hour or so removed from Alana's bone marrow registration drive and what I thought was my most charitable gift ever. But something about the church invader made me resentful. He chose to bully us and make us feel bad if we didn't give. I figured he needed my prayers more than he needed my money. And just as that thought popped into my head, a church usher popped up alongside the pew and escorted the homeless man out the door.

A couple of minutes later the real collection basket came by and I threw five dollars in. I wondered about the beggar, and if I had given him the five bucks, would he have spent it already on booze and drugs? Then I thought he might actually get some of my money indirectly from Catholic Charities. After Mass I walked outside the Cathedral I said to myself, "This day has really tested my faith on so many levels."

Almost as a soon as I said it there was the same guy hitting parishioners up for change as they walked out of church. They were a lot more generous outside church than they were in it. I'm pretty sure they weren't giving from the heart. They gave to avoid a hassle.

CHAPTER THREE

Alana Finds Her Match

JUST A FEW DAYS AFTER HER SECOND BIRTHDAY ALANA Dung's family received the best news they'd heard in months. A preliminary match for Alana had been found. As much as the extended Hawaii family hoped the match would come from a local donor, this call came from Taiwan. Of the 120,000 registrants in the Tzu-Chi Foundation's Bone Marrow Registry, one blinked when Alana's information passed through the computer.

Once the word got out it was almost as if the extended Hawaii community was ready to dig an imu and cook a pig in the ground. But the Dung family knew better and treated the good news with cautious optimism. It was after all a *preliminary* match. The potential donor would have to undergo an extensive physical examination and be largely disease free. Even then he or she could opt out. Fortunately the match turned out to be of good quality and the donor was willing and able to move forward.

As the rest of Hawaii celebrated, Alana was already starting to live a life of semi-isolation. Lots of people wanted to stop by the Dung family home in Nuuanu to wish her well, but with Alana's weakened immune system most people had to stay away for fear of spreading germs. They kept in touch with Alana's parents by phone, and if they couldn't get them on the line, chances were there was an item on the news or in the newspaper to keep track.

Eventually Alana's doctors felt her best chance of survival required a change of venue. The famed Fred Hutchinson Cancer Research Center in Seattle, Washington would be her best option for treatment. Her parents took extended leaves from work so they could be with her. The grandparents went too. The family babysitter came along to look after Alana's six-year-old older brother Spencer. And Alana's

Uncle, Dr. Alvin Chung, left behind a thriving dental practice in Kahala to support his extended family. "My priority is to be here with my family. I can always return to my practice later. Fortunately my patients have been understanding," he told the Honolulu-Star Bulletin.

Hoping to slip out of town relatively unnoticed the Dungs booked a flight on an overnight redeye. Even so, people found out and turned out. Most were family and friends, but there were plenty of strangers. Even with the fuss that Mom and Dad hoped to avoid, Alana embraced it. "She *loved* people and interacted well with friends and strangers. For her I imagine it was just another adventure," mother Adelia Dung said.

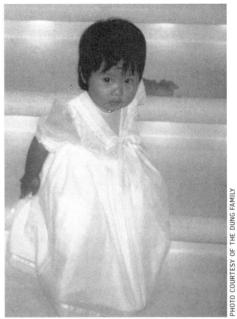

Alana Dung all dressed up and looking beautiful.

It was hardly just another adventure for the flight crew on the Northwest Airlines DC-10. It knew Alana's condition and made accommodations. "We were concerned about germs," Adelia remembers. "We were concerned about exposure to passengers who might be coughing or ill. We boarded last and were given the first few rows of seats."

Quite a few passengers recognized Alana from the news and knew she was going to transplant. Most red eye travelers take the overnight flight because it's quiet, with fewer passengers and usually less drama. This was definitely not the usual red eye. There was a buzz about the plane. Travelers knew they were witness to something special. Alana sat in the first row with her mother by her side. Shortly after wheels up, Alana put her head down in her mother's lap. Adelia stroked her daughter's hair and it wasn't long before the little girl fell asleep.

It had been a long week leading up to the trip filled with lab tests and doctors' office visits. The dark sky over the Pacific and the constant whir of the jet engines was the perfect prescription for rest. As little Alana peacefully slept dreaming of princesses and Sesame Street characters, her parents, her uncle and grandparents anxiously thought about what awaited them on the other end. The pretty flight attendants in their stylish navy blue uniforms came by from time to time with caring smiles, light conversation and the occasional beverage and snack.

The red and gray colored Northwest commercial jet pulled up to the terminal at Seattle/Tacoma Airport right around the time most people were starting their day. Their arrival on the mainland was not unlike their departure from the islands. The Dungs had friends in the Emerald City and plenty of them came to the airport for moral support. Fellow passengers wished the Dungs well before going on their way. After careful hellos and goodbyes, Alana's father Steven and her uncle Alvin went to the baggage carousel to fetch the luggage. Adelia attended to Alana who was waking up and brother Spencer who was starting to stir too.

The Dungs secured ground transportation and made the half-hour drive to Madison Park. Their three bedroom rented condominium was spacious and warm. The view was breathtaking. "We were on Lake Washington. It was beautiful and the neighborhood was charming," Adelia remembers.

The home away from home wasn't so different from Hawaii in a couple of ways. It's damp and humid in both places most mornings. In the islands mauka showers drench the Ko'olau and Waianae Mountains. Thin mist drifts down and the warm, rising tropical sun illuminates it with colors of the rainbow. In Seattle one only has to look over at Mt. Rainier to see a similar sight; rain falling on the higher elevation. What gets wet becomes impossibly green.

There are notable differences. Island rain and mist from the mountains extends only a mile or so away. In Washington, the reach is much farther and longer lasting. Seattle's morning rain often becomes a part of the afternoon lunch and sometimes the dinner hour. Obviously it's much cooler too. Metaphorically speaking the weather in both places is to be drunk like coffee. It adds flavor to the land and the people. In Hawaii it's Lion Kona coffee. In Seattle-Starbucks.

Too young for coffee Alana rested the morning of her arrival on the mainland. Between snoozes she watched children's videos and played with toys. Her doctors did not want to waste any time in beginning the transplant process and were expecting her later in the day. As Alana eased into the day, her mother Adelia and father Steven got the house in order and worked the phones to get a head start on what would be a very busy day.

When afternoon came it was time to go to the hospital, which was just a short drive away. The Dungs knew they would get the latest and the greatest medical treatment at the Fred Hutchinson Cancer Research Center. That is why they came. What they didn't know, but were pleasantly surprised to find out, was that most of the staff could more than empathize with their plight. They really "got" what Alana and her family was going through. "Everyone we met had their own story- a spouse who died of cancer, or a family member who survived. They had a passion for what they did and they always communicated hope," Adelia recalls.

One of the ways doctors and clinicians communicated hope was by looking years into the future, anticipating where Alana would be in terms of recovery and appearance. Alana's Hickman Line, which led to, a chemo port inside her chest needed to be replaced. Adelia could hardly believe the conversation with the doctor who did the swap. "As we were walking to the recovery room he told me they placed it in a different spot than where doctors did in Honolulu. He told me 'When her breasts grow there will be no scar.' I thought to myself I am just worrying about making it to her third birthday and they are talking about *breasts and scars*!" Adelia says with a chuckle.

Humor and conversation of future life experiences like puberty and who knows what else helped the mood. It pushed anxiety farther back in the mind and reminded everyone around Alana that a positive attitude was as critical to the mission as the medicine. When times are bleak, hope is all you have.

The constant tending to Alana was exhausting so the family worked in shifts to ease the burden. Adelia spent the bulk of her time at the hospital, but she would zip back to the rental house in the late afternoon to spend time with son Spencer. When Adelia wasn't with Spencer at home, or with Alana at the hospital, she napped. On a good day she could squeeze in five hours of sleep. Adelia knew if she was going to be able to take care of her daughter and family, she would have to take care of herself. She did when she could.

Norah Chung, Alana's maternal grandmother, pulled some of the longest shifts of all. It wasn't uncommon for her to stay from 11am until 11pm. She did it to give others a break and because she had a special connection with her granddaughter. "No one can comfort Alana like my mom," Alana's Uncle Alvin Chung told the Honolulu Star-Bulletin. "She kind of sings to her and asks her who is popo's (Chinese for grandmother) darling, and Alana will say 'Lana'."

Alana's room was large and cheerful. It had the standard hospital equipment, but plenty of fun stuff. "There was always a balloon or two," Adelia Dung remembers. "We were always engaged. Alana sang, danced, played with stickers, watched videotapes and was read to."

When the music came on, Alana danced with her Elmo doll. Elmo was a gift from a hospital cleaning lady. The cleaner fell in love with the little girl after Alana reached out and said "Hi." The simple "hi" meant so much to the woman that she wanted to give Alana something special. "The woman said in all the years she has been working here, nobody ever did something like that," Alana's grandfather Tai Yau Chung told the Honolulu-Star Bulletin.

Home video cameras recorded Alana dancing. So did the news crews, which made the trip. When the video of Alana swaying back and forth to the sound of Disney's *It's a Small World* played back home in Honolulu, it was as big as any other news story.

A week before the scheduled transplant, Alana underwent radiation treatment in a cage-like crib in the hospital basement twice a day. The radiation was painless, but Alana had to be in the room by herself while it was going on. That was one of the hardest parts of all. Until now her parents had been there to comfort her and hold her hand through therapy and other rough cancer treatments. This time Alana was mostly on her own.

The hospital allowed one exception to the isolation mandate. Alana could bring a stuffed animal friend in with her for comfort. A clever child-life specialist figured out a way to make Barney a part of the treatment process. Before giving Alana a dose of radiation, Lisa Lange cleverly took measurements of the purple dinosaur. Seeing that the process didn't hurt Barney, Alana figured it wouldn't hurt her either. With pediatric medicine it's often a case of whatever works. And in Alana's case, Barney worked wonderfully.

After a week's worth of radiation and chemotherapy, Alana's bone marrow and immune system were completely wiped out. The process left her tired and nauseated. Watching his younger sister was especially rough on six-year-old Spencer Dung as reported by Rod Ohiro in The Honolulu Star Bulletin. "If medicine is good for you, how come Alana is throwing up?" Spencer demanded of Lisa Lange.

"I asked him if all the cells in her body were good cells?" recalls Lisa. "He said 'Not all of them were good.' Then I told him sometimes medicine that is good for us makes us feel bad."

After the transplant prep work there was no turning back. With no bone marrow and white blood cells to fight off disease, Alana's only hope for survival was a successful transplant, one in which Alana's body would accept the donated bone marrow instead of attacking it as a foreign invader.

The donor's marrow wouldn't come for several days and would be personally delivered by one of Alana's physicians. Dr. Jean Sanders would fly to Taiwan to pick it up. Until then Alana would have to wait. There were other children going through similar times at Fred Hutchinson, so Alana had something in common with them. She also had a kinship with adults. The hospital staff did its best to keep things loose. "They were young and energetic," Adelia Dung says.

Some days the nurses wore bright-colored matching socks. On other days they'd wear hats. The key was to make it look and feel less like a hospital and treat the kids like kids, not diseases.

Alana's new bone marrow arrived in a bag similar to what you'd put leftovers in. The plastic was thicker and there was no Ziploc of course. You could see right in. When marrow is extracted from a donor's body it's a thick, rich red. When it settles, it layers. The lighter stem cells rise to the top. Like oil separates from vinegar, stem cells separate from the marrow. It looks like chicken soup on top of red goo.

The delivery process is pretty cool too. The marrow pack rides inside a small cooler carried by an entrusted courier. The marrow is wedged between cold gel packs to keep it fresh. If you're flying commercially you don't check the cooler with the baggage or put it in the overhead bin. It's either under the seat in front of you, or on your lap. If you go to the bathroom it comes with you. The cooler never leaves the courier's side. Many coolers have medical wording and prominent logos stamped on the side. I've carried one before and I can tell you it gets a lot of attention from anyone who sees it. You feel the stares and you just know everyone's playing the guessing game about what's inside.

Dr. Sanders brought the donor's marrow to Alana's side and it wasn't long before the transplant was underway. The bag of marrow was hung on a pole and the contents flowed down through a skinny tube and into the two-year-old's body. Just like a blood transfusion it's simple and profoundly beautiful; an amazing contrast to the complicated science and procedure that leads up to it.

As the bag drained into the plastic tubing which fed Alana, her parents, her brother Spencer and other family members watched in amazement and prayed that it would take. It would take about an hour for the transplant to be complete, but days, if not weeks to see if her body would resist rejection.

The early days following the transplant were an anxious time. There was daily blood work and chest x-rays aplenty. Infection was always a possibility. After two weeks of observation and treatment doctors put her chance of survival near 70 percent. She left the Cancer Center to spend quiet time with her family in the rented home by the lake. After four months of rest and relaxation lakeside it was time for Alana and family to return to their island hale.

Word of the homecoming spread like news of a North Shore winter swell. The wave of excitement was like nothing the islands had ever seen. Honolulu would once again be the scene of a festive celebration, complete with friends, family and the ever-present media. The flashbulbs from cameras popped, but nothing sparkled more than the smile of little Alana. She was front-page news and the lead story on all the television and radio stations. It really didn't get much better, or as they in the islands no ka oi'-the best.

It would be Thanksgiving soon and the Dungs were thankful for their daughter's improving health and just to be home again. So many people wanted to visit with her, but few got close. Alana's immune system was still relatively weak and susceptible to germs. With all the usual holiday hugging and kissing there was a very real concern that someone with a sniffle could leave a part of himself or herself long after they left. Alana couldn't afford to share in any of that, so when visitors came to the house most had to settle for a wave through the window.

By December Alana was beginning to feel much better and could see visitors without a barrier between them. The barriers came down completely on Christmas Day when Alana and family made their first public appearance at the Aloha Bowl. Alana was the game's guest of honor and was brought out to the 50-yard line where she was introduced to thousands of cheering fans, many of whom fought back tears when they saw the toddler standing proud and looking healthy. Alana wore a red and white dress, with a straw hat and sunglasses. She looked adorable and sporty. Then much to her surprise Santa Claus came parachuting from the sky and landed not far away. He came running over and handed her a game ball. Alana loved it and the crowd went wild.

The game wasn't bad either and even ended up as an ESPN Classic. Navy backup quarterback Ben Fay came off the bench and led the Midshipmen to two fourth quarter touchdowns and a 42-38 Navy win over the University of California. It was the last game at Cal for head coach Steve Mariucci, who would later go on to coach the San Francisco 49ers and the Detroit Lions. Few remember all those "little" details, but everyone remembers Alana and Santa.

The New Year would bring new hope for continued health and happiness. Alana was a good patient her mom says, knowledgeable about her condition and willing to give precautionary instruction to anyone who got close. "Wash your hands!" Alana would say.

With Alana seemingly in the clear, the Dungs started to get back into a normal life routine. Aunties, uncles, grandparents and cousins came by for visits, family dinners and Da kine. Eight months after transplant, a check of Alana's blood brought unexpected news. Alana's Aunt, Bridget Dung, wrote about it in the Kapiolani Community College Spectrum. "My brother called and told us that the leukemia had returned. We were devastated. The doctors advised that another transplant would not cure her. It would be too risky."

It was a tough call to make and a tough one to receive. It was strikingly similar to the one Steven Dung made to his younger sister Bridget a year earlier. Both calls were made in the month of March. Both involved an awkward delivery of painful news and an uncomfortable silence on the other end. And both siblings arrived at the same conclusion-they would smother Alana with even more love than she had already. "We spent whatever moments we could with her as we knew she did not have much time left," Bridget said.

The whole family came together for Alana's third birthday party in May. It was a spirited affair with great fun and food. As much fun as it was, few adults could get past the nagging feeling that it could be Alana's last party. The kids were busy with other things-laughing; playing and assembling Alana's newly opened toys.

By October, seven months after relapse, Alana was still doing reasonably well and well enough to tussle with visiting cousins. "Cousins visiting her Monday night wanted to feed her," Steven Dung told Helen Altonn of the Honolulu Star-Bulletin. "She told them, '*Alana feed herself!*'" She also fought with them over candy. "We had to scold her," Steven remembers.

The next day started like any other. Alana woke up early, asked to watch a video, but fell back asleep. Between 8:30 and 9:30 that Tuesday morning Alana took a dramatic turn for the worse. "It caught us by surprise. A total change," Steven said.

Alana woke up a different person from the one who dozed off an hour earlier. She was unresponsive when she awoke but "Waited for everyone to come home," Steven says. Her parents and brother, Spencer, were by her side. Other close family members raced across Oahu to the Dung home in Nuuanu for one last goodbye.

Alana held on for another couple of hours before peacefully slipping away at 12:45pm.

"The loss and pain is always present," says Alana's mother. "You just have to learn to accept the loss and move forward. We recognized we were blessed to have had her. The day she died someone asked, 'If God gave you a choice of having her three years or none at all, what would you choose?'"

It was a question that didn't need to be answered.

CHAPTER FOUR

Chris Pablo Waits and Finally Gets a Match

THE BIG NORTH SHORE SWELLS STARTING ROLLING INTO the Hawaiian Islands a little early, closer to Halloween instead of Christmas. Not that anyone was complaining. And with the early arrival of quality waves there was a sense of anticipation that this could be *the year*. It had been some time since the last Eddie Aikau surfing contest on the North Shore of Oahu, which is only held when conditions are near perfect and waves reach 30 feet, and beyond. You can't really plan for The Eddie because no one really knows when the conditions will be just right. But over the years when the forecast and conditions presented themselves, organizers would put out notice The Eddie Aikau was on.

Word about The Eddie Aikau drifted across the island like the sweet smell of burning sugarcane. You heard it on the radio, people talked about it on The Bus and it was pretty easy to see who at the workplace was looking to pau hana (party after work). Surfers from around the world flew in, hoping to make all the necessary connections and be a part of the granddaddy of all surfing competitions.

There's a saying in Hawaii "Eddie Would Go". It's a spoken honor that speaks to one of Hawaii's favorite and bravest sons. Born in Maui in 1946, Eddie's family moved to Oahu when he was 13. Eddie was a decent student, but the lure of the ocean was too much for him. He dropped out of high school and took a job at the Dole Cannery. When he wasn't picking and packing pineapples he was having his pick of the monstrous waves at Waimea Bay. There are casual surfers and there are big wave riders. The difference is as big as the ocean is wide. The casual surfer might go to Laniakea or Chun's reef; catch a few chest high rights, and sooth in the smooth ride, sun and saltwater bath.

There's nothing soothing about big wave riding. At Waimea Bay one will risk life and appendage to paddle out past a crushing shore break, only to have his nuts in his throat when he drops in on a forty-footer. There's plenty to fear out here and there's no shame in it. You can see it on the faces of those who've paddled out. But that's not what fellow big wave riders saw when Eddie first paddled out and zipped down the face of a massive wave with a smile as big as the wave itself. They saw the next Duke Kahanamoku. Duke was the Hawaiian surfing and swimming legend who essentially introduced the rest of the world to surfing back in the 1920's. Like Duke Eddie didn't need a last name. If you said Eddie everyone knew whom you were talking about.

Eddie became the first professional lifeguard on the North Shore hired by the City and County of Honolulu in 1968. He was in charge of a stretch along King Kamehameha Highway, which was home to some of the most legendary and challenging surf spots in the world; including Pipeline, Waimea, Velzyland and Sunset Beach. Eddie got a good look and first chance to ride the waves each morning, but he was hardly the stereotypical beach/surfing bum. He was a superior waterman who was named lifeguard of the year in 1971. He never lost a person on his watch at the crushing surf of Waimea Bay, which is almost like saying a top cop in Spanish Harlem or the Badlands of North Philadelphia never had a murder on his shift. The saying "Eddie Would Go" was born out of his willingness to pull troubled surfers and swimmers out of treacherous conditions where most others didn't dare go.

The same saying would be applied posthumously after a fateful voyage at sea involving Eddie and the Polynesian Voyaging Society. It was 1978 and Eddie was growing closer to his Hawaiian roots. He wanted to express that by embarking on what was supposed to be a 30-day, 2,500-mile journey retracing the steps his ancestors took when they sailed between Hawaii and Tahiti. The weather was bad on March 16, the day they left Magic Island on the leeward side of Oahu. The crew of the Hokule'a, a modern version of an ancient double-hulled sailing canoe probably should have waited. But there was pressure to go. Governor George Ariyoshi and news crews came out for the launch. Like the Challenger Shuttle disaster in 1985, an already risky journey suddenly became more risky because the participants felt there was a schedule to be met. Eddie Aikau acknowledged as much in his last interview with radio disc jockey Ron Jacobs that was reported in the Honolulu Star-Bulletin, "(The pressure) from the media and all our families was becoming unbelievable from all over. But once we sail out there we'll be all right. We can settle down and be ourselves."

The Hokule'a never really had a chance. It started taking on water almost as soon as it left. It capsized in the Molokai Channel in heavy surf and strong wind. After a night of clinging to the side of the voyager crew members wondered what to do. Flares did nothing to attract the attention of passing ships. Hope like the Hokule'a was sinking fast. Land was still in sight and Eddie estimated the island of Lanai was about twelve miles away. There was never really a doubt about whether Eddie would go. So he climbed on his surfboard and put on a lifejacket. He told the crew he thought he could make it to land in about five hours. Almost as soon as he left the Hokule'a he tossed his lifejacket aside for better mobility. He was never seen again. The U.S. Coast Guard eventually found and saved the rest of the Hokule'a crew.

Chris Pablo would have preferred taking in the spectacle of the Eddie Aikau surfing competition which-had it gone off-would have been a chance to voyage away from the sinking feeling that he might not make it to, or through transplant. But Chris always put on a brave face, or at least tried to when I would see him around town. I remember seeing him at a cocktail fundraiser at Aloha Tower on Honolulu Harbor on a classic fall night. Drinks were flowing and the atmosphere was festive. Chris worked the place like a politician, glad handing anyone and everyone, posing for pictures. You would have thought he was running for office. I couldn't help but notice the contrast of where Chris was in his life and where everyone else seemed to be in theirs. For them life was good, no worries. For Chris, he could never completely ignore the worrying voice that often comes with cancer.

Being the pragmatist that he was, Chris did some estate planning and made revisions to his will. "I didn't want to leave Sandy and the boys in a bad spot if it didn't work out," he said.

Chris even went so far as to have his wife Sandy make sure that his cousin Bobby was in attendance. "Bobby is a funeral director," Chris says. "So he comes over at Aloha Tower and says 'I hear you want to talk to me' and I said yes. And he says 'what about?' And I said you know my funeral in case I don't survive the upcoming transplant. And he said 'I don't want to talk about that' and walked away. He just wouldn't go there. He didn't want me thinking about anything that was negative," Chris remembers.

I watched Chris at the party from a distance, making sure to not let him notice my nosiness. After a couple of hours and a few cocktails later Chris made his way over to Jean and me. "How are you Kevin?" he asked.

"I'm tired," I said. "You look tired too," I told him.

"I am tired. I'm really tired," he huffed. "But I have good news Kevin."

"Really? What's up?" I asked Chris.

"We found a match in Taiwan."

"You did? *Whoa* that's great! When are you going to start getting ready for transplant?" I asked.

"I've already started, but there's a catch. The guy has hepatitis. So I'm trading leukemia for hepatitis, which is a lot more treatable. I've been taking medicine for a couple of weeks to see how well my body will fight it. It's not a perfect situation, but it's better than what I've got now. But, I also just found out there might be *another* potential donor who is disease free! My doctors are trying to track him down to see if he'll do it. I'll call you when I know."

Chris's face and eyes lit up when he told me about the new donor that might come into play. "Oh cool! I'm going to say Saint Jude novenas. St. Jude is the patron saint of hopeless causes, the miracle worker," I told Chris. "He's the guy you pray to when you really need help."

"Well you know I need all the help I can get Kevin. Thank you for coming tonight. I really appreciate it. Keep praying," he said.

Chris was one of the few guys I knew who would let you see him vulnerable. There was no façade. At this point it had been about six months since we'd first met and his appearance and posture had noticeably deteriorated. He was still a handsome guy, but it was clear to me his illness was sapping his energy. As brave as he was, I wasn't really sure in my heart of hearts whether he'd survive the transplant process, if he made it that far. Walking back to the parking garage I told my wife I thought there was a chance that I had seen Chris for the last time. She agreed. "Something about his eyes," Jean said. "They looked glossy. He didn't look well."

The next day we went to Mass at the Cathedral and I prayed for Chris during special intentions. Not long after that weekend the phone rang at my desk at the television station. "Kevin it's Chris Pablo."

"Hi Chris. How are you doing?"

"I'm doing great. Guess what?" he asked.

"What?" I asked sensing something was good from the tone of his voice.

"Remember that other possible match I told you about the other day at Aloha Tower? We tracked the guy down and he's willing to donate."

"That's awesome!" I told him. "How do you feel?"

"I'm just so happy, so happy," he said.

"Well I'm happy too."

The tone of my voice tipped off nosy producers who looked over and gave suggestive shrugs that I should give up the goods. Not yet because the good was getting better.

"How soon are you going to transplant?" I asked.

"I'm leaving for the City of Hope National Medical Center in Duarte, California in two weeks. I'll be there for two months. I just wanted to call and let you know and thank you for all you've done. You've been very good to me Kevin and I really appreciate it."

That phone call made all the difference in what to that point had been a slow news day. Prior to Chris's call I was working on a story about the Honolulu City Council debating the written language in work permit applications. To get what the fuss was all about you had to have an applied understanding of how local politics worked. I didn't. Our usual City Hall reporter Stacy Loe was on vacation and having a malihini like me trying to make sense of the inside baseball at Honolulu Hale made about as much sense as a throwing a soft one right down the middle to Ryan Howard. The City Hall story was boring, complicated and effected very few. It wasn't sexy and had no business airing. But in the news biz sometimes you just have time to fill.

There's an old joke in newsrooms that "someone better be dead" when the phone rings on a slow day. Not this time. Someone was alive, *very much alive* and now had a second chance at life. I covered the receiver with my hand and told the producers sitting nearby that Chris Pablo had found his bone marrow match. As I listened in my ear to Chris I could see the producers, Chris Vandercook and Sharene Saito gathering around the desk next to me with an eye and ear on my conversation. I wasn't about to hang up on the call because I was thrilled to hear about Chris's next step and renewed hope. In addition to the flurry of typing activity erupting from Sharene's fingers I saw the rundown for the 5:00 show drastically changing on my computer screen. I heard a beep, saw the City Hall slug being highlighted and then disappearing. Chris Pablo's match was the new lead and Honolulu Hale was history.

It was like a sudden bolt of energy took over the news operation, which had been limping along fueled only by strong Kona coffee and sliced pineapple that someone brought back to the station after covering a Rotary function. Because I was there with Chris from the beginning with the discovery of his golf ball, I took the lead on his follow up of finding a bone marrow match. There was a script to write, over-the-shoulder graphics to be ordered and old file tape to be pulled. We wanted Chris to come down to the studio for a live interview on the anchor desk but with show time only thirty minutes away, there was no way he'd make it across town in time.

We took a still shot of Chris smiling with the words Good News under his headshot and loaded it into the first ten seconds of the anchor read. I zipped through my reporter library tape to find the video of him and me spending time with his children at Punahou School six months earlier. Glen Foley did a dazzling edit job on short notice and just a few minutes after we aired the update the phones started ringing. People from Kauai to The Big Island called to offer their best wishes to Chris, thinking that because they saw him on TV he must be somewhere in our building. He wasn't but his story would only build on itself from there.

In its totality Chris's journey toward better health would be as lengthy and arduous as a marathon. The lead up though to the transplant would have to come at a sprinter's pace because Chris was fading fast. The delivery of the donor's marrow would have to be coordinated and timed with the start of Chris's pre-transplant chemotherapy and total body radiation. There was a lot to think about, almost too much to do, but it was everything that Chris had asked for just a short time ago.

Chris arrived at the City of Hope in early November and doctors wasted little time getting him ready for transplant. Sandy and the boys came, and someone who had been estranged from the Pablos called out of the blue. "Dad it's Chris. I'm visiting grandpa in Southern California. I'd really like to come by to see you."

"I said that would be nice," the senior Chris remembers while welling up.

The caller was Chris's eldest son who was named after him. The two Chrises hadn't seen each other or spoken for a couple of years. The reasons were related to Chris Senior's divorce from his son's mom. An unfortunate rift grew into a canyon. A family friend had been working behind the scenes to reconnect the father and son. "It was very emotional," the senior Chris remembered when his 21-year-old son walked into the hospital room. "I got my son back. We used to enjoy each other's company so much playing golf. In fact we both started playing the game right around the same time. When he called he said 'Dad do you want me to bring anything?' And I said can you bring me this week's Sports Illustrated with Tiger Woods on the cover?" Chris recalls with a hearty laugh.

The father/son reunion filled Chris up emotionally. Hopes of future rounds of golf with his oldest son, and more quality family time with sons Nate, Zack and Sandy gave Chris the positive attitude he would need before starting full body radiation and chemotherapy. The transplant prep was lengthy, boring and at times tortuous. Although the radiation wasn't painful, what Chris had to do to get ready for it wasn't exactly comfortable. "They kept pumping me full of fluids. I was constantly going to the bathroom," Chris remembers with a laugh.

To take the edge off Chris brought soothing sounds of Hawaii with him. "I had some Kealihi Reichel and The Brothers Cazimero CDs. I was in a room by myself being blasted with radiation I couldn't see or feel. It was boring. The radiation tech, Eric, would play the CDs from another room and pump the sound in. Eric started to like my taste in music, and the sounds of the islands always calmed me down. Then on the last day of a week's worth of radiation Eric told me 'Don't bring any music today. I'm taking care of the music.' So I'm in the room by myself and my wife Sandy and Eric are looking in. And I'm wondering what kind of music Eric is going to play for me. Then I hear that graduation song. You know Pomp and Circumstance? And then I realized it was my last day for radiation. I was graduating from radiation treatments. I started to cry. How Eric got that song I'll never know, but it meant so much to me."

The isolation that came with the radiation may have been tough, but at least it didn't hurt physically. Chemotherapy would take care of that part. "When I saw my nurse, Liz, come into the room one day I knew it wasn't going to be easy," Chris remembers.

The pretty 30-something blonde didn't look like her usual well put together self. "She had on the royal blue gown with these *big* royal blue gloves. I'm like uh oh. Then she hangs the orange chemo bag on the I/V pole and I'm like that stuff must be really nasty."

It was. Chris endured the worst nausea of his life but tried to maintain his sense of humor in it all. "I threw up on my bedroom slippers," he laughs. "Those things were *so ugly*-blue, green, grubby. I was looking for an excuse to get rid of them. If they were rubbuh slippuhs (flip flops) we would have just washed them off. But there's no way we could've cleaned the bedroom slippers."

After two weeks of radiation, chemotherapy and rest Chris was ready for his bone marrow transplant. Looking up at the clear bag hanging from the same pole that the chemo bag once did Chris thought about what awaited him and what he had to go through to get to this point. "I looked at it like this as a journey, a journey I wanted to experience and now it's all happening. It was a helluva ride, something new."

Chris would stay at the City of Hope for two months. He grew stronger by the day, but there was no rush to get back home. In the event of infection, it was better to be in a more sterile environment where he could be better taken care of. The match was so good and Chris had such a positive attitude that few complications resulted. The Pablos celebrated Thanksgiving in the hospital and Christmas too. They had plenty to be thankful for and the best gift of all was Chris's better health.

Chris returned home to Hawaii just after the New Year. It would be some time before things returned to normal, so he concentrated on relaxing, recovering and just feeling better. There were frequent trips to the doctor, but overall Chris hadn't felt this good in several months. He spent the time at home working with Nate and Zack on their homework and helping Sandy with chores around the house. He read The Bible, finding his favorite verse in John Chapter 9. And he thought about his donor, a lot.

After six months Chris and his anonymous donor could exchange letters that would be screened by the Hawaii Bone Marrow Donor Registry to make sure there was no way either party could figure out who the other person was and where they were from. But already some other folks who had been following the Chris Pablo story in the media had figured it out on their own. One was an astute Aloha Airlines flight attendant who noticed a man commuting back and forth between Kauai and Honolulu on the same days she would see updates about Chris and his fight against leukemia on the evening news. She knew most of the passengers on her flights by name and why they came to Honolulu on a regular basis. But she didn't know the business of her now semi-regular 50-something year old man who walked with an unusual gait. One day she told him "You know I bet you're *da guy*. Every time I see you, I later see Chris Pablo on TV talking about his updates. It's gotta be you. You're both Filipino and about the same age."

After the flight attendant said it Roger Ariola started wondering too. He started paying attention to the news coverage around the days he flew to Honolulu. Sure enough there was often an update about Chris on TV. Roger wouldn't know if he was da guy for a year, but in his heart of hearts he suspected it was he indeed.

Roger registered as a potential donor after seeing two-year-old Alana Dung on the news. He didn't know Alana personally, but her leukemia story and her struggle to find a bone marrow match touched him deeply. He saw her massive bone marrow drives at the Blaisdell Arena but couldn't bring himself to be there, because as he would tell you, he doesn't like crowds. Roger felt compelled to register as a bone marrow donor somewhere else, a place a lot more quiet and private with the hope that he might turn up as the match who could save the little girl's life.

By any measure Roger Ariola had a tough life. Thirty years prior life was wonderful. Roger was 19-years-old, engaged to be married, and had a special talent for making cars go fast. Muscle cars were big back then and nobody in the Salt Lake section of Honolulu was better at souping up cars than Roger. His services were in demand; he was in love and the future looked as bright as sun reflecting off the sand.

Roger was a dutiful son to his mother and anyone else in need. On a night that his mother was cooking dinner for him and his fiancé, Roger ran an errand to fetch vegetables from the store. Along the way he noticed a car in a ditch just over a rise in the road. He pulled over and offered to help. The car was stuck and couldn't be driven out. The stranded motorist didn't know what to do. Roger did and he didn't hesitate to put a plan in action. The only option was to tow it out. Roger went to his vehicle to get a tow chain.

As he was attaching the chain to the back of the stuck car, another speeding car came hurtling over the rise in the road and lost control. The car crashed into Roger, pinning him between the bumpers and crushing his legs. He screamed out in pain as witnesses rushed to his side. It was a mighty struggle to pull the heavy cars apart. Rescuers eventually got him out. He didn't make it home for dinner and he would never be the same.

Several hours later Roger woke up in a hospital room confused and in considerable pain. He was still groggy from the heavy meds, but was alert just enough to know something was out of balance. He didn't feel as heavy on the bottom part of the hospital bed, as if his body didn't have the normal sink into the mattress. Part of that could've been the delusional effects of the pain medication, but he wasn't so sure and wanted to take a closer look. When he pulled back the covers he had his answer. Large portions of both legs were gone. Here he was being a Good Samaritan and he lost his legs for the effort.

Not only did Roger lose his legs, he also lost faith. "I turned into the biggest asshole in the world," he told me years later with a hint of shame and certain sarcasm. "I was mad at God and mad at the world."

Who wouldn't understand? Here's a guy trying to do the right thing, *God's work* no less, and he ends up a double amputee. Alana's struggle made Roger take a closer look at his own life. He didn't want her to die, and he didn't want to feel emotionally dead anymore. "I just couldn't keep living the way I was living," he says. "I didn't want that little girl to die."

The next time he flew to Oahu to visit relatives he took a detour over to Queen's Medical Center. He rolled up his sleeve and hoped that he might be the one to match Alana. He didn't match her, but he matched someone else. And that person needed Roger's marrow every bit as much as Alana needed a match too.

Chris Pablo (L) meets Roger Ariola, his bone marrow donor.

PHOTO COURTESY OF CHRIS PABLO

Six months after Chris received his bone marrow transplant he received a letter forwarded from the Hawaii Bone Marrow Donor Registry. It read, "Be well my friend." Chris wrote back with a similar message that was grateful, simple and profound. "I just wanted to say thank you. Thank you for letting me live," Chris remembers fondly.

About a year after Chris's transplant the Hawaii Bone Marrow Donor Registry had a luncheon to honor past bone marrow donors and volunteers who organized bone marrow registration jobs and drew blood among other things. The billed highlight of the day would be the revealing of Chris Pablo's donor. Chris would finally meet his match. All the Hawaii media were there. "I had about five wireless microphones and their transmitter packs on my body. I had to watch what I said-no bad words," he says with a hearty laugh. "And when I had to go to the bathroom I was all tangled up in the wires. It was funny. I don't know how one of those transmitters and microphones didn't end up in the toilet," slapping his knee for effect.

The organizers called several past bone marrow donors to the stage and thanked them for being the ultimate volunteers. The spectacle on stage led to some serious speculation at the Pablo family's table about who their guy was. "I think it's that guy over there in the Aloha shirt," Sandy Pablo said while pointing him out.

"Nah. Nah it's that guy in the shorts and blue shirt," thought Chris and son Zack.

The point is no one in the crowd knew for sure and the drama was building. One-by-one the donors started leaving the stage. The answer would be revealed by who was left alone. And then there was one. It was Roger, standing all alone on his prostheses, but not for long.

"We rushed the stage, *just rushed it,*" Chris told me while cradling a steaming cup of dark roasted Starbuck's Coffee. "We just had to get to him fast. I hugged him and squeezed him so hard I think I may have knocked the wind out of him a little bit. What did I say? I guess I just thanked him for saving my life. Oh and something else. When we were off the stage I pulled him aside and said Roger are you allergic to shrimp? He said 'no' and I was like yeah!"

In taking on Roger's marrow, Chris inherited Roger's allergies or lack of them. Chris had always had a taste for seafood, but would break out in hives if he ate a decent amount of shrimp. On occasion he would slip up and have a shrimp or two, always mindful not to overdo it or run the risk of a most unpleasant itch fest. Now he had license to indulge in all things from the ocean. The next time he ate shrimp it was jumbo, in variety and portion.

Chris likes to say he was blessed with cancer when he was diagnosed with leukemia. And he was blessed with cancer a second time some ten years after transplant. The second go around wasn't nearly as rough as the first, but he still had to have surgery on his neck to make sure the cancer didn't spread down his throat, which it didn't. "Twice is enough to be blessed with cancer. A third time? I don't know if I'd see that as a blessing," he says. "God can bless me in other ways. But you know what? I don't know that I ever would have become the husband and father I am now if it wasn't for cancer. I've been abundantly blessed. I'm a much better person. I'm much more involved in giving back to the community. I want to help people because so many people have been good to me. Cancer shaped who I am."

CHAPTER FIVE

Saying Aloha to Hawaii

ALOHA IS EASILY THE MOST RECOGNIZABLE WORD IN THE
Hawaiian language. In today's translation aloha is a simple greeting with a double
meaning-hello and goodbye. But that one simple word says a lot about who you
are and what you know. If you really have the Aloha Spirit in you, you most certainly will say the word with more passion and understanding than the haole guy
who just walked out of Hilo Hattie in a matching outfit with his wife. Just like the
true kamaaina knows that's a fashion no-no, a person who's true to the Spirit would
never say the word without *feeling* it.

Ancient Hawaiians were very expressive people. When they would greet each
other they'd touch noses and start the conversation a richly warm a-loh-haaa! They
didn't just say the word, they shared it. One would exhale on the final syllable as
the other opened their mouth and breathed in deeply on the haaa part. Aloha in its
ancient interpretation literally means, "sharing the breath of life". You won't see
many people on the streets of Honolulu or Kona macking noses today, but if someone breathily says a-loo-haaa to you, you know they're no malihini.

As much as some folks may have seen me as a malihini haole boy I always
tried my best to honor the culture and live it. I didn't wear leis like necklaces. I
wore them right, on the shoulders-not so much around the neck. I didn't wiggle
my hand while doing the shaka sign. And I always took off my shoes before entering the house. The Aloha Spirit became a part of who I was and who I wanted to
be.

"You're new to the islands yeah?" A pretty woman asked me more in the form
of a statement than a question.

Teri Okita (sunglasses) with the family of fallen Honolulu Police officer and Kevin Walsh. Hilo, Hawaii, 1996.

"Yes," I said. "But I've lived the island culture before. I came here from Guam in Micronesia, so I understand island culture."

I met Iwalani Tseu, a stunning 40-something island woman at Ala Moana Park on the first story I ever did in Hawaii. It was a Saturday morning and she was selling kukui nut leis at a crafts fair. She called me over and gave me and my photographer Marc Delorme leis. She said the kukui nuts had healing powers and would bring me good luck when I needed it most.

"Be good to the islands and the islands will be good to you. Okay Kevin?"

Iwalani's kindness had a lasting impression on me. It made me want to be more than just "there". I immersed myself in island culture-visiting schools, reading and learning about the Hawaiian language and history. I took in all the island music I could find and hear-especially if it was Kalapana or Kapena. It was that emotional investment I made that made it so hard on me when it was finally time to say aloha to Hawaii. And considering it wasn't my choice to leave made a tough thing even tougher.

My co-anchor Teri Okita had left KGMB-9 to take the weekend anchor spot at WUSA in Washington, D.C. For about a month Jade Moon, the 6 & 10 PM anchor came down to the 5:00 show to join me. We worked well together but it was clear that Jade was down on an interim basis. If I've learned anything in my years as a broadcaster it's that other people in the industry love to speculate about mixing up anchor teams.

After Teri left for Washington other reporters and cameramen besieged me in the field pining for my thoughts on whom my new co-anchor would be. I really hadn't given it much thought, but after a month I was starting to get annoyed with the persistent questions. Finally after a month of anchorette limbo I walked into the boss's office.

"Hey Scott, with Teri gone I was wondering how that would effect my future? People keep asking me all the time if I have a say in the selection process. I don't know what to tell them. What can you tell me?"

Scott Picken who had replaced Don Rockwell as news director let out a long sigh and nervously clasped his hands behind his head as he leaned back and rocked in his leather chair. "I'm taking you off the five at the end of the month," he said.

"What? Why?"

"We're looking for someone who's local and could stay forever-a lifer. We don't see you as being that."

"Wait a minute," I interrupted. "Who says I wouldn't have stayed forever? You never asked."

"Look I wasn't put on this earth to make your life miserable," he protested.

"Well you're doing a good job of doing that," I said sarcastically.

"I just don't want you to feel bad. It has nothing to do with your performance."

"Oh that's great!" I said. "I really feel a lot better knowing that you made a decision based on an assumption that I wouldn't want to stick around Hawaii. How could you possibly know what's going on inside my head? You could have asked me about my feelings if you had any doubt."

The boss just more or less took it, shifting nervously in his chair as I unloaded on him. "How long has this been a done deal?" I asked Scott.

"About a month," he said.

That answer made me almost as upset as the previous ones. At the very least it cost me a month in a job search in what was then a pretty tight market. Plus he kept delaying the inevitable because he was nervous about breaking the news. If not heartless I found his withholding of information less than courageous.

"So am I out of job at the end of the month?"

"No, no. You can stay as long as you want. You'll just go back to reporting," he said.

"Look," I said staring squarely into his dark eyes that were lined with unkempt eyebrows, "as soon as I walk out of this office I'm calling my agent, and you will hear from her."

"Okay," he said meekly as I walked out without further word.

Before I picked up the phone and called my agent Liz Sherwin in Palm Springs,

California I took a few deep breaths and looked around the newsroom. The news director had a fishbowl office and I was trying to figure out if the staff saw or heard what was the sinking of my career in Hawaii. I'm sure a couple of them did and probably had prior knowledge of what was coming my way. My pride hurt and so did my gut. Being demoted from a highly visible spot on television is like the being naked in public nightmare. You're doubly screwed. You're embarrassed to be seen without clothes and the public is embarrassed to see you.

"Liz it's Kevin Walsh in Hawaii."

"Hi Kevin. How are you?" Liz Sherwin asked.

"Well not too good. I just got demoted."

"Whaddaya mean?"

"The boss just told me he's taking me off the anchor desk at the end of the month."

"Did he tell you why?"

"Oh yeah."

"Why? What's the reason?"

"He told me they were looking for a local and a lifer."

"How does he know you wouldn't stay for the rest of your life?"

"He doesn't because he didn't ask."

"That's wrong," Liz said. "Give me his number. I'll call him right away."

So I gave my agent his number and said goodbye. A minute later I heard the faint ringing of the phone in the news director's office and saw him pick up the receiver. After a few words I saw him look over at me through his window, a clear indication my agent was reading him the riot act. It was pretty clear to me that Scott was uncomfortable. It wasn't a long conversation, only about five minutes or so. After he hung up, my phone rang. It was Liz.

"So how did it go?" I asked.

"Well not so good. He told me why they were moving in the direction they were going and that was about it."

"What did you say to him?"

"I just told him this really sucks."

"It does suck and I'm really upset."

"Okay look. I know you're upset and you have every reason to be. But you have to think about your career here. If you make a big fuss about it and act up, it will hurt your career. You don't want to be seen as a troublemaker because a lot of people won't want to hire you. You have to think about that," she told me.

News anchors lose jobs and suffer demotions all the time. This was my first time and it shook me up. I promised my agent that I would take the high road in all things, but I made it clear to her to put the word out on the street that I was available. With that done I started to go through the 5:00 scripts.

It wasn't one of my better shows. I got the sense my temporary co-anchor Jade knew that I now knew what my future was at KGMB was. Whatever the case she didn't bring it up as we sat together on the desk during commercial. As much as people might think anchors use the down time to look ahead through scripts it's usually not like that at all. Quite often we use that time to decompress from the stress of live TV and talk about personal things like family and dinner plans. On this night we didn't talk about anything. The floor crew must have known something was up too. The guys behind the cameras are usually a part of the running conversation and cracking jokes. Not tonight. The silence in the studio between reads was deafening. I couldn't wait for the show to be over. When it was I said goodnight to the viewers, Jade and the guys. I walked out desperately in need of some fresh island air and a conversation about something other than TV. I signed off my computer, walked out the door and plunked myself down on a concrete bench at the bus stop on Kapiolani Boulevard.

I looked across the street at Club Femme Nu, a strip bar, and started cracking up. A few months earlier I was in that same establishment doing a story on the Honolulu City Council's attempt to reduce the hours such clubs could operate. There was good statistical evidence that the Honolulu Police Department spent a disproportionate amount of time between the hours of two and four AM responding to disorderly conduct calls at strip joints. It was an easy story to tell in print because newspapers are word driven. In television you need pictures. Obviously much of what goes on inside of strip clubs is not suitable for air.

The safest way to tell the story in pictures was to get a bunch of exterior shots of different clubs around the block. But the Sunday producer didn't want any "boring video" in her show and thought it would be better to go inside a place. That was easy for her to say because she wasn't the one who would have to knock on doors. Most business owners avoid bad publicity like a bad rash so I wasn't hopeful the neighborhood mama sans would be hospitable. I was wrong. The club across the street from the station and my bus stop said come on in.

The plan was to videotape the dancers in such a way that you didn't see the merchandise. I sat in the booth chatting with the club manager and writing the story outline on my notepad. My photographer really seemed to be enjoying his work. He was egging the girls on and they were mugging for the camera. I was operating under the assumption that he'd shoot wide shots of the girls before they disrobed and tight shots from the shoulders up and the knees down afterward. Unless you're looking in the view finder while the recording is going on-almost never happens because your cameraman is doing that-you never really know what you got until you look at the tape later. Boy did I get a surprise when we got back to the station to edit the story!

We were on a tight deadline with the strippers and something else I had to write. After writing and voicing the strip club story I went back to my computer to write the other piece. About five minutes before the show started my photographer/editor said "Come take a look at this," in a mischievous tone.

As soon as he hit the play button in the edit booth I knew it was trouble. The opening shot was of a dancer's butt. She still had her underwear on, but that was hardly the point. You saw more crack than cheek. The camera was so close you would have expected the lens to fog if she broke wind. Even with clothes on it was borderline porn. I thought for sure it shouldn't air like that and told the producer to float the story. "It's not floating," she said. "That's your problem if it looks bad."

So the story aired as is and I braced for the onslaught of viewer calls that I expected to come. The first call came within thirty seconds. It was my wife Jean. "Honey, Oh my God! That woman's butt is right in the camera. Oh my God there's another one. Oh my God! Honey why are you airing this story?" she asked incredulously.

"Honey I know, I know. I feel awful. The pictures should have been a lot less risqué. I gotta go because I want to answer the phones before callers leave a message in the station voice mailbox."

I took one other call that night from another woman who was offended by what she saw, but not nearly as much as my wife. I thought for sure I'd be fired the next day or later that week over the strippers' mess. Nothing ever happened. A few weeks later came the story follow up. The City Council would be voting on whether to reduce strip club hours to curb after hours craziness. Stacy Loe, our City Hall beat reporter announced to the newsroom "Hey anyone have any video inside strip clubs that I can actually use on air?"

Someone said, "Ask Kevin. He did the story the last time and has some stripper video on his reel."

"Oh no," I said. "Stacy, really it's not airable. You probably want to find some other video. Or cover the story another way."

"Wait a minute," she harrumphed. "Why can't I use your video? Yours made air."

"Yeah but it shouldn't have."

"Why is it really that bad?" she asked humorously.

"Yeah it is," I told her. "Let's just be glad management was away or wasn't watching that night."

"I saw it," executive producer Chris Vandercook said as he peered from around his computer. He had an I gotcha grin on his face.

"You did?" I asked.

He nodded.

"I was pretty bad wasn't it?" I asked.

"Yeah it was bad," he said with a wink. "Yeah Stacy you may want to get some other video," Chris he told her before looking back at me and laughing.

"I really got away with that one didn't I?"

"*Oh yes you did,*" he said with a chuckle, suggesting if he and I weren't pals it might have had a different ending.

Just that simple look across the street brought me back to reality. It reminded me that I shouldn't take my career and myself so seriously. I still had a job. Sure I was demoted from a comfortable job with great visibility, but I'd still be reporting and doing something a lot of other people would probably love to try. There were much harder ways to making a living. I only had to look over at Club Femme Nu to be reminded of that.

I had my health and for that I was thankful. Not everyone around me was so lucky. I thought about Alana Dung. I thought about my mother, now five years gone. And I thought about Chris Pablo who spent each and every day fighting for his life. The worst ailment I could complain about was a surfing cut I got stitched up for a few weeks earlier, and they gave me laughing gas, which actually made the repair work fun. Life was not so bad after all. No sooner had I reached something close to an inner peace I heard the sound of a familiar engine and screeching brakes. The doors of The Bus flew open and my favorite wahine bus driver said "Howzit TV guy! Good to see you. Come on in!"

So I guess you could say the bus driver picked me up in more ways than one. Something else lifted my spirits a couple of weeks later. It was a phone call from my agent Liz Sherwin. "Hey there's a main anchor opening in Fresno, California for the CBS affiliate. They've seen your tape and really like you. They want to know if you'd fly out for a visit," Liz told me.

"Sure I can do it. What do you know about Fresno?" I asked her.

"Not much," Liz said. "It's very agricultural there. I guess you'll see for yourself when you get there. Oh one other thing, they want to know if you'll reimburse them for the airfare if you don't accept the job."

"What?" I asked. "What are you saying? Are you saying they offered me the job even though they haven't met me? I mean what if I don't like them and they don't like me?"

"I'll check into it," Liz told me before hanging up.

Turns out the Fresno station was committed and having me come out was more or less a chance for the news director and general manager to introduce me at the station Christmas party as the new hire. I flew direct to Los Angeles and took a commuter flight up to Fresno. I was dressed in a suit because we'd be going straight from the airport to the party at the Airport Piccadilly Inn. My future boss told me he'd already had a couple of glasses of red wine before picking me up at the terminal, and with his purple lips I believed it. He told me the party was in full swing and to expect a festive bunch. My future co-anchor was dressed to the nines in a sequined dress that made her look more like a movie star than a news anchor. The morning news anchor had commandeered the microphone from the DJ and was doing her own version of American Idol and the big boss was doing splits on the dance floor.

When I got back to the hotel room I called my wife Jean back in Honolulu. "How's it going? What are the people like?" she wanted to know.

"You really want to know?" I asked her.

"Yeah."

"They're young and they really like to party," I told her.

"Really? Like how much?"

"Let's put it this way. I haven't been to a party that wild since college. And I think a lot of them are going to be really hung over tomorrow."

"Sounds like fun," she joked. "But really are they nice people?"

"Yes they definitely are," I told her. "I'll visit the station tomorrow morning and the GM is going to drive me around town in the afternoon to get a feel for the city and the suburbs."

The next morning Don Drilling, a second-generation general manager of the station and a real country cowboy picked me up at the hotel. He pulled up in a big, red double axle pickup with the station's call letters KJEO on the license plate. We went to the Peppermill on Blackstone Avenue which was quite popular with the after church brunch crowd. Over a plate of fresh cut fruit he told me the only way KJEO was going to get back into the ratings race was with a commitment to longevity. And if I decided to accept their offer, it would be a five-year contract- long by industry standards. I told him I was ready to put down roots, establish my- self in the community and hopefully start a family. He liked that and said so.

After breakfast we drove around a few of the nicer neighborhoods on the ex- panding north side of town. He asked if I could see myself living here. I thought I could and I asked him what kind of fun there was to be had in Central California. "Well there's plenty of golf, fishing and skiing. In fact you can golf and ski on the same day. Want to take a drive up the mountains?" Don asked.

I could see the snow capped Sierra Nevada Mountains from the valley floor and they looked lovely. "Sure why not," I said. "How far of a drive is it?"

"Only about an hour. Let's go it's a beautiful drive."

So we drove up Friant Road and past the massive dam that held back Millerton Lake. We drove by the Johnny Miller designed Brighton Crest Golf Club in the foothills which was right across the street from the Table Mountain Indian Casino. Within another 15 miles we started a serious climb up the four lane highway that took us into Shaver Lake, a lovely mountain community about eight thousand feet up that looked very much like the picture on a can of Swiss Miss Hot Chocolate. Slow plows were still removing what had been a modest overnight snowfall, and judging from the piles on the side of the road it looked like Shaver Lake had already gotten a couple of feet in just a couple of weeks after Thanksgiving.

I'd seen enough and told the GM to head back to town where I'd do a brief audition in the studio with my future co-anchor. The audition went well although I could tell the crew was still feeling the effects of what had been the wildest of nights. From the studio news director Marc Cotta drove me back to the airport stressing how much they wanted me to be part of their rebuilding process. I told him I was very impressed and would seriously consider the opportunity over the next couple of days. After the half hour puddle jumper flight up to San Francisco I boarded a 747 bound for Honolulu. I landed just before midnight. Waiting to pick me up faithfully was my wife Jean. She was happy to see me, but sad too because she knew our Hawaii story was soon to be over.

Over eggs and bacon the next morning Jean and I talked about moving on to the next opportunity. She asked if Fresno was like Los Angeles or San Diego. Not quite. Aside from palm trees and abundant sunshine, Fresno is a world away in terms of culture and topography. The San Joaquin Valley is a hard-working, agricultural mini bible belt and Fresno is right in the middle of it. Think Kansas and that's pretty much what you have in Fresno. I asked Jean if she could handle that. "That doesn't sound too different than what it was like when we went to college at Purdue in Indiana. I'm okay with it if you are," she answered.

"Okay then it's done. I call them and let them know we're coming," I said while picking through the dregs of the eggs and the crumbs of the toast.

"What about KGMB? What are you going to tell them?" Jean asked.

"I'll just tell them I have a new opportunity and thank then for the time I had here. They did what they thought was right for them in taking me off the 5:00 show. I'm only doing what I think is right for my career and me. I'll be very positive about breaking it to them," I told her.

The next day I reported in for work and went straight to see my news director Scott Picken. "What's up?" he asked.

"I have good news and bad news," I told him while sitting down on his office couch.

"What's the good news?" he wanted to know.

"Well the good news is I have a new main anchoring job in California," I told him.

"And the bad news is you're leaving us," he filled in the blank.

"That's right."

"When do you start the new job?"

"Next month."

With the Christmas Holiday coming up and unused vacation time to be burned off, I was only going to work about two more weeks at KGMB. Scott posted a nice note on the bulletin board about my pending departure and most of the staff found time to pull me aside and wish me well. There would be no lavish on-air sendoff just a simple night on the town for beers with some of the younger staff members. We drank, laughed, danced and sang.

When it came time to leave the islands a good family friend, Dean Fukumoto, drove us to the airport. Dean was my wife's boss at a computer training business. He had been a golf partner of mine, taking me along to play with his Japanese-American Golf Club of Honolulu on different occasions. We went to an airport lounge as we savored the last minutes of our time in the islands. Dean sang a song for us on the karaoke machine. The lyrics spoke of friends flying away on a journey, so the song and Dean really did sing to us. It was touching. Then the call came for boarding. We hugged Dean goodbye, promised to keep in touch, and we headed down the Jetway toward the aircraft.

As we boarded the aircraft one of the Hawaiian Airlines flight attendants recognized me from TV and said what a big fan she was of the 5:00 news on KGMB Channel 9. She asked why she hadn't seen me as lately on the anchor desk, so I told her about the demotion. She was sad about that and even more upset to hear I was leaving the islands. "That's too bad," she said. "Channel 9 doesn't know what it'll be missing."

It was kind and flattering. So were her words on the plane's intercom system as part of the usual flight greeting and safety announcements. "We're also pleased to announce that Mr. Kevin Walsh of KGMB Channel 9 is flying with us today to Los Angeles."

"Auww that's so nice," my wife Jean said as she rubbed my hand.

As the DC-10 taxied toward the runway for takeoff I took in all the scenery and the reflected on the good times. I thought about get-togethers and drinks we shared with friends at Duke Kahanamoku's on the beach in Waikiki listening to the island music of Haumea/Warrington, dinners with the Edwards family in Hawaii Kai, long walks on the beach with my wife. And I thought about Chris Pablo and how I wouldn't be there for his bone marrow transplant. It was an emotional photo album going through my head as the plane raced down the runway. Soon we were climbing, soaring past downtown, Waikiki, Diamond Head and eventually into the clouds. It was a beautiful sendoff. I just wish it hadn't come so soon and on those terms.

CHAPTER SIX

Starting Over

WE FLEW INTO FRESNO IN THE MIDDLE OF JANUARY AND were greeted by the San Joaquin Valley's infamous Tule Fog, named after the Tule Indian Tribe. In general fog is little more than a sinking cloud that forms when the air temperature meets the dew point. But Tule Fog is not your ordinary fog and the San Joaquin Valley is not your ordinary valley.

Exceptionally tall mountains-the Coastal Mountains to the west and the Sierra Nevada to the east surround the valley floor. It's like a bowl. The fog pours in and can't get out. Still and cool conditions make it stick around for hours. Tule fog is blamed for dozens of car accidents each year including the occasional highway pileup. Drivers learn how to drive with their "ears", putting the windows down to listen for traffic they can't see. They might also reset their odometers to monitor precise distance on a familiar route, knowing they have to take a left at sixth tenths of a mile, followed by a right a tenth of a mile later. "Flying blind" is a good analogy and maybe the pilot of our American Eagle Turboprop who flew into the Fresno Yosemite International Airport that day did it with the help of sound or control panels. I know I couldn't see anything from my seat in row two B. When I got off the plane I could hardly see my shoes. "Tule Fog," a fellow passenger told me. "Happens almost everyday between late fall and spring."

It's one thing to be a stranger in a strange land, and something else to not be able to see the land where you are. That's how odd it felt that first day in Fresno. My wife Jean and I fetched our luggage at the baggage claim and hopped a shuttle to the Ramada Inn off Highway 41 and Shaw Avenue. How we got there I'll never know. The best I could tell the driver put the left front tire on the center line of the road, listened for trouble and probably knew the route by heart. Whatever the case he got us there and we checked in.

The Ramada Inn was home for the next week. The station paid for the hotel and a rental car for a week. Before we left from Hawaii Jean secured for us a fully furnished "executive apartment" in downtown Fresno which she saw online. The complex specialized in temporary housing for relocating professionals. It had dishes, silverware, bath towels, etc. You could move right in. We were eager to see it. First we needed wheels and the fog to lift.

Our rental car was waiting for us at the TV station. It was only about a mile away so Jean and I decided to make the walk. The news director welcomed us into the station, introduced us to the newsroom staff, and brought us in his office for conversation. He asked whether we needed help getting settled. I told him about our temporary digs downtown. Based on his raised facial expression, which included wide as pie eyes and arched eyebrows I kind of got the feeling he was surprised to hear about our choice of geography.

"How is the downtown area?" I asked anxiously.

"Well I don't know too many people who live down there," he said with a sigh. "Most of us live on the north side of town, north of Herndon Avenue. When you decide to buy a house you should probably look in the area around Woodward Lake. That's where I live."

After some more small talk we decided to get on with our day. By now it was late morning and most of the fog had burned off. We hopped in our rented Chrysler New Yorker and headed south on Highway 41. The highway would take us right into downtown Fresno. When we got off on the exit by Divisadero Street I knew we weren't home. Drug dealers worked the corners and most of the houses were in obvious disrepair. The apartment complex looked more like a military billet than a residential unit. There was a fence with razor wire around the parking lot and the units didn't have windows. Jean said, "Oh my God! Don't even get out of the car."

It was bad but I thought I'd have a little fun with it. "Okay honey obviously this is not what we thought it would be from what we saw on the internet, but let me see if I can find the apartment manager and at least get our $75 deposit back," I told her.

"Don't even bother. Let's go."

So we went back to the station and talked with the boss about what we found downtown. "Yeah I was kind of wondering about that when you said *Divisadero* Street, but you seemed so enthusiastic about being there that I didn't want to want to hurt your feelings," he said.

"Don't worry about hurting our feelings," I told him. "We're not married to the idea of living in the city. We only considered it because we thought it would be a centralized location before we really settled down. But after driving around downtown we think we'll be better off in the suburbs. Do you know someone who can help us out?"

He did and pretty soon we were settling into a nice two-bedroom apartment on the north side of Fresno. Now that we had a place to live, we needed cars to drive. We sold our only car in Hawaii so we were starting anew. I never had a new car. I'd always driven old, used cars because that's all I could afford. Now for the first time in my life I actually had some money in my pocket and I could upgrade. I wanted something new, something with that fresh new car smell. So I bought a Ford Contour for my wife and a Ford Explorer for me from Decker Ford in nearby Clovis. We didn't futz around. We bought quickly and they treated us like rock stars.

We rented the apartment month-to-month because we really wanted to buy a house fast. A real estate agent took us over to Woodward Lake, a community of about a thousand homes built on and around a manmade Lake. The Woodward Lake Association had a community clubhouse with a swimming pool, and there were several small rowboats, sailboats and canoes that you could use to putter around on the gorgeous lake. What's more, the lake was well stocked with Florida strain largemouth bass and catfish.

Woodward Lake was a desirable place to live, so much so that homeowners had to enter a lottery system when it was being developed ten years earlier. Within a couple of months we settled on a three-bedroom house in a gated subdivision called Americana Shores. The homes were Mediterranean in style and very reasonable in price. We bought a corner lot on a cul de sac with a pool for 114-thousand dollars. In Hawaii, or even where I grew up in Philadelphia a similar home would have easily been five times that amount. It was our first house and our piece of American Pie.

The house was in great shape, with new carpeting and a two-car garage. The backyard and the pool were another story. They would need some work. The pool water was green and looked as if some of the bass from Woodward Lake jumped the fence and splashed the joint. I thought I'd have to drain it. But we had a pro come in and he got it cleaned up with the help of super duper chemicals. It sparkled.

The previous owner must not have liked grass because there wasn't any around the pool. It was all dirt and woodchips-unsightly and very dusty. I cleaned up the mess and put some sod down. Jean put in feminine touches with flowers and plants and I planted some manly tiki torches around the wooden fence. It looked like a luau waiting to break out. We wanted to honor our time in Hawaii with a place that reminded us of the islands. All we had to do was walk out the back door.

We spent a lot of timing hanging out at home, getting to know the neighbors and their children and making sure to invite them over for swims. They appreciated it because the previous owner was not the best of citizens. He shunned the neighbors on the cul de sac, often brought in an entourage from the outside, causing parking nightmares and having parties that lasted well beyond a reasonable hour. My neighbor across the street Marty Mitts told me, "Yeah I told my wife Shirley you guys were going to be okay when I first saw you pull in the driveway in a Ford Explorer. Man I was sick of looking at your previous owner's piece of crap truck parked outside my kitchen window all the time."

We were social people and always found time for fun, but as the main news anchor at a rebuilding news operation there was plenty of work to be done on-air, behind the scenes and at public appearances. The community relations department at KJEO more or less had me on tour the first couple of months. If there was a school career day, the Rotary Club needed a speaker, or anything else that could boost goodwill in the community I was on it. It came with the territory and I was honored that someone thought enough of me to pass along an invite. Plus I figured I could convert anyone I met along the way into a viewer. I was good at it and I liked the schmooze.

In positions with responsibility and visibility there are often perks. We had some good ones at KJEO. Being the main guy on air gave me a certain status. People in the newsroom wanted to help with just about everything-a pronunciation, past history of small town politics, whatever. Much of the staff just seemed to enjoy a conversation with the evening anchor on any subject, whether it was the news of the day, sports or something personal. Showing an interest in their lives and interests made all the difference. By nature anchors love to talk. I think we could all be better listeners.

I had a modest trade agreement with the local men's store. If I wanted tailored clothes all I had to do was walk across the street and see my buddy Bud. Bud Francis was our haberdasher at Gottschalks. He was a handsome grandfatherly type with Santa Claus white hair and a matching mustache. He preferred sports jackets to suits, but he knew I was a dark suit kind of guy. So whenever Bud would get a new shipment of dark suits in he'd always put aside the navy, gray and black 42 regulars for me.

Bud may have been in his 70's but we both shared a love for colorful Jerry Garcia ties. We'd spend almost an hour at times going through the playful patterns, sometimes getting dizzy from looking at them. The wild ties and the conservative suits made for an interesting contrast on TV, but it worked. And if I ever had a particularly good or bad wardrobe night, Bud would be sure to let me know the next time I was in.

We had a golf trade too. I could go to Fig Garden Golf Club on the banks of the San Joaquin River and play as much golf as I wanted. Whatever the tab for golf was at the end of the month, the station would give it back in free advertising. I played two, sometimes even three times a week. I didn't have to be in at work until 3:30 in the afternoon, so that left plenty of time for golf in the morning.

Before long I had my handicap back to scratch, which left me itching to get back in the competitive environment. The golf course also became a social vehicle. I made friends easily with everyday hackers, ringers and even professional athletes. There was a minor league hockey team in town and it wasn't long before I was teeing it up with the boys who played for the Double A Fresno Falcons of the West Coast Hockey League that later merged with the ECHL.

If you're a good golfer word about it spreads fast. Golfers have a sense for who's who around them. It's like the "it" guy or "it" gal at work. We all know who they are. Some like to be around that "it" person hoping whatever "it" is, it's contagious. Others simply have an appreciation for seeing someone do something well. Who doesn't like to be flattered? And when you're on TV, it's magnified.

I met one of my better golfing pals, Rich Rodriguez at Fig Garden. Rich was a trip. He was a man's man in his mid 40s who strutted around the place like he owned it. But he did it in such a way that he didn't come off as a jerk. He was a fun loving, cigar smoking ballbuster who could dish it out, but he could take it too. In fact he probably took more abuse than anyone else at the club. At the time Rich anchored the news on the rival TV station ABC 30, one of the most successful local stations in America. Rich, you could say was the king of Fresno TV.

I introduced myself to Rich one day as he was coming out of the clubhouse with a Coors Light in one hand and a hot dog in the other. He was friendly and said we should play sometime. I got his number and called him a week later. We teed it up the next Friday morning. "Walshy, you know I'm going to kick your butt," he teased as he settled over the ball on the first tee with a cigar hanging out of his mouth and smoke puffing out of the corners.

He let loose a nice little fade, about 220 yards right down the middle. "Good shot Richie," I told him as I placed my new Titleist Pro V1 on the tee and started my preshot routine.

"Walshy, Walshy. Hold on, wait a minute. Let me announce you," Rich interrupted. "Now on the first tee, the new TV anchor from KJEO TV, by way of Hawaii and Philadelphia, Mr. Kevin Walsh!"

His fake announcer voice was funny and dripping with sarcasm. I stopped, gave him an amusing look and proceeded to go about my business. I crushed a drive with a tight draw. It easily flew past Rich's ball and stopped about 280 yards away. I winked at Rich and smiled saying, "You don't want to play me for money."

I made birdie to Rich's bogey. We both made pars the next hole and he started with the needle again. "Hey look, I'm only one down after two. I got you right where I want you," he teased.

I had the honor on the third tee and just let Rich run his mouth for a little while. Then I pulled a 7-iron out of my bag on the par three that measured 163 yards over water. The pin was back left, just over a hump. I hit a sweeping draw that started in the middle of the green and curved its way back to the hole. It landed a couple of feet behind the hole and spun back to within a foot. "You don't want to play me for money," I said giddily as I picked my tee up and flung it at Rich's chest.

"You really are a ringer," Rich said as waggled over his ball. "I guess I'll just have to settle for kicking your butt on TV!"

It was a great zinger with superb timing. The other guys in the group doubled over. It was even funnier when Rich dumped his tee shot into the drink. He was cooked after that and we enjoyed the rest of the round with nonstop insults and stories that would come to define our golfing experience.

Fridays were our golfing days. Even though an 8:00ish tee time was a fast turn-around from the 11:00 news the night before, it was the end of the week and you only had to suck it up for another day. The fun would actually start the night before with a checking in phone call. One would call the other right around 9:00pm between our 6 and 11 o'clock newscasts and after our dinner breaks. "Yo before we play tomorrow I want you to shine my shoes and clean out the grooves of my clubs," Rich would say.

"In your dreams," I'd shoot back. "Listen don't embarrass me tomorrow. Can you at least break 90? It's not good for my image to be seen with a hacker like you."

It was a constant game of one-upmanship and no one was worse for the wear. Rich actually had it in him to play good golf. He got it around in the low to mid 80s most of the time and a few times he flirted with breaking 80. Whenever I shot under par I'd retire the golf ball. I'd take out a Sharpie, sign it and date it and give it to Rich so he'd have to look at it and stew over his own mediocrity. "You're a d___," he'd often say.

"Wait a minute you can't say that. Your family calls you Dickie," I'd remind him. "Look if you ever break 80 I'd gladly take a signed ball from you."

I'm not sure I knew anyone who liked golf as much as Rich. I mean he *loved* the game-loved talking about it and wasn't afraid to ask for help in getting better. Whenever I showed him how to play a shot better he always listened and tried to duplicate it. He was actually a pretty good athlete, but not as good as the hockey players.

Prior to the arrival of the Fresno Grizzlies, the Triple-A baseball affiliate of the San Francisco Giants, the Fresno Falcons were the only professional athletes we had in town. Most of the guys came from Canada with no illusions about going on to bigger and better things. In fact most were on their way down, or had maxed out at Double A Hockey. Still they were professional athletes who easily would have been "the man" on any other level except the elite pro ranks.

Even if the dream of reaching the NHL wasn't meant to be, these guys still had it pretty good. Some made as much money as a starting school teacher playing a game they loved for six months out of the year. They'd practice at the rink each morning for an hour-and-half and pretty much had the rest of the day to themselves. A lot of them played golf to pass the time. With the hand eye coordination it takes to hit a slap shot with a moving puck, it was hardly a slippery transition to hit a ball at rest. These guys were good and they loved to gamble. We never played for much, maybe a five-dollar nassau, but there was always something on the line to make it interesting. Plus whoever won bought drinks. So it was really a wash. It was for bragging rights more than anything.

The Falcons had a trade with Fig Garden too. The guys would play for free and the team would give the club free advertisements on the dashers and the scoreboard. When the guys wanted a change of scenery, knowing my golf connections they'd ask if I could call around and get us on a private course. It was never a problem. And as a kind gesture the players offered game tickets to the pro shop staff.

If there was a game during the week I'd often run down to Selland Arena after the 6:00 news and take couple of periods, if not the whole game, before heading back to do the 11:00 news. It wasn't uncommon to have someone at the game to say "Hey I just saw you on the news! What are you doing here?"

"Same thing as you. Enjoying the game," I'd say.

In fact going to Fresno Falcons games probably helped my ratings. Hockey fans are unbelievably loyal. They really take care of their own. "Highlights at 11 Kev?"

I'd hear it all the time. "Of course," I'd tell them.

"We'll be watching."

The team took me in too. Sometimes after games on the weekends the players would call over the glass as they skated off the ice. "Walshy! Come on down and have a beer, eh?"

So the guard would let me go past the security rail and into the dressing room while my wife, Jean chatted outside with players' wives and girlfriends. I'd be sitting next to a naked dude having a Molson while other guys in various states of undress would walk around and unwind from the game. "Hey Walshy you're coming out with us eh?"

"Walshy. What's going on? We're golfing again soon, eh?"

"Walshy, Walshy, Walshy."

The guys never called me Kevin-ever. Just Walshy. And there was always an eh in there somewhere. We go out to the bars and the guys could really put away some beer. Saturday nights were always big. The whole team would go to the Silver Dollar Hofbrau, Butterfield's or The Elbow Room. They probably sweated out five pounds each night so I guess you could say they were thirsty. They also attracted a lot of women. The married guys knew better and were smart to bring their better halves. The single guys, let's just say they didn't have trouble finding company.

Spending time with the hockey players was nostalgic for me. Growing up in Philadelphia I played hockey on the ponds when they would freeze and on the street in the summertime. After living three years on tropical islands I didn't get to see much hockey, or have anyone to talk about it with. Little did I know I'd find my own hockey Nirvana in Fresno, California.

In a short amount of time I had gone from career crisis in Hawaii to a wonderful life in Central California. It really didn't get much better. I had the exposure I always wanted on television and more. I inherited an extra newscast, the 5:00, to go along with the 6 and 11. More and more people were recognizing at church, in the grocery store and around town. I liked the attention. I don't know that I ever set out with the specific goal to "be famous" like a move star, but there's no doubt I wanted to be someone who stood out from the crowd. TV did that for me. It served my ego. What budding television success I had was just enough to make me feel special without the trappings of being an egotistical big shot. At least that's how I hope I came across.

If there were illusions of grandeur a special addition to our family would soon steal a lot of the spotlight. Even though we lived in a lovely neighborhood and seemingly safe neighborhood my wife Jean would often get scared and lonely at night. So we decided to get a dog. That had always been in my plans because I grew up with dogs. From the time I was born, until the time I moved out of my parents' house, there was always a dog. Once I got out on my own and became a renter I couldn't have a dog because the landlords wouldn't allow it. I had gone years petless and was starting to feel out of balance.

I'd always wanted a German Shepherd. I loved their look, trainability, drive to work and their protection value goes without saying. Jean wasn't so sure about a dog that big and all that comes with it, but I told her in the end she'd probably come to love whatever dog we got more than me. It was the best line I could come up with at the time and she actually bought it.

With the help of The Fresno Bee classified ads we found a German Shepherd puppy living with a young Madera County Sheriff's Deputy named Tony. Tony lived in a small apartment. He had a few pets already and a baby on the way. His fiancée said the dog had to go. Tony was crushed. He loved the dog and was already working with it on training and tricks. But for 75 dollars and the peace that comes with your lover no longer nagging you about getting rid of it, Tony gave the dog to us.

I always wanted a manly man's dog and I had told quite a few people about it. They and I more or less thought I'd come home with Fritz, or another German named burly male. We got Tiffany. I felt like a girly man and the neighbors wouldn't

Walsh family pet, German Shepherd Tiffany with Yellow Lab and play partner Alex. Fresno, California, 2000

let it go. "You can't name a German Shepherd *Tiffany*," my neighbor Ed Crossman teased. "She needs a powerful, or regal name like Duchess, or Sascha. Tiffany? You gotta be kidding me," he said.

Tiffany blossomed into a fine dog. Once clumsy with floppy ears that were easily two sizes too big for her head, she was all the dog you ever wanted. She was sweet as her name with a Golden Retriever's kind disposition. She followed us everywhere. If you took a plop on the toilet she plopped down next to you. If you showered, you had to shoo Tiffany off the bathmat when you got out. I could open the front door and she'd fetch the morning paper from the end of the driveway. She never left your sight, the only dog I've ever had that didn't have wanderlust.

Tiffany also loved to play fetch, especially with golf balls. I'd bring her out front and chip balls across the front yard. Because we lived on a corner, the cross streets generated a good amount of slow-moving traffic which provided a great view of the Dog Olympics. Tiffany wouldn't just run down grounders, I could lob a ball up 30 yards away and she's pluck it right out of the air, turning her head to the side and opening her mouth in a full sprint. When we went for walks people would stop us because they wanted to meet Tiffany. One guy told us, "I've had dogs all my life and seen all sorts of tricks. But that golf ball thing you do with her is the best thing I've ever seen!"

It was a hoot. We actually had a couple of kids from the opposite end of the neighborhood knock on our door one day. "Are you the people with the golf ball dog?" they asked.

"Yes," I told them as Tiffany crawled through my legs and nuzzled up next to them.

"Well can we take her for a walk and over to our house to play?" they asked.

I got the leash and turned her over. An hour later Tiffany and the boys were back, happy as can be. Tiffany was more than a pet; she was a fixture in the neighborhood-real life lawn art. When the Lorbers or the Crossmans were out gardening Tiffany would walk over to their houses, lie down in the grass and watch them work in the dirt. She'd be there for hours, the ultimate hang out dog. When Kevin Lorber went away on business, Tiffany would do sleepovers with his wife Elizabeth. If neighbors thought they heard a strange sound in the house, I'd bring Tiffany over to sniff around and check it out. When I put her "on patrol" it was as if she flipped a switch and became an entirely different dog. I have no doubt if Tiffany ever encountered an intruder they'd be dead, or pretty close to it when she was done with them.

Tiffany understood human nature. She was gentle around the elderly and children. She'd go visit Lolita, a 94-year old woman two doors down who walked with the help of a cane. Tiffany would walk over slowly as if to match the pace of Lolita's gait. She'd sit down and wait to be petted. You could almost tell Tiffany knew not to lean on Lolita because she might fall over.

Tiffany would fetch Frisbees for the twin girls across the street and the two other sisters down the road. With each retrieve she returned it to a different child so each had a turn. She got the concept of sharing. It was beautiful to see. Nobody missed a turn, ever.

I may have been the most recognizable guy in the neighborhood because I was on TV, but we were better known for our dog. And yes Tiffany did make some television appearances. Whenever my station needed video for whatever dog-related story, Tiffany was stock video. The guy across the street was a TV reporter for a competing station. He used Tiffany too.

CHAPTER SEVEN

Demoted Again

IT WAS LIKE ANY OTHER NIGHT. I HAD JUST FINISHED anchoring the five and six o'clock news and was sitting at my desk picking through a plate of noodles. An instant message flashed across my computer screen. "C'mon in big guy."

It was a note from my news director. "What's up?" I asked as I took a seat across from Marc Cotta's desk.

"We need to get more people involved in the anchoring and we can't have anyone do three shows," he told me pushing his face forward suggestively.

I didn't get it at first, but when I did it was a real kick in the balls. I felt numb. I sat in silence for a few moments not wanting to say something too brash too quickly that might end up damaging my career even more. I looked my boss squarely in the eye for a good minute without saying anything. The silence was deafening and growing increasingly more uncomfortable. I wanted it that way because I wanted him to know I wouldn't be pushed around easily. I could sense his growing unease. Eventually someone had to speak.

"So what are you going to do? Take me off the five?" I asked.

More silence and more staring. "The five *and* the eleven," he said with a sigh.

It was like the life was sucked out of me. I could have lived without the 5:00 show because it wasn't mine to begin with. I was brought in from Hawaii to do the 6:00 and 11:00 shows and added the five to the mix when our previous 5:00 anchor, Doug Fernandez, left. But now I had less than what I came for. It was nothing short of a major demotion.

I could almost understand adding another anchor team to the mix because we only had two teams for a total of five shows each weekday. Most stations have three anchor teams; two first stringers and the other team on a lesser show standing by in case a top team tanks. But there would be no addition of a new female anchor, meaning my current co-anchor Molly McMillen would continue to do three shows, contradicting what the boss told me about not being able to have anyone doing three shows. I was upset. And it would only get worse.

"Who's going to take my place?" I asked.

It would be the new guy who had joined us a few months earlier from another market and proved to be a reliable reporter in the field. He worked hard and understood the concept of matching words to pictures. When it came time to deliver a live and unscripted report from the field he got the job done.

When reporters are performing well in the field it's not uncommon for them to get a push on the inside too. Almost all news anchors held in high regard have an appreciable amount of time in the field. When one of the go to reporters is suddenly pitching his stories alongside the anchor and inside the studio, it's a pretty good sign there's grooming going on.

News anchors are very astute to in-house competition around them. Everyone can see whose star is rising with management. When it happens, the entrenched veteran usually feels threatened. But I never felt threatened. In my heart I believed I was the strongest male performer in the house and I knew I had the support of my colleagues.

Television is a strange thing though. What makes sense to many is often foreign for a few. After the news director dropped the demotion bomb on me I pleaded my case. He raised his hands and gestured that he understood what I was saying but couldn't do anything about it.

"Is this your choice or the GM's?" I asked.

He gestured the latter.

"Does this have anything to do with ratings? Or, are you unhappy with my performance?" I asked bluntly.

"No," he said without hesitation.

"Then what is it? You're telling me it's not about ratings and my performance. *What the heck is going on?*"

Marc didn't really have much of an answer, but I think he sympathized with my plight. He was as good to me as he could be considering he was the bearer of bad news. It was my Honolulu hangover all over again

The rub for me was that, as far as I could tell, I became a job casualty without fault. Not once, but twice. That hurt. A lot. I took a walk down the hall, found an open office and closed the door. I picked up the phone and called home.

"Hello," Jean said as she picked up the phone at home.

"Honey you're not going to believe this. The news director just called me in his office and said he was taking me off the five and eleven o'clock shows."

"What! Why?" she asked.

"They're just moving in a different direction," I told her.

As disappointed as I was, to his credit my replacement sought me out and was kind after it all went down. "Walshy I didn't ask for this," he told me as we applied our makeup in the bathroom after my demotion meeting with the boss, and a just few minutes before the start of the 11 o'clock show.

"This isn't between us," I told him between swipes with the Mac sponge. "Sometimes opportunities just find you. What happened to me isn't your fault. You're just taking an opportunity that management has offered you. How could you not take it? You're only following orders."

I think he appreciated what I said. I later found out the reporter sought the counsel of another respected newsroom leader who told me, "The new guy came to me and asked for advice. He said he was concerned about replacing you because of your talents and popularity in the newsroom. I told him to just try to be a good person, keep a low profile and have a talk with you."

The reporter did that and I tried hard not to hold a grudge. We still played golf together semi-regularly and had an occasional beer. It was an uncomfortable situation and I think it was best for both of us not to go there. So we didn't. Others said plenty to me about what happened. I appreciated the sympathy but it didn't change the situation. It stunk and something stunk too. My boss told me "It might be smart to start looking for a new job."

I called my agent Liz Sherwin, and my good friend, now retired Philadelphia news anchor Larry Kane. Liz confirmed what I already knew to be true. The situation really was awful. Larry, as usual, was the voice of reason. He told me to suck it up, to believe that my broadcasting ability and agent would eventually bail me out of a bad situation.

"You know Lar, I'm really upset about what they did to me. It's totally unfair. And you know what? If they only *tried* to convince me of the wisdom in it I might not be as mad. They didn't even try," I rambled.

"Whoa, whoa, whoa! Hold on," Larry interrupted in his huge baritone voice. "Don't ever overestimate the intelligence of people who run television stations. There's an assumption that people who run television stations must be smart. It's not true. You will be continuously disappointed if you believe that. The most important thing you can do right now is calm down because you're mad. And you know what? You're going to be even more pissed off tomorrow. Just take a little time, spend some time with your wife Jean and calm down. You're young. Things are going to work out. The cream always rises to the top. You're good. *You're really good.* They're just too stupid to figure it out. Just do the best you can do and let your agent handle it and try to get you out to something better," he reasoned.

Larry always calmed me down even if he couldn't fix what was broken. I grew up watching him on TV, went to school with his son, interned under Larry in college and have the great fortune to have him as a mentor. There was hardly anything that I could experience that he hadn't already been through himself. He saved me from myself.

CHAPTER EIGHT

New Assignments, New Life Adjustments

MOST OF US AT ONE TIME OR ANOTHER HAVE HAD A ROUGH patch at work. We lost out on a promotion we thought we deserved; we were demoted, or worse yet fired. It happens. Sometimes it is our fault. We simply weren't getting the job done well enough. Other times there's nothing you can do about it. Whatever the case, it sucks. The end result is often a chronic and winless game of "what if"? What if I had done this differently? What if the new guy didn't come, where would I be now? It carves at you.

Suffering a demotion on TV is especially tough because so many people see it. And if they're regular news watchers, they're naturally curious. That curiosity can get the better of them and you. "Hey Kev. I don't see you on the late news anymore. What's going on?"

They might ask such a thing at church, or the grocery store. The thing is you never know when the questions are coming and whom they're coming from. By explaining the situation you end up reliving it. Your uncomfortable tone gives away how you really feel. Your inquisitor naturally feels bad for having brought it up, and then you feel bad for dumping on them. It's a lose-lose-lose situation. "I really miss watching you," they'd say longingly.

"Well I miss doing it too," I'd tell them.

I'd go into work at 3:30 in the afternoon and that would give me a couple of hours to go through the 6:00 rundown. I'd start by opening up the show folder on my computer and page down to see the order. Then I'd read the scripts and whatever Associated Press newswire copy accompanied it. Even though the scripts were mostly written at this point, I'd often rewrite them to match my voice. Someone else's writing may be beautiful on paper, but if it doesn't match how you would say it in tone and word choice-it doesn't fit. It's like wearing shoes. You don't make your feet fit the shoes; you make the shoes fit your feet.

No two anchors are the same in how they prepare. Some like to be left alone with their thoughts and writing in the final two hours before the show. Others like to be on the phone with the reporter in the field crafting a lead-in to the reporter's prepared report, or in constant conversation with the producers about which stories to drop and which ones to move up. I've seen some anchors put their heads down on their desk and take a nap, either because they were lazy, hung over or just wanted to be "fresh" when the time came. I preferred to be busy, hoping the charge from that would lead to good energy on the air. You don't just get out in the studio and read off the TelePrompTer-at least you're not supposed to. Hard work behind the scenes leads to a better product on TV.

But with my new role came new distractions. As I prepared for the 6:00 news each night the assignment desk was already looking ahead to 11. Seeing as I was going to be the featured reporter for the late show, the assignment desk was often busy in the late afternoon preparing a location and crew for where I would go after the 6:00 broadcast. The assignment editors would often come over with a general idea of what my late story from the field would be and ask what I'd need from them. The end result was my mind was often in two places at the same time.

I had to deal with the 6:00 show first and foremost because that was our most important newscast. It was the newscast of record. But I also had to keep an eye on late night responsibilities, because if I pushed that off until after the six, there wouldn't be enough time to turn the story around with the lengthy car rides that often came with covering the spacious San Joaquin Valley.

I tried to make the best of it but it was a grind. I went a lot of nights without dinner and had more close calls with serious car accidents than I can remember. My photographers and I drove our Jeep Cherokees like race car drivers, simply because we had to. It wasn't uncommon to get off the six o'clock news, speed down Highway 99 to the South Valley an hour away, do some interviews, shoot some video, race back to the station to edit the video and then race back to the story location to front a live shot. It was a nothing short of NASCAR each night.

But even with the crazy nights I still had mornings and early afternoons to myself. I filled the time with a lot of golf. Before long my handicap was back down to scratch, as good as it was when I was playing competitively in college. I shot a career low 65 at Fig Garden Golf Club, a round that featured eight birdies and shot-making that made me believe it was time to start competing again-possibly at the professional level.

I played in the Fresno City Amateur, my first competitive event in quite a few years. I was very nervous when they announced my name on the first tee. A gallery was forming and it would walk along with us, watching each and every shot. I made a few bad swings and hit some loose shots, but with excellent chipping and a sizzling putter I settled down. It wasn't long before I found myself in the hunt at a couple under par. I faded toward the end, but considering I was up against some top-notch college players and past professionals I felt encouraged by the effort.

With my competitive drive stoked I started to shop around for which professional mini tour I might try my luck with. There were a couple-The Pepsi Tour and the Golden State Tour. I had friends playing both tours and I knew I could play with them so I figured I could play with the other guys out there. Turning pro would fulfill a lifelong dream of playing professionally, albeit part-time.

Being a golf professional has its advantages. Essentially you're at the top of the food chain and there's a certain status to that. If you can hook up with a manufacturer you can get free equipment. Not just any old equipment-really good, custom-fitted stuff that regular golfers have no shot of getting. It's an embarrassment of riches. You get clubs, balls and maybe even shoes while the manufacturer gets the exposure and writes it off as an expense.

Most golf clubs extend professional courtesy to pro golfers by letting them play for free. It's a fraternity. And of course there's a chance to make some decent prize money. You'll never make Tiger Woods dough on the minor league circuit, but you can make a couple of thousand dollars here and there while satisfying a competitive itch that could never be matched by playing skins with your buds.

With competitive fires burning within, there was an appreciable amount of wear and tear on my body. The twisting motion that is so much a part of the golf backswing is not exactly friendly to the back. By the time I reached the back nine of most rounds, my back was stiff and sore. I'd pop a couple of Advils and be good to go.

I'd battled through back pain before, especially after long practice sessions on the range and putting green. Constant bending over and twisting tweaks your muscles and soft tissue. It's easy now to see that a troubling pattern was developing. The back pain that usually started around the 13th hole was starting earlier and lasting longer. By the time I finished a round I'd probably gone through four Advils. It probably would've been smart to shut it down for a couple of weeks and let the healing begin. But with a qualifying tournament for the United States Amateur Championship coming up, I played through the pain.

Two weeks before the U.S. Amateur qualifier I had an invitation to play at the host course, Visalia Country Club. The Heney family asked if I'd like to play their home course and stay for dinner. It seemed like a perfect opportunity to play a practice round and enjoy time with a most interesting family.

The Heneys were from Dublin, Ireland. Dr. David Heney was a kidney specialist. His wife Agnes was from an eminently prominent family. They were wealthy, worldly people; superbly educated with a zest for life. As sophisticated as the Heneys were, they never let on. They led a pretty simple life. Quite simply they were good people.

Mum was a hoot, a storyteller who made everything seem funny because she put so much effort into the delivery. Every conversation was a performance. The lilt in her voice only added to it. Da on the other hand was almost impossible to understand. His Irish brogue was Guinness-thick. Then there was Charles, the Heney's 26-year-old son. Charles was very Americanized and translated Da's mumbling for me.

Charles was a medical student in the Czech Republic. He was funny, a decent golfer and he'd have a few cold ones with you in the 19th hole. Charles liked to tell funny stories about watching television news in Prague because, as he pointed out, it was quite different than the news coverage I did in the greater Fresno area. "Aside from the language, what's so different about it?" I asked one time.

"Well in Prague the weather girl takes her clothes off during the presentation," he said with a wink.

"Really?" I asked. "Is this legitimate TV news? Or are you watching some kind of porn channel and the hot chick is playing the weather girl fantasy role?"

"No this is real news," Chuck said. "I guess they're trying to pump up ratings. They're not as uptight about nudity in Europe as they are here."

I guess not. During our round of golf that day I shot an even par 71 which gave me a bit of confidence for the U.S. Amateur Qualifier. I left a few birdies out on the course and I figured if I could pick up a few more when it really counted I might make the big show, which really would have been something. But while nursing a pint of Guinness in the bar with Charles and his family, I wasn't just sore; I felt stingers shooting down my back and into my legs.

After finishing my beer and burger I hobbled out of the 19th hole and struggled to climb into my Ford Explorer. It was an hour ride home to Fresno. I adjusted the lumbar support cushion in the bottom of my seat and turned on smooth jazz. The pain only got worse as I headed north. I tried my best not to move, using cruise control as much as possible. When I pulled in my driveway I was in bad shape. I couldn't get out of the car. I honked the horn and my wife Jean came out to help me out of the car and into the house.

I could hardly walk and shuffled my feet just to move the short distance to get into the house. "Honey what happened?" Jean asked. "How did you hurt yourself?"

"I don't know," I told her. "It wasn't any one swing. My back just started getting more and more sore throughout the round. By the time I was getting closer to home my back was screaming."

"Alright let me call my dad and get you some pain medication fast."

We're lucky to have a medical doctor in the family. My father-in-law, Dr. John Gnap, is a family physician in suburban Chicago. Whenever we're sick and need a prescription in a pinch he's just a phone call away.

"Dad it's Kevin. I really hurt myself playing golf and I can hardly move."

"Do you have pain shooting down your legs?" he asked.

"Yes," I told him.

"You probably have a herniated disc. I'll call you in some Vicodin. But make sure you go see your family doctor tomorrow," he told me.

Jean fetched the feel better stuff from the neighborhood grocery store pharmacy and I took a pill as soon as she got home. It helped, but it didn't take all the hurt away. I couldn't stand up straight. The best I could do was about three-quarters-which was better than halfway. When I settled down for the night I didn't know what I would wake up to. It was not a good night's sleep.

I woke up groggy the next morning and called Dr. Michael Montgomery's office. They said to come right away. Jean offered to drive, but I figured if I could get in the car I could make it there on my own. I should have taken her up on the offer. I got to the doctor's office but could hardly climb out of the car. I scooted my butt cheeks over and used my hands to lift my legs, because I couldn't swing them over the edge of the seat. Once I got my feet on the ground I gingerly wedged my arms between the doors to give one last lift before I started walking.

My first step was hardly a step. It was probably more of a slide, followed by a stumble and a wipe out. Good thing I didn't completely let go of the door yet because at least now I had something to pull myself up. As I struggled to my feet, bolts of pain rocketed down my spine and into my right leg and foot. It forced me to shrink back down in a position similar to a baseball catcher's stance. I almost called in for help, but I swallowed my pride, bit my lower lip and sloughed my way into Dr. Montgomery's office.

It was almost the same scenario each time I stopped and started. It was as if my brain told my feet to go and they didn't listen. I had more stops than starts. My back hurt, my leg hurt and my spirit was wounded. I was a mess physically and psychologically. Dr. Montgomery could see the agony in my face and my body when he walked in and started the conversation. "How long has this been going on?" he asked.

"It's been sore for the past couple of months, usually because of playing golf. The pain was mostly lukewarm and manageable. But it went from lukewarm to boiling hot yesterday and overnight. I can hardly walk."

"Alright I'm going to give you some steroids, an anti-inflammatory and more Vicodin for the pain. I want you to go to physical therapy and I want you to see a neurologist," Dr. Montgomery said.

"A neurologist? What for?" I asked.

"Just in case you have to have surgery," he told me.

"Is it really that bad?" I asked.

"I hope we can take care of it with the meds and physical therapy," he told me. "But with the way you're walking and feeling I want to have a surgeon in case that's the way we need to go."

"Wouldn't we want an orthopedic surgeon instead?" I asked.

"Oh no. No, no, no," he said. "The orthopedic guys are bones guys. They like to bang around. The neurosurgeons are soft tissue guys and are gentler. Trust me, you want someone who's going to be very gentle."

He referred me to Dr. Richard Thorp, a respected neurosurgeon just around the corner. Before leaving Dr. Montgomery's office the young ladies behind the counter offered to walk me to the car. I should've taken them up on it because I almost fell on my kiester a couple of times. But I slowly and carefully climbed into the car and rolled down the road to the pharmacy. Later that afternoon I had my first physical therapy appointment.

Physical therapy consisted of light stretching and even lighter weight lifting. I was almost embarrassed by the barbell denominations. I was lifting ten pound dumbbells and forty pounds max with a pull down bar. I was afraid to do further damage so I moved very slowly and carefully. Working with the therapist loosened things up a bit, but I was far from being anywhere close to 100 percent.

After a couple of weeks of treatment there was no appreciable improvement. It was time to see the neurosurgeon. After checking in at the front desk, Dr. Thorp caught me shuffling down the hall to the examining room. "Looks like you have a herniated disc between L4 and L5," he said assuredly as we walked in together.

"Think so?" I asked. "What makes you so sure?"

"I see it all the time. I can tell because of your posture and how you're walking," he told me.

"How long has it been this way?" he asked.

"I've had chronic but manageable back pain for about the last three months. But the last three weeks it's been impossible-unmanageable. I can hardly walk. I mean look at me. I look like The Hunchback of Notre Dame. And you know I can almost deal with the pain. I just can't deal with what this is doing to my mind. I'm feeling depressed and I'm not a depressive person," I said exasperatedly.

"That's when you know," he told me. "That's when you know you have to do whatever it takes to feel better. When you're mind is cooked it's time. Here's what we're going to do. I going to have you get an MRI so we know exactly what we're dealing with. But I'm sure the problem is between L4 and L5. It's been my experience that 50-percent of these hernias end up fixing themselves with two weeks of rest. The disc goes back into place on its own. Now when I tell you to rest I don't mean sitting around on the couch, I mean resting flat on your back in bed, only getting up to eat and go to the bathroom. I'm not kidding. You have to be really still if it's going to work. So take two weeks off from work and try that. In the meantime I want you to go get that MRI tomorrow and come back and see me with the results in a week."

So I called my boss and told him I had to take two weeks off. He understood and asked if there was anything he could do. "No," I said. "Just be patient with me because if the rest doesn't work we're looking at surgery and who knows what else," I told him.

"Okay," he said. "Just do what you have to do to get better."

So I went to the MRI place to get a better picture of what was troubling me. I stripped down and put on a skimpy hospital gown and shuffled over to the tube. Before being slid in a technician asked, "Are you wearing any metal or have any piercings?"

"No. Why?" I asked.

"Because the resonance imaging works with magnets," she said. "If you're wearing anything with metal you'll feel a strong pull and it can be dangerous. We've had a couple of surprises with people and piercings in sensitive places."

"No jewelry and piercings for me," I told her.

Almost as soon as I said that my feet felt really heavy. It was as if something was pulling them down into a hole just in front of the tube's entrance. With the pull on my feet I felt a tug on my back that made it feel like it was going to explode. "OOOWWW!" I shouted trying to get help fast.

The clicking sound of the MRI stopped and the technician ran in the room. "What's wrong?" She asked.

"My feet feel like they're being pulled into a hole," I told her.

"Oh you left your shoes on. Do you have steel reinforced toes?" she asked.

I didn't know, but either way I figured it was the shoes that were holding me back. So I took them off, and in I went. It was a very tight fit with only an inch or two of head room, and even less on the sides. I don't know how a claustrophobe could ever get an MRI. I wasn't claustrophobic going in, but I might have come out a claustrophobe. The fit was so tight and the clicking sound so loud I wasn't sure someone would hear me if I called out for help. Just as I was starting to stir the examination was over. Not a moment too soon either. Another minute and I would have been a mess.

A couple of days later the film was developed and Jean and I picked them up at the imaging center. We brought them over to my neurosurgeon to read. "Feeling any better?" Dr. Richard Thorp asked as I handed him the slides.

"Not really," I told him.

"Remember I said it takes two weeks for these herniated discs to fix themselves when they do. We're not there yet. Just because you still feel bad now doesn't mean you can't get a lot better in the next couple of days. We'll just have to see. In the meantime let's take a look at these and see what's up," he said.

"*Oh,*" he said with obvious concern in his tone and a similar look on his face.

"What? What is it?" I asked.

Dr. Thorp let out a deep sigh and said "Look no amount of rest is going to fix this. Look at this," he said while pointing at the lower part of my spine on the film. "That's the disc. It's way out in the spinal column and it's *black*. See how the other discs are all light in color? There's no other way to fix this other than surgery."

I couldn't believe it. It took my breath away. I looked over at Jean and she was in tears. "Look I know you're very concerned about this but I have to tell you it's not that big of a deal, or at least not as big as some people have probably been telling you," Dr. Thorp said. "I'm going to do micro lumbar surgery. You're not going to be cut wide open. I'll make a small two and-a-half inch incision on the side of your spine, and cut out the part that's in the spinal column and then sew you back up."

"Will I ever be the same," I asked cautiously.

"Probably not," Dr. Thorp said. "But with a good result and your willingness to lose weight and rehab you can probably get back to 80, 90 percent."

I wasn't exactly thrilled by those percentages and Jean was still crying. But I thought about where I was and how I was feeling and you know something? Eighty or 90 percent was a helluva lot better than I was feeling now. "Will I ever play golf again?" I asked.

"Oh yeah," Dr. Thorp said. "You'll be playing again in two months. When you wake up from the surgery you'll walking normally right away."

"And there's no other alternative?" I asked. "Either have the surgery and hope for the best, or continue to live like this?"

"That's pretty much where we're at," Dr. Thorp said.

"Okay I'm pretty sure I'm gonna do it," I told him. "But you have to understand something. I have to talk to my father-in-law who's a family doctor about this first. And he's probably going to want to talk to you. Would you mind if he called?" I asked.

"No not at all," he said. "In fact I'll call him. Give me his number and I'll call him later today."

Later that night my father-in-law called me at home. "Kev it's Dad. Listen I talked to the surgeon and you really ought to go ahead with the surgery," he said.

"Are you sure?" I asked. "I thought you'd be against it," I told him.

"Well normally I would be. Back surgery is really a last resort. But after talking with Dr. Thorp he's right. There really is no other option but to operate. Just relax and let him take care of it. You're going to be just fine when it's all done," he assured.

Having my father-in-law's blessing gave me the peace of mind I needed. Until then whole experience of living in pain and visiting doctors and therapists left me wounded and confused. Prior to meeting with Dr. Thorp and having the MRI done there was a lot of guessing about what was specifically wrong with me and what to do about it. Once the film came back there was no doubt about what was broken and how we were going to fix it.

"I can probably get you scheduled for surgery next Tuesday," Dr. Thorp offered.

It was Thursday morning and a lot was happening fast. I thought something as serious as surgery would take more time to prepare for. Not here. It was a relatively simple procedure from Dr. Thorp's standpoint. "Just show up," he told me before wishing me well and moving on to other patients.

I booked the surgery with his staff and called the insurance company. The agent said she'd have to run the surgery by a consulting doctor to see if it was covered. "Wait a minute!" I shouted into the phone. "Why wouldn't this be covered?"

"Because it's an elective procedure," she said.

"Whaddayya mean elective?"

"Well there are alternative treatments and therapies to herniated discs. I have to consult with the medical advisor to see if your surgery is a viable option and it could take a couple of days," she said.

"Ma'am surgery is my *only* option. I've done the therapies and medication. Nothing has worked," I said exasperatedly. "My doctor says surgery is the only thing that can fix this. I've seen the MRI and my disc isn't just bulging out, it's in the spinal column. I can hardly walk and I'm in unimaginable pain. Really I can't take it anymore. You're killing me with this red tape crap. I pay for insurance for the assurance that these things will be taken care of. Now I have to deal with this? This is heartless. This isn't what I signed up for," I told her.

"I understand," she said sympathetically. "But our medical director is actually away on vacation and won't be back until next Wednesday. So that's the earliest I can have an answer for you."

"Look my surgery is on *Tuesday!*" I barked. "What if I had a heart condition and my life was threatened? You wouldn't hold that up! Don't you have a back up to the medical director? This is absurd! What the hell is wrong with you people? Interrupt your medical director's vacation, tell him to call me and I'll under no uncertain terms explain to him the absolute agony I'm in. This is shameful," I scolded.

"I'm sorry about how you feel. I will do my best to get in contact with him.

You could always go ahead with the surgery and hope he approves the coverage. But I can't guarantee that," she said.

"I am going ahead with the procedure and you will cover it. Anything less would be unacceptable."

"I'll get back to you as soon as I can," she said before saying goodbye and wishing me well.

Without insurance coverage I would have been on the hook for a little more than $11,000. I didn't have that kind of money in the bank at that time in my life, but I decided to move ahead with the surgery on schedule because I just couldn't live like I was living much longer. I would have done the surgery that same day if I could have because the physical and mental anguish had reached a breaking point.

The next day the phone rang. It was the insurance company. The consulting doctor had gotten word about my predicament and signed off on it. I was good to go. But the whole thing made me lose a lot of faith in insurance and it brought back painful memories of when my Mom died of brain cancer. I had to listen to my father haggle with the insurance company over the bills. One day I asked him about it and he told me, "Remember when your Mom had her second brain surgery to remove the tumor? The insurance company only wanted to pay for *one* day in the hospital after major cranial surgery. Her doctor wanted her to stay for at least a week."

And we wonder why healthcare is a mess in this country?

On the day of surgery Jean took me to the Fresno Surgery Center right around 7 AM. I stripped down out of my clothes and put on the standard hospital gown. I was in a waiting room adjacent to the OR having a conversation with my wife when Dr. Thorp came barging in with an excited expression on his face. "Kevin!" he said excitedly. "Great party last night. Great party!"

I didn't know what a jokester Dr. Thorp was, but the line about being at an all night shaker the night before my surgery was a great icebreaker. He must have sensed how anxious I was and fired off the zinger. I shot back. "Yeah great. You better have steady hands party boy. This is only my *life* we're dealing with here," I said sarcastically.

"Listen. Don't worry about a thing. I know exactly where I'm going and what to do. The surgery will only last about half an hour. You'll wake up a couple of hours later and you'll climb off the table and walk away. It's a lot easier than you think. Just relax," he said assuredly.

His words and demeanor helped a lot, but I was still a little bit nervous. Within minutes I was in the OR under general anesthesia and my damaged back was being fixed. I woke up two hours later with a dry throat and Dr. Thorp standing bedside tugging at my toe. "Kevin you did great. I cut the bad part out and you didn't have any complications. Why don't you get up and take a walk," he suggested.

Cautiously I slid my legs over the side of bed careful not to get tangled up in the IV that was attached to my arm and rolling stand. I let my feet hit the floor and I slowly started to stand, not completely erect, about three quarters up. "Stand up straight," Dr. Thorp encouraged. "You're going off memory. The damaged part of the disc is gone. Nothing is in the way of you standing erect."

I stood up straight, enjoying the elevated view and trying to remember what better posture felt like. It felt great. "Now start walking," Dr. Thorp ordered.

Muscle memory took over again. I started to shuffle my feet, afraid that a stinger was going to shoot down my leg if I moved too fast. "Just walk," the doctor coached. "There's nothing holding you back anymore. Just stand up straight and walk like you always have your whole life."

Standing tall I took my first big step, almost expecting to topple over after months of compensating for the pain and walking lopsided. I didn't stumble. I took another step. Didn't stumble. Another step. Same thing. "Now just start walking like you're taking a walk in the park," Dr. Thorp said.

Now I took off. I strolled down the hallway and came back. I couldn't believe the freedom of finally being able to swing my legs without worry and without pain. The simple walk down the hall brought tears to my tears and Jean's too. "You're all fixed," Dr. Thorp said happily. "Now come see me at the office next week and we'll catch up."

"I don't know how to thank you enough," I said with my voice cracking and my eyes welling up while shaking his hand.

"Just seeing where you are now, walking down that hall now compared to where you were when you could barely walk into my office. That's all the thanks I need," he said smiling before taking off and heading out the door.

My recovery at home consisted of rest and short walks. I took the dog for a walk around the neighborhood making sure she didn't pull too hard on the leash. I planned on taking two weeks off from work, but I went back earlier, simply because I felt well enough to do it. I had already used quite a few sick and personal days leading up to the surgery and I didn't want to be without time off when the holidays rolled around.

When I came back to work I did so with the commitment that I was going to put my health and my happiness first. I would celebrate each day, enjoying the simple pleasures in life, the most important of which was better health. I wasn't going to let my job status define how I felt about myself as a person. That's one of the things I discovered in my health crisis. So much of my self-worth and self-esteem were wrapped up in my work. Being demoted and other negativity in the workplace chipped away at who I was.

I don't know remember the exact moment of my epiphany, but somewhere in my recovery I had an aha! moment. My work, however visible it was, shouldn't have to define how I felt about myself as a person. Anchoring the news was what I did, not who I was. First and foremost I was a good person and a good husband. I was kind to others and had the respect of colleagues, friends and family. Rediscovering myself gave me a lift similar to the one Chris had when he found the *beat leukemia* golf ball in the basket. And like Chris, my discovery more or less found me, instead of the other way around.

Two weeks after surgery I discovered the gym. Like our golf trade at a local course, our sales staff secured a trade at a local health club. I lifted weights, did cardio and worked hard to strengthen my abdominals with carefully executed sit-ups. I got stronger, looked better, felt better and lost weight. I was fully embracing Dr. Thorp's strong urging to be fit, or risk returning to his operating table. Dr. Thorp was a nice guy but I really didn't want to see him again.

Whatever sacrifice I had to make to make that early morning workout was well worth it. It made the day seem so much easier. The way I looked at it, the hardest of my work for the day was done after I left the gym. I didn't so much like the workout itself, but I always enjoyed the result.

Two months to the day after my back surgery, I made plans to play golf. I called my pal Rich Rodriguez. "Richie you up for some golf tomorrow?" I asked.

"Walshy, you sure you can do it?" he asked. "I have a friend who's an orthopedic surgeon and he said that was major surgery you had. I don't want to see you get hurt again."

"No it's not a problem," I told him. "My doctor gave me the go ahead. He said it might hurt a bit, but I'm not going to break what's been fixed. Let's do it. It'd be great to be out again."

So we got together on a breezy September morning and played as a twosome. The first couple of shots were shaky. I could definitely feel some twitching right above my tailbone where Dr. Thorp cut me. But I kept playing, giving it the smoothest buttery swing I could. I didn't care about score. I just enjoyed the day, the walk, seeing squirrels gathering nuts and enjoying Rich's joy as he got on a roll and almost shot a personal best.

When I got to the 18th tee I realized I was even par for the day. Not bad for not having touched a club in three months. "Walshy you're actually playing pretty good golf," Rich told me.

"I know. I think it's just the simple fact that I'm not trying so hard. I'm just glad to be out here playing for fun," I said.

With that I teed up my Titleist Pro V1 and hit a solid fade down the right center of the fairway, giving myself a shot to go for the par five in two. The narrow 18th green was guarded by water in front and on the left side of the green.

"You gonna go for it? Or you gonna wuss out and lay up?" Rich teased.

"Oh no, I'm going for it. You kidding me?" I asked sarcastically. "After what I've been through, I don't really care if I hit it in the water. I've been worse."

I pulled out an eight iron and aimed at the pin, which was in the back center of the green. I caught it flush and the left to right ball flight left no doubt it would stay dry. The ball landed about fifteen feet right of the hole, took one hop and checked up. It left a reasonable look at eagle. The putt was flat and relatively straight. I put a good stroke on it and I knew it was in halfway there. With the perfect speed the ball was dead center. Eagle three, two under par 70 for the day.

"Walshy that was beautiful," Rich said. "You played so well. I'm really proud of you."

The round and everything about it did wonders for my spirit. My back was a little sore, but a few Advils took care of that. Later that afternoon I went into work feeling good about life. And that's when the boss called me into his office again. "Starting next week you're going to do the noon show," he said.

"Okay," I said nervously. "Anything else?" I asked.

"Yeah. We're taking you off the six, completely out of the evening rotation. I might be a good idea to start looking for another job," he warned with a look of concern on his face.

It was the other shoe dropping. I was more than crushed, I was angry. "Does this have to do with the same issues we discussed when you took me off the five and eleven? I asked.

He indicated it was.

"This is wrong and I won't stand for it! I did you a favor last time and didn't make a big deal out of it. You tell the GM if he takes me off the six, I'm not going to make it easy on you, and I will talk to an attorney about it," I yelled, as the news director's eyes got wide.

"Okay I'll get back to you," he said nervously, clearly shaken up by my anger and threats.

It didn't take long to have a resolution. The station caved in and kept me on the six. I fought and won the battle to stay on the newscast of record. I also inherited a new show-the noon news-that was our ratings winner at time. But it was bittersweet news. Even though I won that battle, there was no question I was at war with the GM. It made me feel insecure all over again. Just when I was starting to feel a sense of inner peace, the pieces of my life fell apart again. It was a tough time.

CHAPTER NINE

Magical Phone Calls and Miracle Matches

I CAME HOME FROM A ROUGH DAY AT WORK. IN A MOTION similar to the ergonomic weave of McDonald's employees at lunch hour, I walked a loop around the kitchen, grabbing a beer, turning on the stove and hitting the button on the answering machine. "You have one new message," the annoying female voice said as I took a swig from a Butterfield's Bridal Veil Ale.

The next voice was more familiar. It was my father-in-law. "Kevin it's Dad. I just got a phone call from the Hawaii Bone Marrow Donor Registry. Apparently you've turned up as a potential bone marrow match for someone. You may want to give this woman Renee a call."

I had the volume turned up so my wife Jean heard her dad's voice too. I turned to her and said, *"Honey do you realize what this means?"*

"No," she said, but she could tell how excited I was.

"Remember we went to that bone marrow drive in Hawaii for that little girl Alana? This means I matched someone else. I told you it would happen! This means I could save someone's life!"

The Hawaii Bone Marrow Donor Registry contacted my father-in-law because I put him down as a backup contact in case we moved. As a medical doctor my father-in-law knew what the call from the registry meant from a clinical standpoint, but he had no idea how I got wrapped up in such a thing. Judging from the tone of his voice he seemed worried. So I picked up the phone to fill him in. "Dad it's Kev."

"Are you alright?" he interrupted hurriedly.

"Oh yeah I'm fine," I told him.

"What's going on?" he wanted to know. "This bone marrow thing is pretty serious stuff. Is someone in the family sick?"

"No, no, no," I assured him. "Everything's cool. When Jean and I lived in Hawaii we went to a bone marrow registration drive in the hopes of matching a little Chinese girl who had leukemia. We didn't match her, but once you're in the registry you could end up matching someone else and they could call and ask you to be a part of the transplant. That's what's going on here. At least I think so," I told him.

"Oh that's great Kev. Let me know how it goes. That's really exciting, really exciting," he said before we said goodbye.

By now the water for the pasta was boiling, my beer was empty and I was buzzing with excitement. Suddenly that crappy day at work didn't seem to matter. Jean was aglow and Tiffany kept an eye and ear on the conversation giving the occasional goofy dog head tilt as if she understood what we were saying.

I dumped the Del Ecco macaroni into the pot and started the Three Cheeses Marinara Sauce on the other burner. I also poured a glass of CLOS DU BOIS Cabernet Sauvignon. Jean already had a glass of Riesling on the counter and she was rolling the meatballs in her hands. We toasted the day's wonderful reversal of fortune and wondered what was next. Not wanting to delay I picked up the phone and I called Hawaii.

"Hawaii Bone Marrow Donor Registry this is Renee," the woman said as she answered the phone.

"Hi. This is Kevin Walsh calling from Fresno, California. I got a call that I turned up as a potential bone marrow match. I just want to let you know I'm here and available if you need me."

"Okay that's good," the woman said. "It's always nice to hear that someone is willing to be a donor because there's a lot involved in the donation process and we don't recommend people get involved until they understand how big of a commitment it really is."

"Oh I *know* how big of a commitment it is and I want you to know I'll go anywhere, anytime. I'm all in. I'll do it right now if you want. I'm not kidding. I'll do it right now!" I told her happily.

"*Ah wonderful*," she said with her Pidgin English accent dripping with aloha.

"Now what can you tell me about the person who's sick?" I asked.

"Well you know I can't tell you his name and where he lives because of confidentiality reasons yeah?" Renee asked.

"Yes I understand."

"I can tell you it's a boy. He's 16 years old and has leukemia. He's very sick and his cased was marked urgent, meaning we would have to move fast. You're a five out of six match, not perfect but that's pretty good. You're the only known match in the world right now. In the days leading up to the transplant there's always a chance a six out of six match might turn up and be taken instead. But right now you're all we got."

To hear that you're the only person in the world who can save another person's life is a life-changing message. It's an interesting cocktail that gives you a lift but floors you at the same time with humility. In an instant you realize there is a place and purpose for you in the world above who you think you are and what you do. First and foremost you feel special. To be told there's only one of you in the world is to feel blessed almost beyond comprehension. It's almost like a warm, comfortable tingle penetrates every cell of your body. You feel larger than life. But right after that immediate euphoria, you soon feel small; as if what you've been doing your whole life is little more than a brush stroke on a grand canvas. But with each single stroke, the painting masterpiece comes to life.

Almost like Michelangelo said God worked through his hands in painting the ceiling of the Sistine Chapel, you just get out of the way and let the hand of God guide you. That's all I did. I didn't create anything. I was just there and available when a call for help came. There's no sudden pressure to elevate yourself, you know you are exactly where you need to be and that you have been selected for a most meaningful mission. What a wonderful gift it is to be chosen.

I was told I didn't have to go through donation process if I didn't want to, and that donors for other people had backed out before. "Really?" I asked. "What for?"

"Some people just had a change of heart," Renee said. "Others didn't have the time for it. Some were scared. We don't always know why, but we have to respect their wishes to not want to get involved."

"Oh I can't respect that at all," I told her. "How could you live with yourself knowing you let someone die because your day to day activities were more important than saving a life? I couldn't live with myself. But you won't have to worry about that with me. I'm doing it Renee."

"Okay great. Glad to hear it," she said. "Because you live in California I'm going to try to set you up with the Sacramento Medical Foundation Blood Center which handles the collection process. Is Sacramento fairly close?" Renee asked.

"It's about three hours away. That's close enough for me," I told her.

"Okay. I'll contact them and maybe they can work with you on doing some of the pre-blood work at your neighborhood blood center in Fresno. But for the bigger things like the full body physical, X-rays and the bone marrow extraction, you'll probably have to drive to Sacramento to have that done."

As the phone call was winding down I asked Renee for a little background on what I thought I knew about the donation process. "Hey Renee give me a little bone marrow 101 here. Isn't it almost impossible to match someone outside your race and ethnicity?" I asked.

"That's true," she said. "But there have been exceptions."

"Oh I know there have been exceptions because when I worked in Honolulu at KGMB Channel 9 I did a story on a woman who was Japanese turned out to be a perfect match for a white guy in Tennessee," I told her.

The line went silent for a little while. "That was me you did that story on!" she screamed into the phone.

"What? Whoa, hold on a minute here. You're Renee *Adaniya?* Oh my God! I didn't know that was you!" I told her.

"Oh my God! *I have chicken skin!*" she told me.

Chicken skin is island talk for goosebumps. My skin was bumpy too and the hair on my arms was standing up. When Renee Adaniya picked up the phone she only knew me as a name in a pile of numbers. The thought that we'd met before didn't even cross her mind. My registration form didn't identify me as a television personality. For all she knew I was just a regular guy from California who maybe lived or visited Hawaii previously. But when I mentioned that I worked on TV in Honolulu it all came back to her.

"Remember we met at Ala Moana Park and sat at the picnic table and you told me about your recipient?" I asked.

"Yes I remember. You were fairly new to the islands and you were a golfer. You really understood how important Chris Pablo's golf ball find was to the story of leukemia awareness. You were very helpful in getting the word out," she told me.

Speaking of Chris Pablo, it'd had been a while since I last spoke to him and I asked Renee if she'd seen or heard from him.

"Oh yes!" she said with a giggle. "Chris comes around here all the time. He's very active with bone marrow registration and awareness."

"And Alana Dung's family? How are they?"

"They're doing pretty good. It was hard for them losing Alana. But they are still very active in the community and encouraging people to register as potential donors," Renee said.

"Well next time you see Adelia and Steve Dung please send them my regards. And when you see Chris Pablo tell him I said hi and let him know that I'm a potential match. I think he'd like to know that. If it weren't for Chris, you and Alana Dung I never would have registered to be a donor. I didn't know anything about bone marrow donation before I met you all. Chris's story with the golf ball, meeting you and seeing how being a donor meant so much to you, and the huge turnouts for Alana's drives gave me the inspiration to register. Really without you guys we're not having this conversation today," I told her.

"Well when did you register?" Renee wanted to know.

"I registered on the last day of Alana Dung's drive at Blaisdell Arena. When I was covering your story, Chris's story and Alana's story on the air I was really pushy in telling people to do the right thing-get out, roll your sleeve up and register. Then I thought 'wait a minute, what kind of a hypocrite am I?' I'm telling them to do it and I haven't done it myself. I guess I had a crisis of conscience. My marrow was as good as theirs and who knows? Somebody might need me just like the man in Tennessee needed you. And I wanted to have what you had, a chance to save someone's life and hopefully meet them sometime down the road."

"Well maybe you will get the chance Kevin. I sure hope so. It's a wonderful feeling to connect with the person on the other end and I'm so glad you have volunteered to help," Renee said.

"It just means so much to me to be asked to be a part of something so special and important. This is the best news I've gotten in a long, long time," I told her.

And with that we said goodbye. Dinner had been made for some time and it had to be reheated in the microwave oven. Once Jean and I got it all together we sat down at our dining room table, said grace and talked about what the next few weeks would hold. "So how do they get the bone marrow out of you and into them?" Jean asked.

"It's almost like pumping oil," I told her. "They drill a hole in your pelvis and they pump out the marrow."

The verbal visual made Jean squirm.

"How do they pump it out?"

"They aspirate it. They put a thick needle in the hole and suck it out with an oversized syringe."

Jean squirmed and took a sip of Riesling. "Doesn't that hurt?"

"I guess so. I know it hurt a lot years ago. But what can you do? There's no easy way really to get the marrow out of the bones," I told her.

"I don't get how marrow is in bones. Bones are hard."

"Bones are hard on the outside, but they're hollow," I told her. "You know how when we give Tiffany a fresh bone from the butcher there's the dried red stuff that she tries to lick out? That's the marrow. It lives in the bones. Now your pelvis holds more marrow than any other bone in your body. It's like a big reservoir. That's why they go there to get it."

Ever the pragmatist Jean wondered if my effort to help someone else might end up hurting me. "Honey are you sure you're okay to do this?" she asked.

"Yeah. Why wouldn't I be?"

"Well you just had back surgery a year ago and they're going to drill right around the same place where your back connects to your pelvis. Aren't you worried that that's too much trauma in the same place?"

"I don't know. I guess I haven't really thought about it yet," I told her. "But either way I don't really think I have a choice. I have to do it. If I don't, this kid is going to die."

"I know. But honey you have to think about yourself too. I know you want to do the right thing and be helpful, but you can't do something that could leave you hurt. I don't want to see you like you were before you had back surgery. That's no way to live."

"I know honey," I told her. "But sometimes you have to put the greater good above yourself. I really want to do this for the boy and for me. I need this too. With all the work and health problems I've had in the past several months this makes me feel like there's something bigger out there for me. Who knows? This could be my greatest life's work. Like I told Renee on the phone, I don't know if I could live with myself if I didn't do it. Let's not worry about it now. Having these decisions to make is a good problem to have, don't you think? Let's just enjoy dinner and we'll address whatever issues we have when they come up, okay?"

"Okay," Jean said, as we settled into our pasta, our wine and other conversation.

A couple of weeks after learning I was a potential match, I was asked to emcee a Catholic evangelist event at my church, Holy Spirit. The evangelists were brought in from Los Angeles by the Catholic Professional Business Breakfast Club of Fresno. The CPBBC was like a Catholic Rotary. It was a networking, socializing, faith-based service vehicle. I was asked to speak about my Catholic experience to the CPBBC about a year earlier, and afterward I joined the club.

When you're a member of a professional organization, if there's a need for your services, you're going to be asked. In my case, that meant the phone rang whenever someone needed an emcee, host or auctioneer. I was slightly amused at the opportunity to watch Catholic evangelists in action because I'd never met one. In fact I didn't even know they existed. Catholicism has always been the quiet, calm, stable faith. Except for abortion and the death penalty, I don't think I've ever seen a Catholic get ramped up about anything.

One of the featured speakers that day was Tim Staples. Long removed from the Baptist and Assembly of God denominations, Tim still had a flair for Protestant drama. He was loud, passionate and demonstrative. He talked about what the Catholic faith brought him that others couldn't-namely peace of mind, and the consecration of Christ by receiving communion. Tim moved around a lot. He was persuasive, entertaining and got the crowd involved too. Many of his speaking points were punctuated by the audience that nodded and shouted verbal acknowledgement back. "That's right! You got it! Keep on it Brother Tim!" a large black man shouted repeatedly.

I didn't know who this man was, but he stood out. There just aren't a whole lot of blacks in the Catholic Church, so to see one in a sea of white draws your attention. He was tall, a bit chubby, funny, engaging and loud. He had so much enthusiasm that you wished some of it would rub off on you. The people sitting near him were clearly entertained by him. He wasn't just working the crowd. He was working me. He kept shooting me funny looks, winks and finger points all with the brightest of smiles. And I wondered, "Who is this guy?" "Had we met before?" I couldn't put it together but there was no doubt we were connecting for reasons I didn't understand. For a second or two I wondered if he was a plant.

When Tim Staples was done speaking it was time for lunch. Before sending everyone off to the church kitchen I thought I should say something pithy to recap what we'd seen and heard during the morning hours. "The best Catholics are converted Catholics," I said. "You know why? Because most converts made the choice to become Catholic. The rest of us were just born into it."

"Thaaaaat's Riiiight!!!!" screamed my black friend.

As the flock filtered out of the church hall and into the kitchen I approached the man who made watching a crowd so interesting. "Hi my name is Kevin," I said extending my hand. "Obviously you're a convert by the way you reacted when I said the best Catholics are converts. What's your name?" I asked.

"I'm Earl Neal," he responded.

"And so how did you become a Catholic Earl?" I asked.

"Well a few years back when I found out my son had leukemia I just hit my knees and prayed to God not to take my boy, to help us find a bone marrow donor."

No sooner had Earl said that I felt the air being sucked out of my body. I couldn't breathe and I had shivers throughout my body. My scalped tingled and the hairs on my arms stood up. It was the same feeling I had when I got the phone call three weeks ago that I was a potential bone marrow match for a teenaged boy with leukemia. Earl could tell something was up by my reaction. *"What is it Kevin?"* he asked with a concerned look on his face.

It took me a moment to get my composure back and then I said shaking my head, "Earl you're not going to believe this, but I'm in a situation similar to the one you went through with your son."

"Really? You have a son with leukemia?"

"No, no it's not that. A couple of weeks ago I turned up as a potential match for a 16-year-old boy I'd never met. He got sick and nobody in his family matched him. They prayed someone else would and it looks like I might be the only match in the world."

"Oh that's amazing," Earl said. "I'm sure his family really appreciates you trying to help."

"You know Earl the whole time we were listening to the evangelists I felt as if you were reaching out to me with all your showmanship. I felt like we *had* to meet for some reason. Now I know why. This is just too weird," I told him.

"Ah man, you're giving me the chills!" Earl said.

"I have them too!" I told him. "So your son gets sick and you start praying. How does that lead to becoming Catholic?"

"Well I wasn't exactly a practicing Christian of any kind at the time my son got sick, but my neighbors in Coarsegold were. I told them about my son and I asked them to take me to church. They said 'Well you can come to our church if you want Earl. But it is a *Catholic* Church.'"

Earl got the hint. It wasn't as if his neighbors didn't want him there, it was just that they thought he might be more comfortable at a traditional black church. "I said I don't care as long as God's there."

That's how Earl became a Catholic.

"What about your son? Is he okay?" I asked.

"Oh yes we found a bone marrow match and thank God my son's doing very well today," Earl told me.

With Renee Adaniya, the woman who I did a news story on a few years earlier reaching out to me with news that I was a potential match, and my stumbling upon a man so different, but so similar to me in other ways, I started to wonder if my bone marrow journey was a product of a predetermined fate with Godly connections.

CHAPTER TEN

Getting Down to Business: The Only Match in the World

WHEN SOMEONE IS SICK WITH LEUKEMIA AND BONE marrow transplant is their only option, the first place doctors look for a match is within the family. Siblings are the best option, but even then there's only a 25 percent chance they will match well enough to go to transplant. Parents and offspring might get a look too, but they will be half matches at best because of how antigens are inherited. So, more than likely, if they find a match, it will come from a stranger.

Today the chance of finding a match on the outside is between 60-88 percent. It's higher for whites than minorities because minorities are underrepresented on donor rolls. If you're lucky enough to find a match and go to transplant, there's only about a 40-percent chance of survival. Rejection and infection are common. There's no easy way around it. The lead up and the aftereffects are absolutely brutal. Going the transplant route is the ultimate display of how much the patient wants to live.

It was no sure deal that I would be the actual match that went to transplant for my 16-year-old mystery patient. To get to the point of consideration I had done well. Any regular guy or gal who registers at a local bone marrow registration drive has a one in 200 chance of turning up as a potential match and going to transplant. To put it another way, chances are you'll never get a call.

A lot happens along the way on the journey to transplant. Better potential donors with more exact tissue type deep inside their marrow may turn up and you may be bumped. This is what I faced. I was a close match, but not a perfect one. The boy's doctors were hopeful they could find someone else at 100 percent.

Matching bone marrow markers is much more precise than matching blood. A donor may or may not have the same blood type as their recipient, but it's quite common for the bone marrow recipient to have their blood type change to that of the donor after transplant. Deep inside the marrow there are key structural tissue markers. The goal is to match them all, to be perfect. Perfect isn't always possible. You work with what you have. It's like a contractor who repairs the column that crumbled. There may be a piece or two of marble missing, but if most of the pieces are there you might be able to restore the column and save the overall structure. Same is true with a less than perfect bone marrow match. It goes without saying the better the match, the better the chance of survival.

"Kevin it's Mark Kalstad from the Sacramento Medical Foundation Blood Center. Do you have a couple of minutes to talk?"

It was the call I was waiting for. "Yes I do. What's going on Mark?"

"Well I know you spoke to Hawaii about your turning up as a potential bone marrow match and donor. Are you still interested in being a donor if we need you?" Mark asked.

"Most definitely. I'll do anything you need. What's the next step?" I asked Mark.

"Well we'll have to get some preliminary blood work done and eventually we're going to need you to come to Sacramento for more extensive tests. Let's start with the blood work. Do you know where the Central California Blood Center is?" he asked.

"Yes it's right down the street from where I work. I'm a regular blood donor there," I told him.

"Okay good. I'm going to overnight the testing kit which has a bunch of vials and other medical related stuff in it. I'll make you an appointment at the blood center for tomorrow. I know you know the case has been marked extremely urgent so we have to move fast. Just bring the testing kit with you to

Kevin at Central California Blood Center holding his own bone marrow testing kit.

the blood center tomorrow. They'll know what to do with it. I'll be back in touch soon okay?" he asked.

"Yes we're good to go," I told him.

The next day I walked into the Central California Blood Center on Dakota Street. The receptionists knew me because I came in to donate my Type O Positive blood every two months or so. "Hi Kevin," one of the ladies said to me as I walked in the door and sat down. "Are you here to give blood again today?" she asked.

"No I'm here for bone marrow testing. I turned up as a match in a computer for a 16-year-old boy who has leukemia. I have to do some lab work here before we do further testing in Sacramento."

"Oh *you're* the guy! Yeah the Sacramento Medical Foundation Blood Center called yesterday and said a potential bone marrow donor would be coming in today, but they didn't say it was you. Oh this is so exciting! We haven't had a potential bone marrow match in a few years and it's a pretty big deal for us when we get one. Everyone is excited about it, especially Dean Eller. Oh wait until I tell him you're the one."

Dean Eller was the CEO of the Central California Blood Center. He was an Army medic in Vietnam and saw a lot of blood there. When he returned from the war he decided he'd had his medical fill and wanted to try something else. He chose real estate, which turned out to be a wise choice. Back then the Central San Joaquin Valley real estate market was exploding. Land was cheap, so was labor. The result was a home building boom. Dean got in at the right time, made smart decisions and did quite well for himself.

But a major family tragedy brought Dean back to his medical and blood specific roots when his 18-year-old daughter was diagnosed with a blood related cancer. Jenny Eller had come back to the family mountain house in Shaver Lake after a day of skiing at Sierra Summit. While changing into more comfortable clothes, Jenny noticed substantial bruising on her backside and around her hips. It didn't seem to make sense. Jenny was a good skier and hardly ever fell. Despite the exceptionally black and blue marks on her body, she felt no pain.

A family friend who was also a dermatologist checked her out. The bruising was far from his specialty, but he knew without an obvious injury and a known

Jeff, Claudia, Dean and Jennifer Eller. Shaver Lake, California.

preexisting condition, such dark bruising should not be taken lightly. Soon thereafter with consultations and tests run by their family doctor and specialists, Jenny was diagnosed with an aggressive form of adult leukemia. "I just remember walking out of Valley Children's Hospital after we got the news," Dean remembers. "I was so stunned I could hardly walk. And I just remember me and Claudia were on each side of Jenny with an arm on each of her shoulders. Jenny was holding us up."

Dean held his daughter's hand, as doctors would take marrow biopsies out of her hip. The needle going in was plenty painful, the aspiration—having the marrow sucked out was something else. "It just killed me to see my child have to go through something like that. I just told her to hold my hands and she squeezed," Dean remembers emotionally.

Dean and Jenny were very close. They shared a love of sports. She was a tomboy, but still girly girl enough to do princess things with her mom, Claudia, and her friends. On Dean's wall in his large office is a framed picture of Jenny in

Jennifer Eller. Died from complications of leukemia at the age of 21.

The Fresno Bee newspaper blocking the plate on a close play at home during an All Star softball game. It's a portrait of courage from what would be her last softball game.

Unable to find a potentially life saving bone marrow match, Jenny was warned by her leukemia specialist Dr. David Shorr to avoid playing sports because, if she suffered a bloodletting injury, her blood was so thin she'd probably bleed to death. Dr. Shorr didn't exactly like the fact that Jenny rollerbladed to her doctors' appointments and platelet transfusions. When he saw Jenny's picture in the paper he confronted her. "You see Jenny this is what I'm talking about," pointing angrily at the picture in the newspaper.

Jenny would have none of it. "You gave me a death sentence," she politely scolded him. "I have to live my life."

After that they were good. Dr. Shorr realized no prescription he could write, or medical advice he could give would slow down Jenny's zest for life. He would manage what would become of her condition instead trying to cure it. Sports and

Jennifer Eller's final softball game. The front page shot in the sports section of the Fresno Bee caused alarm for her oncologist.

PHOTO COURTESY OF THE FRESNO BEE

recreation made Jenny feel alive, even if she didn't have the energy she once did. She took more trips up to the mountain house in her beloved Jeep, and even had a late life romance with a young man who could've been long term potential if Jenny had longer to live. A few days shy of her 21st birthday Jenny suffered a series of strokes related to her leukemia. She slipped into a coma and died surrounded by her mother, father and brother.

Dean Eller honored Jenny's memory when he accepted the opportunity to be the chief executive officer at the Central California Blood Center. It was at the blood center where Jenny received several platelet donations that improved her quality of life and extended it. After the initial diagnosis, doctors thought Jenny would probably only live a few months. She lived almost three years. Dean was so grateful for what the center did for his daughter that he just had to have the job. Under his leadership and with Jenny's legacy, the Central California Blood Center increased its marketability and donations on all fronts. Dean couldn't save his own daughter's life, but he ultimately played a role in saving the lives of so many other people.

"Have you ever had sex with a man? Have you ever paid for sex, even once? Have you ever had a tattoo? Have you ever visited Haiti or sub Sahara Africa? Have you ever taken drugs intravenously?"

On and on the young man in the semi-private cubicle asked the prerequisite questions that made up the prescreening process. "No, no, no, no and no," I told him as he checked off those and two dozens other boxes.

"Give me your finger and you'll feel a little stick," he said as I turned my left index finger over.

He pricked my center of my finger right where the prints come together in a swirl. He squeezed a few drops of blood into a skinny glass tube filled with a clear liquid to check my iron levels. As he was filling out the paperwork my mind started to wander. I started thinking about the 16-year-old boy who needed a bone marrow transplant. I wondered what he looked like, what he did for fun and whether he had brothers and sisters. I thought about his parents and how worried they must be. It was almost as if I checked out of the interview with the screener for a few moments.

"Are you alright?" he asked noticing that I lost my focus on him.

"Oh yes I'm fine," I told him as I put my head in my hands. "It's just the enormity of this all is suddenly hitting me."

"I understand. We tell people all the time that by being a regular blood donor, you are helping to save a life. Everybody needs blood after surgery. With blood, as long as it matches, somebody else's blood is just as good as yours. They just happen to pull your blood off the shelf. In your case though it's much deeper than that. You may be only person in the world who can save this one person's life. That's deep man."

And that's really how I felt. To hear someone else describe my emotions so accurately was amazing. I got the goose bumps.

After that I was on a recliner chair waiting to be stuck with additional needles for more detailed blood analysis. Just as Angie the blood technician was steadying the two and-a-half inch needle to plunge into a fat vein in the crook of my left arm, I felt a heavy hand on my right shoulder and a familiar baritone voice.

"This is really going to hurt," laughed Dean Eller interrupting the moment.

"Hey Dean how are you?" I asked. "Have a heart will ya? Some of us are wimps when it comes to needles. But don't worry. I'm not so wimpy that I'm gonna run away."

"Good because that's what we need. So good to see you Kevin," he told me sincerely. "I just wish there was someone like you around when my daughter needed a match."

It was a touching moment. Dean complimented me on being generous and having courage. But when he sensed my anxiety he did what most guys do when showing macho affection-he made fun of me. Even though he was being specific about what was coming, it was just the right diversion to divert my attention and eyes away from the cold, steel needle that was about to plunge into my arm. And

Dean allowed me and the other technicians to hear about a very personal part of his life. Our conversation revealed his still grieving his daughter's loss years later. There was no question that my being in his blood center was a bittersweet moment for Dean. What I was about to go through was everything he wished for, hoped for and prayed for when Jenny got sick. He was heartsick, but his comments, however prickly they were; were truly from the heart.

Dean was an ordained minister. He wasn't raised overly religious, it just sort of found him later in life. He was easy to talk to because you never had to dilute the faith elements of conversation like you do with other folks. He wasn't a bible thumper who always seemed to work scripture into regular conversation. Dean was just a regular guy with a regular job, wife and family. If you wanted to talk about God he would. But he could just as easily talk about sports.

As sophisticated as the Central California Blood Center was, it couldn't handle all the blood and marrow testing that I would need. There was Qwest Laboratory down the street that would handle the rest. During an appointment a young lab technician named Dee Dee Brown did the blood draws. Dee Dee was a pretty black woman in her early 20's, with her hair pulled back in a knot and a blinding smile. She was a proud young mother with pictures of her newborn baby boy scattered around the office. "Are you feeling okay Mr. Walsh?" she asked politely.

"Yes I'm fine," I told her. "These tests are not really for me. My blood and marrow are being tested for someone else."

"Really? What for?" Dee Dee wanted to know.

"I've turned up as a potential bone marrow match for a 16-year-old boy who has leukemia. If everything tests out right, I could have bone marrow harvested from my pelvis and transplanted into him."

"Ooooh," she said with wide eyes. "That's cool!"

"Well we're not there yet. There could be a better match that turns up and is used instead. But so far, I'm the only match in the world."

Dee Dee smiled before she took a strip of surgical tubing and tightened it around my left arm just above the elbow, causing my veins to plump up. As she readied the needle and roughly a dozens vials to be filled she asked, "Are you nervous, or have you ever had a bad reaction while giving blood or having your blood sampled?"

"Yes I have," I told her.

"Really? What happened?"

"Well I'm always nervous about needles, but I always give blood anyway. No sense chickening out. A couple of times I've felt light-headed and fainted."

"Did you eat a good meal before coming today?" Dee Dee asked.

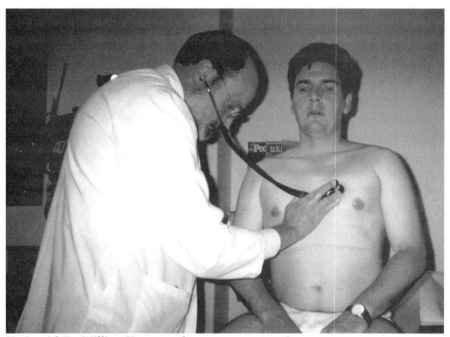

Kevin with Dr. William Keane, pre-bone marrow extraction surgery. Sacramento, California.

"Yes I had a big breakfast so we should be okay. But you never know," I told her.

Things were going okay until the fourth or fifth vial. My scalp started tingling and I felt my hair standing on end. Hot flashes reddened my cheeks and made it feel unbearably hot in the otherwise cool, air-conditioned testing room. As I watched Dee Dee switching the vials from the back of the suction needle I felt sweat beading up on my face. The room started to spin and I was quickly becoming nauseated. "Are you okay?" Dee Dee asked.

"I'm not sure. Why?" I asked deliriously.

Her eyes bulged and her hand covered her mouth. She was obviously afraid. "You're white as a ghost, like you're getting sick. Oh my God. Your shirt is soaked!"

"You know I just think I need to stop and lie down for a second. Are you okay with that?" I asked.

"Yes."

About five minutes later I felt great and we finished up with the rest of the blood draws. "Was I really that bad?" I asked Dee Dee before walking out the door.

"Yes," she said. "I don't think I've ever seen quite a reaction like that. Are you sure you can drive home?"

"I'll be fine. Thanks Dee Dee," I told her before walking out the door.

It would take a couple of weeks before my blood analysis was done and the tissue markers in my marrow were compared to the boy on the other end. I also had to make a six-hour round trip to Sutter General Hospital in Sacramento for a chest X-Ray and a physical. I was expecting the usual height and weight checks, but when I saw Dr. William Keane putting lubricant jelly on the surgical glove I really started getting nervous. When Dr. Keane asked my wife and station cameraman Jacob Jenkins who tagged along to get some video to leave the room, I knew Dr. Keane and I were about to have our Chevy Chase Moon River moment from Fletch. Jean and Jake laughed while walking out the door. I cried on the inside and pretty soon Dr. Keane knew my insides as well as my outside.

Awaiting results of all my medical tests made me nervous on two fronts. Considering the boy's grave condition I was worried he wouldn't be well enough to go to transplant, and selfishly I was concerned I'd be bumped for a better match. There was little I could do other than wait and pray. I wanted what was best for the boy, but I'd be less than honest if I didn't admit I would've been sad to come so close to being a part of such a profound, life-changing experience and then be bumped in the final hours.

I got on my knees plenty of times, but I also doled out much of the prayer duties to prayerful friends. My first call was to Claudia Smolda. Claudia is my best friend Steve's mother. She grew up on the mean streets of the Germantown section of Philadelphia. She had a city girl's edge, but the spirituality of a saint. Claudia was married to Wayne, who had a brief stay in the seminary before deciding the priesthood wasn't for him. On Monday nights Wayne and Claudia would drive from the suburbs back into the city to say novenas at Claudia's childhood church in Germantown. I asked her to include me in her intentions and that in the end I would be the bone marrow match that would go to transplant.

"I'll pray that God does what's best for the situation," she explained. "You see Kev sometimes what we want, what we hope for, what we pray for is not always what God wants and what's best for the situation. We may *think* we know what's best, but we need to let God decide that. He knows best. When will you know if you're the one who does the bone marrow stuff?" Claudia asked.

"No more than a couple of weeks because the boy is in bad shape and they can't wait much longer without going to transplant. I'll let you know when I know," I told her.

"Okay Kev. God bless you. I'm proud of you. But remember I'm going to pray for what's best."

Next I called Father Richard Smith. Originally from Orange County California, Father Richard was a priest at a small church in the vineyards of Selma, California. In addition to his love of God, Father Richard loved to play golf. One of his parishioners who was also a news producer at my television station introduced us. From time to time I would set up golf dates. Father Richard was a ringer. He was a single digit handicap and had all the latest and greatest equipment including Callaway Irons and Titleist Pro V1 balls. He was all in when I asked him to pray for the boy and me.

I called Sue Reilly in Huntingdon Valley, Pennsylvania. Mrs. Reilly played guitar and sang at St. Albert the Great Church. She also sang spiritual songs in the aisles of the Bethayres Shop-N-Bag while gathering groceries for her seven children. She reminds me of Sister Katherine, a very loving nun who taught my CCD classes. Interestingly Mrs. Reilly almost ended up in the convent before she met Hugh Reilly and became prolific. Like her husband, three of her sons became golf professionals. I knew her because I played golf with her sons, Will, Hughie and Michael.

"You know Kev God is calling out to you," she told me. "You are being touched by God. Do you know how special that is?" she asked.

"I think so," I responded. "That's been one of most humbling and wonderful parts of this. I haven't done anything yet, but to be told I might be a part of a life saving mission I guess it just makes you feel like a special person-like there's something special about you. That might sound weird but that's how I feel. I can't really think of any other way to describe it."

"You are special Kevin. We're all special in our own way. This is God's way of revealing it to you," Mrs. Reilly said. "I will definitely pray for you and the boy."

My final prayer request went to Luz Bergstrom. Luz was a Puerto Rican lady in her mid fifties. She was devoutly Catholic and would always seek my wife Jean and me out for conversation after Mass at Holy Spirit Church in Fresno, California.

Luz was a sonic boom, full of energy and zest. Like Mrs. Reilly Luz sang in front of our church. Her positive attitude was contagious, her kindness to others legendary and to hear her sing and speak in accented English just made Luz even more adorable. She did adoration, prayed the rosary and was easily one of the most persuasive and passionate people I knew in making a case for religion.

In my case she happily accepted my prayer request that I turn out to be the preferred bone marrow match for the boy and even offered to say a rosary for him and me. Those are no small steps. Saying a rosary can take a half hour or more.

It was a Monday afternoon. I had just gotten back to the television station from a long lunch. I was feeling sleepy and sore, the result of a heavy morning workout at Dan Gamel's Health Club followed by pasta overindulgence at DeCicco's Italian Restaurant. Looking to perk up I fetched a cup of Armen's legendary strong coffee from the front office before settling into my desk in the newsroom. The message light on my phone was blinking. I dialed up the voice mail and punched in my password as I took a sip of the bitter black coffee. This is the actual message from Sharon Redding of the Sacramento Medical Foundation Blood Center. "You were tested in March for a particular recipient. The transplant center has asked us to contact you to see if you'd be willing to be a donor for this person and proceed with information sessions toward becoming the bone marrow donor. I need to let you know this is an urgent request and so we're going to try to move on this rather rapidly. If you would give me a call as soon as you can I'd appreciate it."

As soon as I heard those words I felt my lips quiver and my pulse race. My heart climbed into my throat and tears poured from my eyes. I was numb and I sobbed like a small child. I didn't have any tissues in my desk so I used leftover napkins to wipe my eyes. Because the napkins were dimpled and rough, the constant rubbing and dabbing left my eyelids chafed and sore. But it was a good kind of sore. My co-anchor Molly McMillen looked from around her computer terminal and saw the pile of napkins on my desk. Aware of what I was going through to this point Molly asked, "Was that the phone call you were waiting for?"

"Yes it was," I told her.

"Maybe these would work a little better than what you've got," she said handing over a few soft Kleenex tissues.

Molly wasn't the only one who noticed my meltdown. Tony Kirkpatrick, a handsome, deeply religious, heavily muscled news photographer did too. The former gangbanger from Pasadena had turned his life around in his twenties by getting married and quickly pumping out enough kids to field a basketball team. Dedicated to his work and having a flair for everything he did in life Tony was nicknamed "Prime Time". Seeing him at that moment made me smile, because Tony really was a special guy.

Tony and I became lasting friends despite being different in so many ways. He was black, a rough-and-tumble city kid from Southern California. He was the picture of good fitness and healthy eating. He was always scarfing down something, usually freshly cut pieces of fruit. But occasionally I'd catch him eating Twizzler's Licorice Sticks. Prime Time never missed a workout and probably could have been a bodybuilder, or an actor. With his clean-shaven head, bulging muscles, shaved arms and a collection of gold around his neck, wrists and fingers Prime Time looked like a cross between a black Mr. Clean and Mr. T.

As striking as Tony's physical appearance was it really was his personality that made him stand out even though he couldn't have stood more than 5'8". Whenever we'd go to a sporting event, or someplace else where there were a lot of people, inevitably someone would pipe up and yell *"Prime Time!"* Tony would go over and engage, shaking hands and making new friends along the way. For a guy who carried a camera, you would have thought he made his living in front of it. He was recognized everywhere he went. I've never seen anyone better than Tony at working a crowd, and I've been around Presidents, Vice-Presidents and other world and sports leaders. Prime Time knew how to make quality time with everyone, even if it was for only a brief moment.

Tony liked me because I wasn't afraid to indulge in black culture. I could go into the rough parts of town and talk the language of the land in word and tone. One night Prime and I had to get viewer reaction to the cold, foggy winter weather. On the west side of Fresno I saw two black guys dressed like pimps pumping gas into their car late at night. They just looked like trouble by the way they dressed and their body language. Hardly anyone was out that night except these guys. "Pull over Prime. Let's go talk to those guys," I instructed.

"Oh I don't know cuddy," Prime said in protest. "Those are my peoples and I don't even know if I want go over there."

"Whaddaya afraid?" I asked him teasingly.

"Yeah," he said.

"C'mon Prime. Don't be such a wussy. Those aren't just your peoples. They're my peoples too. They're *our* peoples. Just relax. I know just what to say and how to say it," I told him.

So we pulled up next to the guys. Prime got the camera out of the back of the car and I walked up to the guys with my microphone in hand. "Sup fellas?" I asked in my most jazzy, brotherly tone. "Dang I can hardly see in this fog. How did you ever make it down the road driving in this fog?"

It was obvious the guys were not only in foggy weather, but also in a chemical fog from booze or drugs. "Well you know I just put my left tire on the yellow line and follow it down the road. So long as nobody comin' the other way, I just make it where I gotta go," the driver told me through bloodshot eyes.

"Really?" I asked.

"What about you cuz?" I asked his partner.

"The fog doesn't really bother me 'cause I'm mostly blind anyway. I just go where he go. Hope we don't bump into nothin'. So far I haven't seen anyone. Not that I could see them anyway if they were there," he laughed with the smell of cigarettes and liquor wafting from his mouth that was filled with sores and sorely in need of dental care.

"Right on guys," I said as I backed away and thanked them for their time. "Be safe now okay?"

"You got it," the driver said before climbing into his older model four door Oldsmobile and dinging a garbage can on the way out of the station lot.

"*You're crazy,*" Prime told me as we watched that spectacle and loaded up our Jeep Cherokee for the ride back to the station.

"See that Prime. Just talk to people calmly and friendly and they'll respond. You got all that on tape didn't you?"

"I hope so," he said. "The video may be a little shaky. I was so nervous at first, but then I was laughing at how you talked to them. That was so funny. Especially when you said sup? I can't believe you actually got them to talk. Those guys were so wasted."

Moments like that and so many others let Prime know he and I could do anything and talk about anything together. We picked each other up when the other was feeling down. When he saw me in tears at my desk dabbing at my eyes he put his strong hand on my shoulder, invaded my personal space and asked "Cuddy buddy. You alright?"

And I told him, "Prime, I've never been better."

We both smiled and I told him I'd explain the fuss when we rolled on the town later that night. "Can't wait cuddy. God Bless."

As I finished cleaning up my slobber, I carefully wrote down the number of Sharon Redding at the Sacramento Medical Foundation Blood Center before kicking back and enjoying the natural high of such joy.

When I got myself back in working order I picked up the phone and called Sharon Redding. No sooner had I introduced myself she interrupted. *"You're the one!"* You're the lottery winner and the preferred match!"

I tried to match Sharon's excitement, but when I opened my mouth to speak no words came out. I couldn't talk but I sure could cry. The tissues Molly gave me earlier were no match for the emotional overflow, so she gave me the whole box. "Kevin? Kevin? Are you there? Kevin it's Sharon Redding, are you okay?"

I managed a meek "Uh huh."

"Kevin is there someone in your family who had an experience with leukemia?" Sharon asked.

"No," I told her. "But this is so deeply personal and special to me. I'm so glad you called."

"Do you want to take some time and call me back in five minutes?" Sharon asked.

"Yes let me do that. I'll call you right back."

In the time I took to gather myself together I thought about where I had been and how this bone marrow journey of mine was evolving so splendidly. I thought about Chris Pablo and his golf ball. I thought about little Alana Dung and her massive bone marrow registration drive turnouts. I thought about Renee Adaniya, a past marrow donor who I did a news story about years earlier calling with the early news that I too was a potential match. And then there was Earl Neal; the black man whom I'd met at church who became a Catholic after his son became sick with leukemia. Everything seemed to be falling into place.

After catching my breath and cleaning up I picked up the phone and called Sharon Redding back. "Oh you sound so much better," she told me during the reconnection. "I've never had quite that reaction from a donor."

"It surprised me too. I don't know. I knew it would be special to be chosen, I just didn't know it would be so emotional," I said.

"Well it's nice to know how much it means to you because it means a lot to us and certainly to the family of the boy who needs your marrow," she told me.

Over the phone we worked out logistical details, some of which involved curbing my alcohol and caffeine intake. I'm no lush, but I like an occasional libation and I *need* coffee to get me going in the morning. Without my morning Joe I'm grouchy, even to myself.

Cutting out my beverages of choice led to cravings for other things-namely sweets. All things considered I wanted to give the healthiest possible marrow I could. I may have fudged on the diet, but diehard workouts made up for it. I dropped a couple of pounds and matched the boy's weight at 184. The last time I weighed that little I was the same age as him.

A couple of days after getting the call that I was the preferred match to go to transplant I got another call. It was word the boy had developed shingles and wasn't well enough to start the grueling pre-transplant process. Chemotherapy and radiation would destroy the boy's diseased bone marrow and his body's immune system making him very vulnerable to infection. It's as close as you can come to death's door without opening it. Once there something as simple as the sniffles could do you in.

Doctors diagnosed the boy's shingles virus before they went too far with the aggressive prep work. Had they not one can only imagine what would have happened. But in trying to get the shingles under control they feared they might weaken an already ravaged body making the risky transplant a non-option. We set another transplant date for three weeks later. More than a few of us were concerned we might not make it that far. It was 21 days of agony for the boy and his family. I was worried sick. I took all that grief and anxiety and applied it to prayer reminding St. Jude in novena after novena that we didn't come this far not to give transplant a shot.

Three weeks later I got the call we were *on*. The boy was good enough to go and I was to get to the hospital for my end of the extraction deal. Talk about relief! I was thrilled and beginning to feel as if this was going to have a happy ending despite the odds. We'd had enough close calls and survived them all. By now I figured there was nothing stopping us. We just had to do the deed.

CHAPTER ELEVEN

The Surgery

THE ROAD TO MY BONE MARROW EXTRACTION SURGERY didn't get off the ground without something dogging us. On Highway 99 about a half hour north of our Fresno home we realized we didn't leave the house open for The Worm. Worm's real name was Matthew Lievre. He was a coworker who was taking care of our German Shepherd, Tiffany. We pulled over at a mini mart and my wife Jean called our neighbor Elizabeth Lorber who laughed at our forgetfulness, but offered to crawl through the doggy door and unlock the front of the house for Worm.

During the 160-mile evening drive Jean and I talked about the news of the day, our family and friends, and how this journey of ours just might change our lives. We didn't know how, but there was no doubt we were going to be different people on the ride home. "Honey is there a chance that you could really get really hurt during the surgery?" Jean asked

"There's always a risk being under general anesthesia. But I really think we're going to be fine. Besides what's the alternative? We can't turn back out now. I couldn't live with myself if I did. Plus the boy will die. There's no other choice," I told her.

"How long will it take before you feel normal again? I mean are you going to be in pain when it's over?" Jean wanted to know.

"I think I might have pain in my pelvis for about a week, but I really don't know. I've never done it before so I guess there are a lot of unknowns. Let's not worry about what we don't know and concentrate on what we know for sure. We know it's the right thing to do. Someone needs our help and God wants us to do it. There's no way we'd be in this situation if neither were true. Let's just enjoy it for what it is. We've been wonderfully blessed," I told her.

The conversation made the three hour drive seem like half that. We checked in to the downtown Holiday Inn just after 10:30. Room 1119 had a dark, faux wood décor, a soft king-sized bed and a view of Interstate 5 and Denny's. We unpacked our bags and I quickly found my St. Jude statue and prayer card. I wanted to fall asleep fast because it had been a long day. But I didn't want to crash before saying a novena. After prayers I slipped under the covers, closed my eyes and tossed and turned for at least an hour. I nudged Jean but she was sound asleep.

With the clock approaching midnight I was starting to worry I might never fall asleep. With the wakeup call coming at 4 A.M. I knew at best I'd have half my usual amount of sleep. Feeling fidgety I went in search of sweets. Dressed in a robe I wandered down the hall looking for the vending machine. Along the way I bumped into two lovers coming off the elevator, partially disrobed and desperately in need of privacy. We shared a laugh before I fetched some peanut M&M's and went back to my room.

While settling into the corner table to eat my snack I looked back out the window and up in the early morning sky. The moon was almost full and the stars were shining brightly. Traffic was brisk at the late hour and there was a steady stream of young adults moving in and out of Denny's across the street. I wondered who are these people? And what are they doing out so late? Then I thought about the boy who would receive my bone marrow later that day. Would he grow older and have the same chance to do something as simple as staying out late with his friends and searching out a greasy spoon after a few cold ones? It was a good thought to ponder and the last one I had before the Zs set in.

It wasn't a long rest. In fact the three hours or so of sleep I had felt like a few minutes at best. Jean tickled me like she always does to take the edge off and it wasn't long before I put my feet on the floor and got moving. I knew it would be a couple of days before I could exercise after the bone marrow extraction so I did some stretching and abdominal crunches. I worked up a light sweat during the hotel room workout and retreated to the bathroom to shower and shave. Before dressing I did a couple of things. I made sure I had on clean underwear and I taped a small picture of St. Jude over my heart.

I checked into Sutter General Hospital right on time at six and was quickly handed a hospital gown with orders to strip off everything underneath. The gown hardly covered the undercarriage. A thoughtful nurse tried to help me cover up, by retying the loosening strings in the back. Nothing seemed to work. As a result there was a pretty good view of my backside.

After the requisite height and weight checks I settled into a pre-surgery bed near a television. The bed was about as comfortable as a cabin cot and to hear my wife brag about how comfortable she was in the recliner next to me made me want to switch spots. Just as I was about to ask for the swap a nurse came in to draw some blood. "More blood?" I asked. "I thought I was done with that," I told her.

"No we need a little more for cross-referencing. We need to make sure the blood we're giving you back is actually your own," she said.

A few weeks earlier I donated a few units of blood that were stored and to be used for me to replenish the blood and marrow I would lose in the extraction process. There's no better blood than your own so I told the nurse, "Go ahead and poke away. Let's get it right."

By 7:30 a representative of the Sacramento Blood came by. "Hi Kevin. I'm Mary Allen from the blood center. How are you doing?" she asked.

"I'm good and I'm ready," I told her.

"That's great," she said. "We're so thankful for what you're doing."

Mary took a few pictures with a disposable camera and gave me a reassuring pep talk. I don't remember everything that was said, but I remember Mary was very comforting, almost motherly.

"Mary I get to write a letter to be sent with the marrow if I wish to, right?" I asked.

"That's right. You can write whatever you want so long as you don't give any indication of who you are and where you live. We'll make sure it rides in the cooler along with the marrow," Mary said.

Jean handed me a yellow legal pad and I bummed a pen from an orderly tending to the next patient over in the pre-surgery holding area.

6/22/00

Hello Friend,

I know you're a football player. I played quarterback years ago. I've given you the ball, now I want you to run with it. I'll be waiting for you in the end zone. Take care, be strong and be healthy.

— Your Donor

Shortly after writing the letter, a heavily muscled black man with a spirit as warm as freshly baked cookies came by my bed rolling a gurney. For a second I thought it was Prime Time—my cameraman pal from Fresno. Considering my television station wanted to document my procedure, it wasn't a stretch to think it

Jean Walsh placing note Kevin wrote to his bone marrow recipient in envelope that would ride along with the cooler.

might send an extra cameraman to get extra footage. Prime could pull a prank or two and I wouldn't put it past him to bum surgical scrubs from an orderly, steal his cart and then roll up to me with a gotcha grin. But it wasn't Prime rolling up the meat table, it was a guy named Larry.

"Kevin Walsh?" he asked in a friendly voice.

"That's me," I answered.

"It's time to go. Climb aboard," he said.

As Larry pushed me down the hall I felt myself letting go of all the tension I had building inside of me for weeks. It wasn't so much my doing as it was Larry's. He didn't say much along the way, but there was something about him that made you instinctively trust him. He was so big, so strong and so friendly I thought there's no way this protective man would roll me into a situation that wasn't meant to be.

"Mr. Walsh, you have a nice day now and good luck. I'll be thinking about you today," he said before turning me over to the OR nurses in a pre-op room next to the larger room where the surgical extraction would be done.

"Thanks Larry," I told him. "I'll keep you in my thoughts and prayers too," I told him in return.

In addition to the surgical staff, also waiting in the pre-op room was Jacob Jenkins. He was the cameraman assigned to shoot video of doctors harvesting my marrow. "Hey Kev just to let you know, I brought some eyehooks that I'll give to the doctors when they're done the drilling," he said with a cackle.

Some of the staff probably didn't appreciate or get Jake's barbaric wit, but I did. Jake and I had a running joke that when this procedure was all said and done he was going to string me up. It took big ones to make that kind of a joke in such company, but that's what made Jake who he was. He'd say anything in front of anyone.

Jake took as much as he gave. While his joke had me howling, I took a stab at his headwear. Jake is a Native American and normally wears his hair long and braided. On this day he had to curl it up and stuff it under a surgical cap. It looked ridiculous. "What did you go to the local meat market, buy a sausage and then let the thing curl up on the top of your head?" I asked acerbically.

That got the crew laughing including Jeni Tyler, a station producer who tagged along to watch the surgery and help Jake with his equipment. Jeni gave Jake a friendly punch in the arm after my hair comment driving home the point that I got him good.

All kidding aside Jake was a pro's pro when it came to shooting video. He didn't just make it look like you were looking in on a procedure, he made it seem like you were looking right over the surgeon's shoulder-which of course you were because Jake's camera was right behind the doc's head. And Jake was a master of capturing natural sound. Before they wheeled me off into the big room Jake made sure to clip a wireless mic on my gown to pick up conversation and any other pertinent sound.

Lead surgeon Dr. William Keane came in and gave me a briefing on what to expect. "We'll take about two pints worth of marrow from the top of your pelvis," he said.

The anesthesiologist, Dr. Cho came by and we briefly discussed the possibility

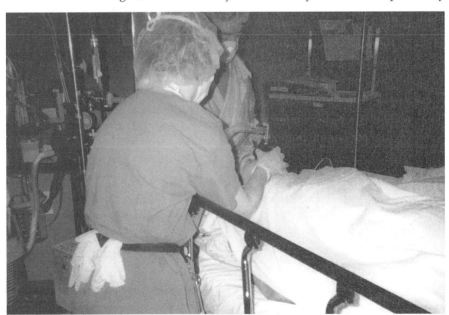

Kevin undergoing anesthesia treatment prior to bone marrow extraction surgery.

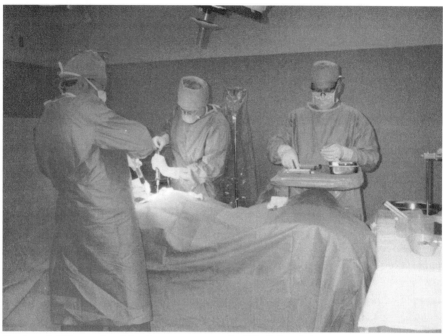

Doctors drilling and sucking bone marrow out of Kevin's pelvis.
Sutter General Hospital, Sacramento, California.

of me staying awake during the procedure. Medically it was possible and I wanted to experience the extraction for all that it was. "I don't think that's such a good idea," Dr.Cho said. "Your blood pressure might drop and make you feel really nauseated. I just think you'd be a lot more comfortable if you were completely out."

"Okay that's enough for me. I'd rather not throw up in the middle of the procedure and God forbid have Jake capture it on camera. Let's go general. Knock me out," I told him.

"Have you ever had general surgery before?" Dr. Cho wanted to know.

"Yes. I had back surgery a year ago," I told him.

"How did you feel when you woke up?"

"It was like the mother of all hangovers. I felt awful. I couldn't stop vomiting."

"I'm glad you told me beforehand because we can take care of that," Dr. Cho said before handing me a small cup of a sour-tasting antacid that I drank while being rolled into the operating room.

My first impression of the OR was that it looked really *old*. If I had to guess, it was probably 50 years old with blue and green tiles that you might find in your grandparents' bathroom. But it was bright, impossibly clean and having full confidence in the surgical team it wouldn't have mattered to me if we did the surgery in the hospital parking lot.

The surgical table was bent almost like something a masseuse works on. It had a bump in the middle to fit the curvature of my body. But it was a tray of tools next to the surgical table that really got my attention. Lined up like little soldiers on a green surgical cloth were pokers, mallet-like hammers and large syringes. It didn't take a brain surgeon to figure out what everything was for. The docs would hammer away on the pokers, stick the syringes in the holes and give a mighty pull to suck my marrow out. It was a visual that I could have done without, but I knew I could laugh about it later. What I really wanted was a dose of Lidocaine to knock me out and get the poking party started.

Just as I was thinking about drugs Dr. Cho poked a syringe into the port of my I/V.

"Yo doc. How long before I start feeling sleepy?" I asked.

"Oh not long. Probably less than 15 seconds," he said.

I tested the doctor's prediction by lifting my head off the gurney and finding the clock across the room. I counted five seconds and planned to put my head down for just a second before checking the clock again. I never got a second look.

Here's what I missed. Doctor William Keane and Dr. Antoine Sayegh spent the better part of 40 minutes drilling and banging into my pelvis with the pokers. Once they pierced the bone deeply they replaced the pokers with large syringes that had heavy gauged needles. Threaded inside the thick needles were thinner needles, which plunged deep into the hollow center of my pelvis. I've seen the video and it's hardly delicate. Piercing bone takes some serious muscle power and once you're there you're hardly done. Sucking the marrow out takes a mighty pull on the plunger. If you didn't see my ass and know doctors were performing surgery, you might have thought they were trying to remove a car's engine block.

In the end the doctors got what they wanted, about a freezer bag's worth of thick, rich marrow that was speckled with flecks of white that were chips of bone. They packed it in the cooler along with my note. Almost as soon as they were rolling me out of the OR, my marrow was on the road to its final destination, the 16-year-old boy.

CHAPTER TWELVE

Waking Up
and Moving On

THE FIRST THING I SAW WHEN I WOKE UP A COUPLE OF hours after surgery was my wife Jean. Her face is always a great sight, but especially then. "Hi honey," she said. "How are you feeling?"

"You know I feel pretty good," I told her. "I feel refreshed, like I just took a nap. I definitely feel better than I did when I woke up from back surgery."

The bed in the recovery room wasn't too comfortable so I asked Jean if we could switch places. The recliner she was sitting in was much softer, and considering the banging around my backside underwent a couple of hours earlier it was a better fit. As easily as I settled into the recliner, Jean was doing the same in the bed. In fact she fell asleep. When doctors and nurses stopped by the room to check in they weren't sure who the patient was with Jean being in the bed instead of me. I assured them Jean was just fine. I was too.

Jacob the cameraman and Jeni the producer stopped by for a chat. Jeni pinned the lavaliere microphone on my gown and asked a few questions that would be used for a later story. Jake was talking about how barbaric the surgery was. "Really? What happened?" I asked.

"Oh yeah it was really something," he joked. "For a moment I didn't think you were going to make it."

I played along asking Jake if he took a swing with one of the hammers, or a poke with a poker. "No but I tried to convince them they ought to let me screw in the eyehooks," he said.

"And they didn't go for it? Jake you gotta be more assertive," I told him.

It was all a goof and it was the best medicine I could've had at the time. Jake and I connected by pulling tricks on each other and busting balls. He got me good, but we both knew I would get him back eventually. At the heart of the matter he was proud of me and the fact that he offered to shoot the surgery when some of the other cameramen got squeamish about it spoke volumes about Jake's courage. It couldn't have been easy to have a steady hand considering the graphic nature of the extraction procedure. But I was sure Jake's video would turn out to be as steady as a lead ball rolling on a smooth track.

Jake's joking around actually piqued my curiosity about what my surgical wounds looked like. So I excused myself to the bathroom to have a look for myself. When I closed the door behind me I realized I was alone for the first time in several hours. I took a deep breath and realized for just a moment I didn't have to be anything or anyone to the many people who were following me around and catering to my every need since arriving at the hospital early in the morning. It was just me, the toilet and the smell of hospital bleach.

As well as I felt, the reflection in the mirror didn't match it. The guy I saw looked like he'd been out all night on a bender. My hair was disheveled and dark circles had formed under my eyes. But there's just something about looking in the mirror after you know you've done something good. You see more than your reflection, you see deep inside your being and into your soul.

I closed my eyes and breathed deeply through my nose hardly getting a whiff of the bleach that smelled so strong just a minute earlier. I was too busy getting in touch with what I couldn't see. I felt the weight of my lungs expanding and contracting. I listened to my breath; the pitch higher going in than coming out. The simple rhythm of life's simplest reflex breathed life deep into my body and inside of the bones. I felt enriched, as if I needed spiritual and emotional replenishment before my body regenerated and replenished what was taken in the bone marrow extraction.

Whenever I experience profound life moments I always place my hand over my heart. It's a "feel" thing. A simple touch on the outside helps me to get in touch with the inside. Imagine saying the saying the Pledge of Allegiance or singing the national anthem with your hands at your side. It just wouldn't feel the same.

When I touched my chest I felt something lumpy under my gown. I had forgotten that someone special was with me since early morning and with me now. The paper cutout of St. Jude was still taped over my heart. It had been almost nine hours since surgery and his picture still stuck. I half expected he would have fallen off by now, but even with his sides curling up he was hanging in there in what was the most seminal moment of my life. I peeled him off and held him in my hand as I said his novena once more. I felt a rush of warmth coming over me, and the hair on my body standing up. Then a more primal instinct called. After hours of being pumped with intravenous fluids, nature replaced spiritual nurture. I had to pee.

While washing up and getting ready to head back to the friends and family that awaited me I realized I had neglected to do what I entered the bathroom for in the first place. Gingerly I peeled the adhesive tape that was holding a large dressing in place over my puncture wounds. The bandage was soaked and slippery. The fact that it was stuck to a part of my body that had a healthy patch of peach fuzz didn't make it any easier. In peeling the bandage back I not only did a makeshift grooming, I may have even taken off a few dermal layers. It hurt-a lot. The slow peel was going nowhere and if anything seemed to be prolonging the agony. Having had enough I clenched my teeth and braced myself for what would be one mighty final pull. Riiiipppp it went and finally I had a chance to see the evidence of what was left of the most important thing I'd done in my life.

I couldn't get a good look at the holes along the top of my butt crack because, like the back of your head, it's one of those spots you can't really see. The only way to get a good look was with the help of a mirror. Even that was no simple task because the mirror above the sink was too high to get a good look at anything below my chest. Needing to elevate myself I used the toilet as a step to climb up on top of the sink. Then I turned my backside to the mirror and peered over my shoulder while doing a delicate balancing act. I saw four dark holes with dark, almost black blood oozing out. I wasn't sure if it was a beautiful sight, or simply gross.

While posing like a lawn jockey on the sink top I thought about St. Thomas. He was the one who didn't believe it when the other apostles said Christ had risen from the dead and appeared before them. He would only believe if given the chance to see Jesus himself and place his fingers in the holes left behind from the crucifixion. The story of Thomas is where the expression "Doubting Thomas" comes from. Like Thomas I thought poking my finger in my own holes would further help me realize how real what I just went through really was.

I washed my hands carefully making sure to scrub the tops and bottoms and between the fingers. I took my right index finger and circled it around the hole on the far right side of my pelvis. When I tried to gently slide it in the hole I braced myself for what I thought could be pain or something else unsettling. The plunge didn't go far because my finger didn't fit. So I tried my pinky instead. It went right in. Next hole, same thing, and so on. It was wet and warm, and yes I was a little grossed out. But like Thomas I had no doubt when I was done that what I did was real and it really was God's work being done through me. You have to have faith to believe that and an affirmation would certainly help. That would come later.

I climbed off the sink, cleaned up and rejoined the party of friends, family and coworkers clogging up my hospital room. "You were in there a long time," my wife noticed. "Is everything okay?"

"Yeah I'm fine. I just wanted to see the puncture wounds," I told her.

"Really? Why?"

"I guess I just wanted validation. I wanted to know that what I gave really was

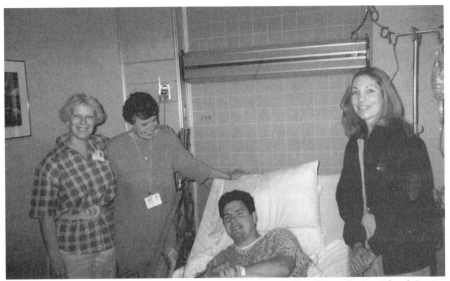

Kevin post op with representatives of the Sacramento Medical Foundation Blood Center and wife Jean.

of flesh and bone. I didn't want to have to guess about anything. Now I don't have to. I know what I did and I know how it felt," I said with satisfaction.

Because I fasted for 12 hours prior to the surgery, I needed to satisfy some hunger. I rang the nurse who ordered food from the kitchen. The hospital faire took the edge off, but looking forward to a better meal later I made sure not to eat it all. Mary Allen from the Sacramento Medical Foundation Blood Center stopped by and we had a nice conversation.

"How soon will the boy who's receiving my marrow have his transplant?" I asked.

"He's having it today," Mary said. "As soon as you were done, the marrow was sent on its way with your note in the cooler."

"That's so cool. I can't believe I've been a part of this," I told her as tears welled up in my eyes. "I don't think I've ever felt so good about something I've done. I'm just proud to have been a part of it."

"And you know something Kevin?" Mary added, "you may not be done yet. This will always be a part of who you are. You've expressed interest in knowing the results and someday having contact with your recipient. If he and his family agree to it there's no telling what could happen. It could be really special."

"I hope so. I can't imagine not knowing the results because I'm not good with uncertainty. I want to know what happened one way or another. I just hope he does well and feels better," I told her before we said goodbye.

Soon after my conversation, Dr. Antoine Sayegh stopped by for a second visit. "Kevin how are you feeling?" he asked.

"I feel fine."

"Are you in any pain?"

"A little, but nothing unmanageable."

"You know you can stay here tonight if you want, or even longer. But if you think you'd be more comfortable at home I can release you this early this afternoon."

"I've had a good stay, but I think I'm ready to go home. Plus we have dinner plans with some friends in town later tonight," I told him.

"Oh great. Yeah let's get you out of here then. I'll get the paperwork started downstairs. In the meantime let me write you a prescription just in case you need something for any pain. You can stop by our pharmacy on the way out."

"Thanks Doc I really appreciate it," I told him as he walked out.

Jean and I packed up the room and left the hospital with a vial of pink Vicoprofin pills. It was just after one in the afternoon and we were hungry. "What do you feel like?" I asked Jean.

"Italian," she said.

"Yeah me too. And I could really use some wine," I told her.

We didn't have to go far as we found a nice semi-upscale place right around the corner. Jean ordered Fettuccine Alfredo and a glass of white wine. I had veal parmigiana and a glass of Cabernet Sauvignon. The wine was wonderful and the food fabulous. The lunch crowd was mostly gone so we pretty much had the place to ourselves. We talked about the day and how much fun we expected to have later that night catching up with an old friend that we hadn't seen in six years. Before I knew it my glass of wine was empty. So I had another one, and one more after that. My heart was happy and light and so was my head. Jean drove back to the hotel.

After a mid afternoon nap and shower we headed over to Stephanie Nishikawa's house. She and I used to work together at Guam Cable News in the U.S. Territory of Guam in the Western Pacific. She taught me how to put on

Jean Walsh and Stephanie Nishikawa over dinner.
Tumon, Guam 1994

pancake makeup. When Stephanie came over, she and Jean would sit on the couch and pluck each other's eyebrows. Jean and Stephanie were beach and shopping pals too. Stephanie left Guam about a year before we did for a job upgrade in Kansas City. From there she made it back to her California home, settling in at KOVR TV as a weathercaster. She had a new man in her life, who just happened to be the son of Sacramento's mayor. Leslie Botos, who did marketing for the Sacramento Medical Foundation Blood Center came over too. There was a lot to talk about.

We arrived at Stephanie's house around six and she proudly introduced us to her new boyfriend Ken Yee. Ken was very pleasant and we could tell they were very much in love. Sammy, Stephanie's little white terrier was sporting a new grooming job and bows in his hair. Stephanie and Jean went to the kitchen to tend to pupus on the stove. Ken and I concentrated on cocktails. My afternoon buzz had worn off, but I figured with the glass or two of red wine I'd be right back in the saddle.

The doorbell rang and it was Leslie Botos. Leslie was a pretty lady in her early fifties with a dazzling smile and a spirit as warm as a San Joaquin Valley summer. "I still can't believe this happened with you Kevin," she said as she gave me a hug and kiss.

"I can't either," I told her.

Leslie worked in Fresno a few years prior as the spokesperson for the Central California Blood Center. Our paths had crossed before because she was always working the Fresno media for publicity, especially when blood supplies at the local blood center were low. When she left Fresno for a similar position in Sacramento a few years later, never could we have imagined we'd meet again.

Being that Fresno is something of a small town when Leslie got word the Sacramento Medical Foundation would be handling a bone marrow donor coming up from Fresno, she wondered if she knew who it was. As we all made small talk in the kitchen with drinks in hand she told the story. "When I saw the name of the donor I remembered there's a news guy in Fresno by that same name, but then I thought nah couldn't be him. Then I called down to the Central California Blood Center and they said 'Yep it's him.' I just couldn't believe it. I thought this is going to be really cool. And here we are," she said.

Like Jean, Stephanie and me, Leslie had connections to Guam. Leslie had been a flight attendant for Alaska Airlines and Continental Micronesia. Her travels eventually took her out to Guam and other Micronesia islands. She told funny stories, including the one about how native islanders in Yap were scared of the Alaska Airlines company logo-an Eskimo head painted on the tail of the plane.

Prior to entering the television world Stephanie was a flight attendant with Northwest Airlines. Putting two flight attendants together in a social setting is instant comedy. They tell the funniest stories about people at their best and worst.

They see it all. I didn't hear all the details of Stephanie and Leslie's conversation, but it was clear from the raucous laughter they were having a ball reminiscing.

Sipping on a glass of Cabernet in Stephanie's kitchen I started a mental building process of how we all came together to be here on this night. The common denominator was Guam. Starting my career in Guam seven years earlier set the table for Hawaii. It was the work I did in Guam that impressed the television executives in Hawaii to move me from Micronesia to Polynesia. Without my tour in Hawaii I never would have met Chris Pablo and two-year-old Alana Dung, the two most important people who started my bone marrow journey. And as I drank the good wine I savored the taste of friendship, faith and fate, all of which brought us here on this night.

More visitors came by that night including the Honorable Mayor of Sacramento, Jim Yee, who was most kind in conversation and in thanking me for putting someone else's health ahead of mine. The company and food were great and spirits flowed. I don't know if it was from all that standing or the drinking, but I started to bleed a bit more. After excusing myself from the kitchen cocktail conversation to change the bandages someone asked if they could see the holes. So I lifted the back of my shirt, unbuckled my pants and peeled back a sliver of the bandage. "Whoa! Don't those hurt?" he asked.

"Dude I'm on my third glass of wine. I'm feeling no pain," I said with a hearty laugh.

The loud laughter turned the attention from the kitchen to where the guy and I were standing outside the bathroom. "Honey pull your pants up!" Jean ordered with a laugh as she and Stephanie about doubled over.

"He wanted to see my holes," I protested as if exposure was a perfectly acceptable part of any dinner and cocktail party.

"Just don't be showing us the hole that you were born with!" someone screamed as the house howled with laughter.

"No that's not on display tonight, at least not yet," I said. "Maybe later."

"No. No. No." Stephanie said, laughing so hard she hard to grab onto Jean for support.

It was a great night and a great way to end one of the best days of my life. And as Jean safely drove us back to the downtown Holiday Inn, I thought about the boy who received my marrow earlier in the day. I wondered if someday he might celebrate life the way we did that night.

CHAPTER THIRTEEN

The Newsman
Becomes News

WORKING IN TELEVISION FOR SO LONG I'VE LEARNED you're only as good as your promotion. If you don't get the word out, it hardly matters. Some promotions are better than others. Remember those Double Your Pleasure Doublemint commercials? They drove my mother crazy. Years ago she met the creator of the spots and told him how much they annoyed her while she sang to him the Doublemint song. "You see they work," he chastised her. "You're singing the jingle. It doesn't matter that they bother you. You remember the ad. I've done my job."

He had a point. We chewed plenty of Doublemint Gum in my house growing up. But my mom was right too. What's effective advertising isn't always pleasurable. Same was true with the promotion of my bone marrow story, which was set to air a couple of weeks after a promotional blitz. My station went to great lengths to promote my story and present me as a hero who just about risked his life in the process. There was a life hanging in the balance, but it was more my recipient's life than mine.

The promotions department at KGPE Channel 47 took some of the more graphic pictures of my bone marrow extraction surgery and married them with dramatic headlines that made for a real cliffhanger. As I watched the spot I saw in slow motion the anesthesiologist lowering an oxygen mask on my face. Graphics with words like *"to save a life"*... and *"a most personal journey"*... flew into the television screen. More video clips showed my face turning toward the clock, the I/V dripping, a breathing machine and my heart monitor going up and down. What's more, Sarah MacLachlan's tear-your-heart out sappy song *I Will Remember You* played in the background.

Music sells like nothing else. And when people sing a line that is attached to a person or product it's gold. Like the old Doublemint jingle that annoyed my mom, friends and coworkers started singing Sarah McLachlan to me mockingly. *"I will remember you, do to do to... will you remember me? Do do do do do... don't let your life pass you by, weep not for the memories."*

Their teasing drove me crazy but I knew I could count on them. They would watch. And in TV that's what matters. Location means a lot with TV too. It may not be scientific, but I believe I can tell the impact a story or a commercial has based on what people say to me in line at the grocery store, or at church.

"I saw you on TV with the bone marrow surgery," a grandmotherly lady said to me as the checker scanned my items at Save Mart. "Are you going to make it?" she wanted to know.

"I hope so," I told her.

"Hey I saw your commercial on TV," an older man outside church told me. "What kind of cancer do you have? Are you terminal?"

"Cancer? I don't have cancer. No, no, no I'm fine," I told him.

"Then what did I see on TV?" he asked.

"That's the promotion for a story about a bone marrow donation I gave to a 16-year-old boy. He's the one with cancer. He has leukemia, cancer of the blood."

"Is he going to make?" the man asked.

"I hope so," I told him. "Without the bone marrow transplant he didn't have a chance. So hopefully it takes in his body and he gets better. He was very sick beforehand. I wish I knew more, but because it was an anonymous donation I won't know for six months whether it worked. That's just part of it."

"That must be tough not knowing. Either way you've done a very good thing," he said before stepping inside for Mass.

On the way out of Mass a lady who appeared very concerned approached and grabbed me by the arm while asking, "I saw you on TV. Did you die?"

"No. As you can see I'm still alive," I answered with a chuckle. "I'll die someday eventually, but not anytime soon. At least I hope not."

As crazy as the questions and confrontations were, the people were always kind. I appreciated their concern, but a part of me was still troubled about the endless self-promotion. I thought it was immodest and suggested to my current news director Alex McGehee that maybe we should temper it.

"Why?" he asked incredulously.

"Because it kind of creeps me out. I just think good deeds should be done quietly. It's kind of shameless self promotion," I told him.

"Look let me remind you of something," Alex protested. "When both you and I were working in Hawaii what was the result of all the media attention given to the golf ball guy Chris Pablo and the little girl Alana Dung? Thirty thousand people turned out for bone marrow drives. That's the power of the media. That's the media doing something good. Those people never would have turned out if it wasn't for the media telling personal stories like Chris's and Alana's. If you really want to help people tell your story. Whatever's making you uncomfortable get over it," he said.

I thought about it for a few seconds before telling him, "You know you're right. I'm all right with the story airing. I just don't want to write it and tell it myself. That's just too much. I hope you understand."

"I do. You don't have to write it. We'll have Molly do it," Alex said.

Dates were set for the two-part story but not before there another life saving opportunity presented itself. "Kevin? It's Leslie Botos from the Sacramento Medical Foundation Blood Center," the familiar voice on the phone said.

"Hi Leslie! What's going on?" I asked.

"Well there's an opportunity to be a part of a very important life saving mission. Typically when we have bone marrow being transplanted, we have someone from the medical foundation hand-deliver it. That's what we did with you. It's really a special honor to be the courier. I've done it before and it's very rewarding. Every now and then we also extend the privilege to past donors and some of them involved traveling to interesting places. Would you like to do it?" she asked.

"I'd love to," I told Leslie.

"Okay. This is going to be a cool one. The donor is actually from the Fresno area. He's the maintenance man at Fresno City College. Do you know Mike Yelinick?" Leslie asked.

"No I don't."

"Well he appears to be a little nervous. Do you think you could talk to him and maybe calm him down a bit?" she asked.

"Sure give me his number and I'll give him a call."

"One more thing," Leslie added before saying goodbye. "You can't tell Mike or anyone other than your spouse where you're going. There are legal and privacy issues similar to what you went through with your donation. Neither you nor Mike can know the results of the transplant for six months, and Mike can't know the name and location of his recipient for a year. Let me know how your conversation with him goes."

I called Mike the maintenance man the next day. Someone told him I'd be calling and what I did for a living, so he checked me out on the news the night before. Immediately I could tell Mike was my kind of guy because he made fun of my clothes. "Where did you get that tie you wore last night?" he asked sarcastically.

"Why you don't like the multi-colored Jerry Garcias?"

Kevin Walsh with fellow bone marrow donor Mike Yelinick on the set of KGPE TV, Fresno, California. Kevin was the courier of Mike's marrow on a long trip to a woman in need.

"I like Jerry Garcia," he said. "But that tie was *awful*," he teased.

"Great!" I told him. "I'm sure it'll look better on you. When I come to see you at the hospital remind me to bring it."

After the good-natured ribbing we got down to the business of what Mike was about to go through. He consented to the extraction surgery, but underneath his tough talk and workingman's exterior I sensed some fear.

"Look Mike it's okay to be afraid. I'm not gonna kid you. I was too. I'm afraid of needles, so you can imagine. Trust the doctors. I know those guys; they did the same thing to me that they're going to do to you. You're going to be fine. Plus, aside from waking up with a sore ass you're going to feel so good about yourself and what you did for the woman who needs your marrow. I wish I could share with others how profound the satisfaction is. I don't just have those thoughts in my head; I feel them in my body-in my heart, in my bones. Wait till you feel it. It's amazing."

I told Mike I'd see him and his family soon at the hospital. But before I did I had the tricky task of making sure I could get a few days off from work to take the important courier mission. Considering what was at stake it would seem like getting time off would be simple. But nothing's easy in the world of television, especially in the critical November ratings period. Short of being dead or having a terribly contagious illness you are not to call in sick. And taking time off is pretty much out of the question. When I asked Alex McGehee he was reluctant. "I don't know Kevin. It's ratings and I'm not sure Barry (new station GM) would go for that."

"I know it's ratings time Alex but this is a chance to be a part of a life saving mission," I told him.

"I understand that," he said. "But do you really have to be the courier? Can't someone else do it? It really doesn't matter who carries it as long as it gets there right?"

"Yes that's true, but they've asked me and it's such an honor. I'd really like to do it. Look we can make it work to our benefit as part of the storyline with my donation. Not only have I been the donor, now I have a chance to be a major player in someone else's story. Let's put what's right and what's charitable ahead of business. It's the right thing to do."

"Let me think about it. I'll talk to Barry."

"Okay don't take too long because I have to make the travel arrangements, or tell them to find someone else if not me. Then they would have to make arrangements too."

"Okay I'll let you know by the end of the week," Alex said.

I wasn't too hopeful that I'd be free to go, but a couple of days later Alex came to me with good news. "I talked to Barry and he said it's okay for you to go," he said.

"Great. I'll tell the folks at the Blood Center and I'll make sure to bring along a video camera to get footage of the trip."

The timing of my courier duty was very close to the six-month anniversary of my own bone marrow donation. That meant I might have an update on the boy who received my marrow in addition to the new bone marrow journey. But before we got that far I had to fetch a camcorder and take a shooting lesson from our chief photographer. Soon after that I was on a train heading north.

The Amtrak brought me to Sacramento and a taxi took me across town to Sutter General Hospital once again. I was hoping to catch Mike Yelinick before he started his surgery preparation to put him at ease with a few good jokes I'd ripped off from somebody else. I missed him by a few minutes, but I took his wife Deanna and young daughter Jillian to the hospital cafeteria for breakfast and conversation. A little more than an hour later the surgery was done.

One of the assisting nurses came to find Mike's wife and me. "Your husband is fine," the nurse told Deanna. "He should be awake in a couple of hours. Kevin we need to get you going on the courier training because there's more to it than just carrying the cooler, you may actually have to handle the marrow. Plus you have a flight to catch in about and hour and a half and it's a good 45 minute drive to the airport."

I said goodbye to Deanna and Jillian and went with the nurse to fetch Mike's marrow. As we were walking down the hallway another nurse carrying a small cooler intercepted us. "Here's the marrow," she said while opening the lid.

It was in a thick plastic bag and wedged in between pieces of cardboard, small surgical towels and cool gel packs. The nurse pulled the marrow out and rocked it back and forth between her hands. "The marrow needs to be massaged every so often so it doesn't get stagnant. Just gently squeeze the bag so the marrow gets moving around. And never let the gel packs actually touch the side of the marrow because it's very delicate. That's why we always keep the cardboard and the towels between them. Here you try it," she said.

My first thought when she handed me Mike's marrow was that it was much heavier than I imagined it would be. It must've weighed a couple of pounds and you could feel its density through the plastic. It was fascinating to look at because I knew I held in my hands a most generous gift and a sick woman's best chance at life. But at the same time I felt a little queasy. I've fainted over much less. As I rocked the bag back and forth I saw the thick marrow circulating and bone chips squishing around. Once I got the hang of how to handle it, I repacked the cooler making sure to keep the marrow away from the cold stuff. It was a tight fit.

"A couple of more things," the nurse said. "When you get to the airport tell the gate agent and then the flight crew who you are. They're expecting you. No one is to handle the cooler other than you. It never leaves your sight and side. You don't check it with the baggage and it doesn't ride in the overhead bin. It's either in your lap, or between your feet under the seat in front of you. If you go to the bathroom the cooler comes with you. In fact the bathroom is probably the best place for you to massage the marrow because it may be uncomfortable for the passengers on board to see you handling a big bloody bag."

We had a laugh over that one, but there was no doubt this was serious business. A tremendous amount of responsibility had been given to me. If I missed a connection or mishandled the marrow the consequence could literally be life and death. And with my flight departure from Sacramento quickly approaching, I wanted to get moving. Before leaving the hospital a Medical Foundation coordinator gave me several hundred dollars in cash and a backup ticket on another airline just in case of flight cancellations and alterations to my original travel plans. I said goodbye to everyone in the hall, stopped by the cafeteria to say goodbye to Deanna and Jillian and hopped in a cab for the airport.

"So where are you going my man?" the black 50-something driver asked looking in his rear view mirror.

"I can't tell you. It's kind of secret," I told him.

"Well is everything okay?" he wanted to know.

"Oh yeah, I'm fine. I'm bringing a healthy man's bone marrow to a sick woman who needs a transplant. I'm the courier. Because of legal and privacy reasons we're not to tell anyone where we're going exactly," I said.

"Well that's a nice thing you're doing. What time is your flight?"

"It leaves at 10:45."

Kevin starting the journey to deliver Mike Yelinick's bone marrow.

"Oh. In that case we better get moving," he said with a sense of urgency.

So the cabbie stepped on it and pretty soon the rest of the cars on the road and highway looked pedestrian. It was an older cab with a speedometer that only went up to 85, but the needle was pinned past that as we zigzagged through traffic. By my estimate we must have hit 90, 95 at a couple of points in the ride. As wild as the ride was the cabbie had a good handle on the car and got the marrow and me to the airport safely.

When I got to the ticket counter to collect my boarding pass, the agent had no idea who I was and that I was a courier on a medical mission. "What are you carrying?" she asked.

"Human bone marrow," I answered.

Her eyes bugged out of her head and she said, "Oh. I didn't know. Do you need anything from me?"

"Well if you can let me pre-board that would help because I need to tell the flight crew just in case we need to expedite things."

"Okay as soon as I make the initial announcement you just go right down the Jetway and tell the flight attendants what's going on. We're about 15 minutes till boarding."

I took my seat in the waiting area and placed the cooler on the ground in front of me. I opened up Khalil Gibran's The Prophet. I had read it a couple of times before and it always brought me peace. *You give but little when you give of your*

143

possessions. It is when you give of yourself that you truly give. See first that you your-self deserve to be a giver, and an instrument of giving. For in truth it is life that gives unto life - while you, who deem yourself a giver, are but a witness.

It was the Lebanese-American philosopher's wisdom from the 1920s that spoke so personally to me in word almost a century later. As a bone marrow donor I gave a part of myself months earlier and felt far more satisfied than I ever did writing a check or volunteering my time to charity. It wasn't as if I sought the opportunities to be a donor and now a courier, those privileges more or less presented themselves to me. And in each mission there was as much for me to watch as there was for me to do. As I looked up from the pages and pondered the profundity, I noticed quite a few people in the terminal noticing me. It wasn't so much me as it was the cooler.

The stampings and logo on the side of the cooler made it pretty obvious it was for medical purposes. I could see the looks of wonder and horror on their faces and knew instinctively they were trying to figure out what was inside the box. I heard whispers around me. And when I turned my head to see whom the whisperers were they looked away trying not to be noticed.

When the pre-boarding call came I was the first to stand up and walk toward the gate. I could feel the eyes following me. I gave the gate agent my boarding pass and walked down the Jetway to the aircraft. I told the lead flight attendant who I was and what I was doing and she brought me to the cockpit. "Okay let me call ahead and let them know that we should have priority upon landing," the co-pilot said to me. "What you're carrying is time sensitive right?"

"Yes it is," I told him.

"Okay. If we don't tell the control tower here and there what we're doing, they'll never know and we'll be treated like any other flight. By calling ahead we'll go to the front of the line for take off and landing."

"Okay great," I told him.

"After we get in the air I'll come back and check up with you to see if there's anything you need or any update on my end okay?"

"Sounds good."

And with that I wandered back into the plane to find my seat. I placed the cooler on the seat as I loaded my small carry-on bag into the overhead compart-ment. In the short time it took me to close the overhead bin and settle into my seat the woman across the aisle had locked in on the cooler. "What's inside?" she wanted to know while pointing at the blue and white box.

"Bone marrow," I told her.

"Is it yours?"

"No it's someone else's. I'm just bringing it to someone who needs a bone marrow transplant."

"Where are they?"

"I can't tell you. It's a privacy thing. Obviously you know where this flight is landing, but I'm making a connection and going somewhere else."

"Oh okay. So how does the transplant work? Do you put the marrow inside their bones?"

"No, no, no," I told her. "It's like a simple blood transfusion. They get it intravenously."

"And once the marrow's inside them they get better?" she asked.

"That's the hope," I said.

Our conversation across the aisle attracted quite a crowd in the center of the aircraft. Because people heard me talking openly about my mission they were less discreet about listening in. A few children even came over for a closer look. Not long after take off the co-pilot came back to see me as promised. "Usually we land from the east, but to save a few minutes where just going to fly straight in from the west. Air traffic control has cleared everyone out of our way in the air and on the ground. When we land we're going to go directly to the gate next to your connection. Your connecting flight was at a different terminal but we moved it to save time. Once we land we're going to really hump it to the gate. It won't be your usual landing and slow ride to the gate. We'll be taxiing pretty quick okay?"

"Yeah that's good with me," I told him.

The conversation with the nosy woman stirred the plane up. The visit from the pilot took it to another level. Hoping to unwind I tucked the cooler under the seat in front of me and pulled out *The Prophet* once more. The reading soothed me and it wasn't long before I nodded off with the help of the whir of the plane's engines. Waking up about 45 minutes later it was time to massage the marrow. I retreated to the lavatory with the cooler in one hand, my video camera in the other, and eyes following.

Inside the bathroom I took great care to wash my hands. Before I reached in I memorized the location of all the contents in the cooler so I could repack it properly. I even shot some video in case I forgot. I pulled the bag out and held it in my hands feeling the full weight of the contents and the mission I was entrusted to do. Massaging the marrow was as simple as kneading dough in your hands. You squeeze it and rotate it. I could hear a soft swoosh and the marrow swishing around inside the bag. The rich, heavier red marrow blended with the chicken soup-looking stem cells and the occasional bone chip floated by. With Mike's marrow in my hands I thought about him and how he was probably just waking up from surgery and seeing his family. I thought about the person who would be receiving Mike's marrow later that day and whether her family would be beside when it happened. And I thought about the 16-year-old boy who had received my marrow a few months earlier, wondering if he was well enough to play sports again. My heart climbed in my throat as high as the aircraft in the sky.

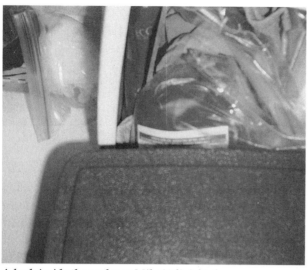

A look inside the cooler at Mike Yelinick's bone marrow. Every couple of hours the bag of marrow needed to be taken out and massaged.

After repacking the cooler and taking special care to make sure the cold gel packs didn't rub against the bag of marrow, I left the bathroom and headed back to my seat. "I can't help myself," the young man sitting next to me said. "But after you got up and left, everyone around the plane started asking 'Who is that guy and what's he doing?'"

"Really?" I asked.

"Oh yeah. It was wild," he said.

"What did you tell them?"

"I said I think he's a doctor carrying a heart or something."

"I'm not a doctor and it's not a heart."

"What do you do and what's inside?" he wanted to know, missing out on the earlier conversation I had with the woman across the aisle.

"I'm a television news anchor and it's bone marrow."

"Oh. That's cool."

I craned my head and looked around and sure enough lots of people we're looking our way. It really was turning into a most interesting flight. I asked my seatmate why he was traveling and it turns out he was a pretty interesting fellow who made computer-animated games. He was on his way to a business meeting to present a new smash, bang-up racing video to a major entertainment company.

After talking for a few minutes he returned to his work on his laptop computer and I jumped back into my book. With about five minutes left in the flight the captain came on the intercom and said, "Ladies and gentlemen we're going to be landing shortly. We've had a special guest on board who's taking part in an important medical mission. When we land we're going to taxi very quickly to the gate. When we arrive please stay seated and let him get off the aircraft first."

The pilot was right; it was a fast ride to the gate. By my estimate we must have been going 50-60 miles per hour as the plane bounced around. When the plane stopped I gathered the cooler and my carry on bags and started walking to the front of the aircraft. Almost every head in front of my row turned around and looked to see who was coming. With heads on both sides of the aisle turning back for a look I almost had to run the gauntlet to get to the exit. "Hey thanks a lot. I really appreciate you guys working so hard to make the trip faster and easier," I said to the flight crew, which had gathered around the door for my send off. "You got it," the captain said. "Just get that to where it needs to go and we'll all be happy."

"I'll make it happen," I said as I stepped out and made my way to the connecting flight.

When I got to the next aircraft most of the passengers had already boarded. Like the previous flight I told the lead flight attendant what I was up to. "We've been expecting you," she said. "Go to your assigned seat and settle in for a while. But I think there's a spot that's going to be open in Business Class. Because we're proud of what you're doing we're probably going to move you up there once we close the door."

"Oh that's not necessary," I told her. "I'm fine in coach."

"No, no, no. We insist. You'll be a lot more comfortable there and we want to take good care of you," she said.

Just as she said, someone didn't show up for the flight and just before we took off I got upgraded. Most of the people in Business Class were busy working on their laptops so my slipping into the rear seat of the Business section hardly attracted a ripple of attention. That was fine with me because I was starting to tire from what had been a long day. The engines whirred and the 757 barreled down the runway for takeoff. As it did I took a few deep breaths and settled in for the ride.

After we got to cruising altitude I massaged the marrow in the bathroom a couple of times and videotaped the effort with the camera in one hand and the bag of marrow in the other. Because there were no more flight connections and air traffic was relatively light around the final destination there was no reason for the pilot to rush. I kicked back with a soda and watched the movie.

Upon arrival I grabbed the cooler and my bag and headed for ground transportation. I gave the cabbie directions to the hospital and pretty soon we were doing about 90 miles an hour on the highway. There really was no need to rush and I told him so. He paid no attention and continued his assault on the speed limit. We made it to the hospital in no time, free of injury and with tires that smelled of burning rubber.

I had specific directions to the office of the oncologist who would receive the bone marrow. The hospital was old and didn't have an elevator. So I took the steps to the second floor. The hospital was also a teaching facility so I could see medical students at work in labs as I walked down the hall. When I got to the oncologist's office I found the door open and the doctor sitting inside a cramped office that looked more like an English Literature Professor's office than that of a medical doctor. There were books and files stacked everywhere. The doctor was sharing a cup of tea with another man. He took the cooler and signed the necessary paperwork. "Thank you," he said while waving goodbye.

"Is there anything else you need from me?" I asked.

"No."

"The patient will get the marrow today?" I asked.

"Oh yes," he said while nibbling on a cracker.

"Okay then. Have a great day," I told him as I walked out.

The doctor's nonchalance was something of a letdown for me. I had come a long way and I guess I expected something bigger on the receiving end. Everything up to this point had been pretty big. But I quickly realized while this was a huge mission for me, Mike and the woman who would receive Mike's marrow, it was no big deal for the doctor. This, quite simply, was what he did regularly.

I took a cab to a hotel desperately in need of sleep in the prone position. I checked in and snoozed for a couple of hours. When I woke up I went in search of a neighborhood pub for some good eats and beer. As a courier you're not allowed to consume alcohol when in possession of the cooler. With my mission complete I was ready for a few cold ones. I found a place about a 15-minute walk from the hotel in the center of the small town. I had spaghetti and meatballs and washed it down with a few draft beers while watching the town drunk smoke an unlit cigarette across the bar.

The next day I was on the return flight, thankful to be a part of such a meaningful mission and just as happy to be heading home. I connected through Los Angeles and my wife picked me up at the Fresno airport. "How was the trip?" Jean asked.

"It was really special, really special," I told her.

"Are you hungry?"

"Yes."

"Wanna go to In-N-Out Burger?"

"Definitely."

The next week I returned to work. I showed my co-anchor Molly McMillen the new video from the trip and we talked about how to combine the new video with that from my bone marrow surgery. Part one would be about me and the people who inspired me to register as a potential donor-Chris Pablo, Alana Dung and the 16-year-old recipient of my bone marrow. Part two, the privilege of carrying someone else's bone marrow on a similar life saving journey.

I didn't watch the pieces as they were being edited because I didn't want to steer the content. It was Molly's story and I trusted her to do it right. I was very nervous the night part one aired. As she read the lead seated next to me I could feel a lump in my throat and my face blushing. The story ran about two minutes and was filled with drama and emotion, but I didn't cry. When it was done we were on a two shot and Molly said to me, "Kevin that was a really nice thing you did."

"Thanks Mol. But I don't think I had any other choice. It was the right thing to do and the only thing to do."

She handed me a piece of paper and said "You wrote a note to the boy who received your marrow. Do you remember what you wrote?"

"Yeah most of it," I said.

"Well that's a copy of the note you put in the cooler that carried his marrow. Why don't you read it to us?"

Hello Friend,

I know you're a football player. I played quarterback years ago. I've given you the ball, now I want you to run with it. I'll be waiting for you in the end zone. Take care, be strong and be healthy.

— Your Donor

It was live television and I broke down in tears. Molly did too. Being the tough guy that I am I wasn't exactly thrilled to be bawling like a baby because I knew my buddies would totally bust my balls over it. But in the end it was a good release and honest TV-raw and real.

Part two was just as good bringing viewers much closer to the end game of bone marrow transplant. Because we didn't shoot Mike Yelinick with his family prior to, or just after his bone marrow surgery, Molly and me took Mike and his family out for dinner to get cover video. With his reddish hair and beard, Mike looked the part of a

News anchors Molly McMillen and Kevin Walsh on newspaper billboard shot, Fresno, California.

Viking devouring a meal at a king's banquet. His personality and regular Joe disposition made him as loveable as pizza pie, which is what we had at Luna's in Clovis.

After a few slices and beers we got Mike to talk about how special it was for him to become a bone marrow donor for a woman he's never met. "I just know she's a woman in her 40s and I just wonder whether she's a mother," he said. "I know how important it is to have a mother in your life. I look at my daughter Jillian and how she responds to my wife. There are certain things that Jillian needs in her life that only a mother can provide. I can only imagine what it's like for my recipient and her family."

Molly told Mike's story in an "I still can't believe this is happening" kind of context. Mike went to a bone marrow registration drive at Fresno City College and never really expected to be called. And he certainly never could have imagined his match and donation would spark this kind of publicity. Suddenly the guy who was best known for fixing stuff around campus had a new calling card. Students and faculty who saw his story on TV chatted him up. "I mean it's great and everything to have been a part of trying to save someone's life, but this TV stuff that you guys have to go through...Kevin look at you, you're a guy and you're wearing *makeup*, I could've lived without that."

That's how Mike was, a loveable ballbreaker and a new pseudo celebrity.

CHAPTER FOURTEEN

A Marathon Tribute

IN ADDITION TO BEING ONLY AS GOOD AS YOUR PROMOTION, another TV truism is be prepared for anyone to approach you at any time with a comment or a request. Many of my colleagues don't do well with that part because they want their "privacy". Me? I love it. I'm flattered that someone finds me worth talking to.

Not long after the stories of my and Mike's bone marrow donations aired my encounters with the public increased about tenfold. "It's nice to finally see some *good news* on TV," a woman at Fig Garden Books said while I shopped for something to read.

"We saw what you did," a woman outside the Edwards Movie Cineplex told me and my wife Jean after we walked out of an afternoon matinee. "Me and my husband went to the blood center and we registered as potential bone marrow donors because of what you did."

It was comments like those that made me proud of the stories we did. It convinced me that my boss was right about the power of the media. Had we not aired the stories of Mike Yelinick and me I'm sure the couple outside the movie theater never would have known about bone marrow donation. Now they're in the system, and they'll be ready to go if the right person ever gets sick and they get a call.

The Fresno chapter of the Leukemia and Lymphoma Society saw the stories and sought me out. On my way into a morning workout at Dan Gamel's Health and Fitness Club, Becky Renee about tackled me as I walked by. "Kevin!" she said.

"Yes?" I answered, somewhat startled by hearing my name shouted.

"I saw what you did on TV with the bone marrow story. You know you ought to run in a marathon with us at Team in Training. Do you know who we are?

"No I'm sorry I don't," I answered.

"We're a fundraising group with the Leukemia and Lymphoma Society. We run in marathons to raise money for research and treatment. It's a worthy cause and it's a lot of fun. Someone with your story and stature could really help us," Becky said.

"Wait a minute," I said. "You want me to run in a marathon? Like one of those 26.2 mile things?"

"Yeah you'll love it."

"I can't. I'm not in shape for it."

"Yes you are. I see you coming here everyday. You're in shape."

"Maybe gym and treadmill shape, but long distance running shape? I probably couldn't even run two miles," I told her.

"We've trained 300 pound women to run and walk in marathons. Believe me, if they can do it. You can do it. I'm telling you it's fun."

I thought about it for a moment and asked, "So I don't have to run the whole time?"

"No. You can do whatever you want. Some people walk the whole thing. A lot of our people do a combination of running and walking. We have professional trainers and a three and-a-half month long program that can make anybody ready to do a marathon-even people who've never worked out before. Believe me you're way ahead of the game than most people we train."

"Let me think about it," I told Becky before heading into the men's locker room to change my clothes for a workout.

As I climbed on the elliptical machine in the cardio room I started to mull the idea over. The idea of running in a marathon was once *on the list*. Flying in a fighter jet was on the list, so was skydiving, hang gliding and driving a race car. These were all things I wanted to do once, so I could get my adrenaline rush and cross them off the list. However, achy knees and a surgically repaired back pushed the marathon idea farther down the list, if not off of it entirely. Considering I could walk if I had to, and the fact that 300 pound women did it, the idea of me doing it suddenly didn't seem so impossible.

For years I carried my golf bag while walking 36 holes a day. And when I wasn't carrying for myself I caddied for members at Huntingdon Valley Country Club in Huntingdon Valley, Pennsylvania. I often went doubles, carrying a bag on each shoulder while walking the famously hilly landscape. It wasn't uncommon to lug ten plus miles a day looping. I figured if I could do that weighted down; there was no telling what I could do baggage free.

With the "idea" of participating in a marathon no longer out of the question I had a sudden charge of energy in my workout. I increased the resistance on the elliptical machine from 15 to 19 and picked up the pace. I could feel my heart rate increasing and beads of sweat popping up on my forehead. I imagined myself crossing the marathon finish line and how good it would make me feel. I upped the elliptical resistance to 20, the maximum, putting all my effort into the exercise. I went another five minutes, finishing soaked with sweat and my appetite whet for a new adventure.

Darya Oreizi, Clovis, California. Darya was one of Kevin's Honolulu Marathon honorees.

After a quick shower and a change of clothes I found Becky Renee in the health club lobby clutching a cup of coffee. "You know Becky I thought about the marathon and I *might* be able to do it," I told her. "But I have conditions. I only want to run in the Honolulu Marathon because that's where my bone marrow journey started. It would be like a homecoming."

"Oh that's fine," she said beaming. "You can do any marathon you want. I'm just glad you're interested. This will be really good for you and really good for Team in Training and the Leukemia and Lymphoma Society."

To train with TNT and compete in the Honolulu Marathon I would have to raise about three thousand dollars. In selecting my honorees I went back to the beginning of my own leukemia journey in making the selections. Chris Pablo, the man with the golf ball who essentially got my bone marrow donation journey going was one honoree. So was Alana Dung. It was at her massive drive that I became a part of the Hawaii Bone Marrow Donor Registry. Seven-year-old Darya Oreizi of Clovis, California, would become an honoree too. Darya was recovering from leukemia treatment and his father would join me in marathon training. But more than anyone else, my top honoree was the 16-year-old boy who received my bone marrow transplant. Without him on my mind and in my heart, competing in a marathon at this point in my life was not an option.

I signed up for the Honolulu Marathon about three and-a-half months before the actual event. That didn't seem like a lot of time to get ready for a 26.2-mile journey, but Team in Training had a sophisticated training regimen that, if you followed it correctly, you'd be ready for the big day. I had my doubts, but at the same time I figured TNT wouldn't be so established if it didn't have a proven track record.

The first day of training involved a getting to know you session with our trainers in a group setting at Holy Spirit Church. There were about 50 people, half of which would be doing their first marathon. Most of the rookies looked anxious, as if they still couldn't imagine themselves finishing a marathon. The trainers assured everyone they would finish so long as they followed the training manual religiously and didn't rush on race day. The seasoned runners would be done in about three or four hours, the beginners perhaps as long as 10. Few in the bunch were focused on finishing in competitive time. Most, like me, would be happy just to finish.

To get a feel of our general state of fitness the trainers took us to the basketball courts behind the church. They led us through a series of calisthenics on the hot pavement. The air temperature was probably close to 90 degrees and the asphalt was even hotter. Aside from the physicality of exercise, doing pushups and sit-ups on the ground wasn't exactly pleasant because touching the pavement was almost like touching the stove. But most of us made it through the drills.

After that we were sent on a run around Woodward Lake. I used the two and-a-half mile warm up to check out a few of my favorite fishing holes. I finished the jog huffing and puffing and covered in sweat. I was exhausted. Some of the people still weren't back a half hour later. I was a bit discouraged and I wasn't the only one. But the trainers assured us it was just the beginning and endurance could be developed quickly. I hoped so because my initial optimism at being able to the finish the marathon was almost dashed.

Later that night I looked through the training manual as Jean rubbed my sore feet. I was hurting, but not injured. It was my body's way of saying "that was a good workout, now it's time to rest and recover." The training manual said much the same thing—initial soreness in the beginning days was absolutely normal for marathon newbies. Eventually the soreness would go away and the muscles would loosen up. The manual was right, I was far less sore after the next couple of runs and I could feel my stamina building quickly.

We practiced every other day to let our bodies recover in between. We would meet in the parking lot of Holy Spirit Church at 5:30am and set out on runs in nearby Woodward Park and surrounding neighborhoods. Running early had its advantages. It was much cooler, the roads were clear, and you never had your workout hanging over your head the rest of the day. The hardest part was rolling out of bed at such a ridiculous hour.

I ran mostly with women. The men in TNT were pretty serious runners and I couldn't keep up with them. Running with the gals was just fine with me because they talked a lot and that helped pass the time. Sheryl Bavoso, Becky Renee and Sheila Meyers became my regular running pals. They liked to talk about current events and used me as their personal news almanac whenever they needed additional details for the yarn they spun. "Kevin you just have a lot more intelligent things to talk about than most guys your age," Becky told me as we ran four aside one morning.

"Really?" I asked. "What do the guys you know talk about?"

"Not much. Other than sports most of them can't talk about anything," she answered.

"What's wrong with talking about sports?" I asked jokingly.

"Nothing," she said. "But it gets boring after a while. You have to move on to other things."

That part I got. It was easy for me to be comfortable and social in different circles because I read so much and lived in so many different places. Those experiences gave me a deep reservoir of conversational topics from which to draw upon. "What are some of the cool things you liked to do when you lived in Hawaii Kevin?" Sheryl asked.

"One of my favorite things was to get out of town and take a drive to the North Shore. It took about an hour. It was long enough that you felt like you went somewhere, but not so far away that you really had to do any planning. If the surf was up we'd check out Waimea Bay and Pipeline. The surfing and people watching were incredible. On the way back we'd stop for lunch at Kua Aina Sandwich on Kamehameha Highway. It has the best bread in the islands and the French fries are terrific. After lunch we'd grab a shave ice at Matsumoto's for the ride home," I told them.

"What's shaved ice?" Sheryl wanted to know.

"Shave without the d. It's like a snow cone, but much smoother and tastier. A descending, spinning blade shaves a micro thin layer off the top of a block of ice. When there's a pile of snow on top of the block they scoop it off and put it in a paper cone. You have something like 40 flavors to choose from — pina colada, mango, pineapple, grape, cherry, whatever. Because the ice is like snow the syrup soaks in consistently. There's not a lake at the bottom. The top is as good as the middle and the bottom. Never do you have those hard, crunchy, tasteless spots like you do when you buy a snow cone from the county fair. My favorite flavor is grape. It's ono."

"What's ono?"

"Ono means delicious in Hawaiian. And Kua Aina Sandwich, that's no ka 'oi - the best."

"You see what I mean about having intelligent things to talk about? You just used a different language and made a sandwich place and shave ice sound *fascinating,*" Becky gushed. "How many guys other guys could do that?"

I didn't know what to say so I just shrugged. We talked about everything during our runs-work, family, friends and life. There was no pecking order in our group. No one person dominated the conversation, or the pace that we ran. There was equal opportunity to speak and listen. Some days I was chatty. Other days I let everyone else do the talking. As much as we all enjoyed the conversation I know the women liked the visual part of having me around too. "Kevin we need a better view. Why don't you run out in front?"

"Why? What does that have to do with improving the view?" I asked naively.

"We get to check out your ass!" they howled.

"You see that's the thing about being outnumbered by women," I scolded them. "When there's only one guy and a bunch of women, the women gang up on the guy and say things they'd never say if they were alone."

"That's right!" they said in laughter.

"I just wanted you to know that I'm now fully aware of your ulterior motives. Don't worry, I won't sue anybody. I can handle your harassment," I laughed back.

It was this kind of fun, ribbing and camaraderie that made the early morning runs worth waking up for. Within six weeks we were running double-digit mileage in one shot. That was a pretty fast training curve considering it wasn't all that long ago I could hardly run a couple of miles around Woodward Lake without being winded. "So Kevin, are you already thinking about the next marathon you're going to run in?" Becky asked.

"What do you mean next marathon?" I responded.

"You know after Honolulu. Which marathon are you going to run in-Vegas, San Diego or New Orleans?"

"Oh no. I'm one and done. I'm never running in another one after Honolulu. I told you guys that," I said in between breaths.

"Oh don't act like you're not *loving* this," she said.

"Love *what,* all this running? I don't love all this running; in fact I don't like the running part at all. I like the discipline of the activity, I like spending time with you ladies and I'm certainly proud to be running for my honorees. But I really can't say I love it and would love to do it again. Really once is *enough,*" I told her.

"We'll see," she said with a chuckle. "You're not the only one who's said you'd only do one marathon. We have other TNTers who said the same thing and you know what? Some of those guys are on their fourth or fifth one."

"Trust me. You won't see me on the jogging trails after this one. I'll catch up with you guys for breakfast and coffee afterward. I'd much rather stay in bed until 6:30 instead of waking up at 4:30."

Generally speaking we'd add two miles each week to the long runs, which always took place on Saturdays. During the week we'd have shorter runs, usually single digit mileage supplemented by track work at Clovis West High School, and individual weightlifting. In addition to building endurance, I lost almost 20 pounds.

It was obvious how I and other runners lost weight. We simply couldn't eat enough food to sustain our weight with the level of training and number of miles we were putting in. Not that anyone was complaining. Oh wait, the women were. They complained they weren't losing as much weight as the men. I wasn't about to get into a gender war; I was too busy running, lifting, working and eating ridiculous amounts of ice cream without worry. There was nothing I couldn't eat and run off the next day. My ice cream consumption became a something of a joke at Save Mart. "What's up with the ice cream binging?" the manager wanted to know.

"I know it looks pathetic doesn't it? I can't stop eating the stuff," I said with a laugh.

"But you're not gaining weight. In fact you're almost starting to look emaciated. Are you okay?" he asked.

"Oh I'm fine. I've been training for a marathon and we're running so much that we burn it all off. Yeah I'm perfectly healthy. But the weight loss thing I know. I look different and my pants are starting to slip off my waist. I'm getting concerned and sympathetic looks from people. My buddy Rich asked me the other day if I had a virus."

To give you an idea of how absurd my sweet tooth had become I didn't even bother to put my chocolate and peanut butter ice cream in a dish. I ate it right out of the carton because I usually ate the whole thing. I'd buy three or four pints each time. I would've bought more, but they wouldn't fit in the freezer.

As much as I overindulged in ice cream and sweets I cut back consumption in other areas. Friday nights after work were usually a good time to hit the Silver Dollar Hofbrau on Shaw Avenue and Highway 41 for frozen mugs of Newcastle Brown Ale, or to sing a few karaoke songs at Tokyo Gardens downtown. But knowing a 15 to 20 mile run awaited me at 5:30 the next morning made party nights a one and done affair. If you've never gone on a long run hung over, I certainly don't advise you try. I would further recommend you not stuff yourself with Mexican food the night before too. Based on personal experience, if you do the beer and beef burrito combo I guarantee you will have the runs at some point during your run. Mine happened right as I ran by Noah's Bagels in Fig Garden Village Shopping Center. I dashed into the bathroom moments before a gastrointestinal eruption. I was lucky to have made it to the john. Whoever used the bathroom after me was very *unlucky*. I still have nightmares about it to this day. I'm sure the cleaning person who scrubbed the toilet later that day does too.

We were near the end of training and close to the six-month anniversary of my bone marrow donation when the phone rang at my work desk. I was sore after what had been a pretty grueling morning workout. Reaching for the receiver was enough to make me wince. I was hoping that I'd be getting a call soon about my bone marrow recipient's condition and secretly I was hoping he'd find out I was running a marathon to honor him. "Kevin it's Lupe Valdez from the Sacramento Medical Foundation Blood Center."

"Hi Lupe, how are you?" I asked with great anticipation.

"Oh Kevin you have no idea of how much I didn't want to have to make this phone call," she said.

I could feel me heart sinking and the air slowly retreating from my lungs.

"You had requested to be informed about the result of the transplant and I have them for you. Unfortunately it's not the result any of us wanted. The boy who received your bone marrow is no longer living," Lupe said quietly but directly.

Her words felt like a dagger to the heart. Tears filled my eyes, my nose burned and I felt completely hopeless.

"What happened? Did his body reject my marrow?"

"No it wasn't that at all. It took, but he developed an infection. His body was already so weak and damaged from the disease and the massive chemo and radiation he had before transplant. You didn't do anything wrong Kevin. It just wasn't meant to be," Lupe said.

"How long did he live?" I asked.

"Three weeks. The important thing is you gave him a chance and his family will always be grateful for that."

"Well listen, I'm glad it was you that called even if it wasn't what I wanted to hear. You were very sympathetic in delivering a tough message," I told Lupe.

"Thank you Kevin. You take care," she said.

"You too," I said before hanging up.

Fortunately for me it was around the lunch hour and the newsroom was pretty empty. I fished a couple of tissues out of my desk and cleaned up before heading outside for some fresh air. I plunked myself down on an air conditioning unit and sat quietly alone. A few minutes later Tony Kirkpatrick—"Prime Time"-came bouncing across the parking lot heading for the newsroom's backdoor. "Cuddy Buddy!" Prime called out with his usual warmth and pizzazz. "What's up Cuddy Buddy?" Tony said extending both his hands for a double shake.

"Not a good day Prime," I told him.

"*Why?* What happened Cuddy?" as a look of concern took over his normally smiley face.

"Remember the boy I donated my bone marrow to a few months back?"

"Yeah, yeah I remember. How's he doing?"

"That's the problem. I just found out he died."

"Oh Cuddy, Oh man! That's so sad. I'm so sorry to hear that," he said as tears filled his eyes.

"When did it happen?" Tony wanted to know.

"It actually happened a while back but I just got a call about it today. I had to wait six months after transplant before I would be told the results. He lived just three weeks after transplant," I told Prime.

As we were talking our boss, Alex McGehee was coming back to the station after lunch. "What's wrong guys?" he asked.

"I just found out about the boy who received my bone marrow transplant," I told Alex.

"It didn't go well?" he asked imploringly.

"He didn't make it. He lived just three weeks afterward," I told him.

"That's too bad Kevin. But you really did a good thing in trying to help. Always remember that," Alex said.

"Thanks Alex. Hey by the way, can I take the rest of the day off?" I asked him.

"What for?"

"Well I'm just broken up about it all and I'm not sure I can concentrate so well. I'd really just like to go home and unwind," I told him.

"No I don't think I can let you do that Kevin. We really need you here. Look I'm sorry about your loss, but we really need you here," Alex said.

As Alex walked away Prime gave me another handshake and pulled me into a one-arm man hug. "Hang in there Cuddy Buddy. I'll pray for you," he said before walking into the newsroom too.

Alone again I dropped my head down and thought about all the different moments and people who inspired me to become a bone marrow donor-Chris Pablo, Alana Dung, Darya Oreizi and my now deceased friend. I gently kicked my legs back and forth like a metronome, letting the repetitiveness of the motion rock me into reflection. I was proud of what I had done and thankful for the opportunity to have been a part of something so special, but I was sickened by the result. I knew this could happen, but I never really thought it *would*.

Prior to my bone marrow extraction I tried to see the end result and the future as I wished it would be. I would someday meet the young man who received my bone marrow and we would become lasting friends, if not family. We'd exchange Christmas cards and maybe I'd see him at important times in his life-graduation, marriage, whatever. I wanted to see him in the flesh and blood, so I could know my blood was doing his flesh well.

I wanted him to have everything I had. A chance to play sports again, a chance to graduate from high school, a chance to go college, a chance to fall in love and chance to start a family of his own. I wanted so much for this young man to live. Selfishly I wanted him to be well for me. Like a parent, part of me would live vicariously through him. And just like the parent who feels a part of them dies when their child precedes them in death, I felt a part of me died that day too.

His loss left me lost. I still didn't know who the boy was, or where he lived. I couldn't send a sympathy card to his family. I had nothing but my thoughts and grief. I didn't want to do anything for the rest of that day other than get home and crawl in bed. And I certainly didn't feel like waking up at 4:30 the next morning to train for the Honolulu Marathon. My biggest inspiration was gone, and so too now was my motivation.

When I got home later that night I went straight to bed. I lay on my back staring at the ceiling as my wife Jean tickled my arm and sat quietly on the side of the bed. "Honey I'm proud of you. You should feel good about what you did. You gave that boy and his family a chance. That was all you could do," she said lovingly.

"I know, I know, I know. It's just... I guess I never really thought it would end this way. I prayed so hard and really in my heart of hearts I just took it as a given he was going to get better. So... so I guess I'm not prepared for this. I didn't know you could ever feel this sad. This is different. My stomach hurts, my scalp is tingling and the rest of my body is numb. I don't like how my body feels right now. It's just awful. I can't imagine what he went through and how his family felt-especially his mom. I just want to fall asleep so I don't have to think about it."

I closed my eyes but I couldn't sleep. My mind raced as my body lay still. I thought about the boy and his final moments. Did family and friends surround him when he died? Was he in pain? Was he mentally and spiritually ready? The questions kept coming but the answers didn't. It was a mental marathon and it was exhausting.

"Honey it's time to get up for marathon training," Jean said into my ear while gently rocking my shoulders.

"What? What time is it?" I asked.

"It's 4:30," Jean said.

"I didn't even know I fell asleep. How long have I been asleep?"

"You dozed off at about eight o'clock last night. I went to get you something to drink and when I came back you were out cold. I tried to wake you up so you could change out of your clothes and brush your teeth but you wouldn't budge," Jean said.

"So how long was I actually in bed before I fell asleep?"

"At least two hours," Jean told me. "Are you going to get up and go run?"

"I don't know. I still don't feel so well. And I'm not sure I want to do the marathon anymore," I told her.

"Why not?"

"Because the main reason I was running in the first place was because of the boy. Now that he's gone I just don't feel like I have the same motivation."

"What do you mean? You're going to quit?"

"I don't know, maybe. I mean what's the point? My whole point was I wanted to run to honor him and let him know I would push myself in the hopes that he'd do the same toward better health."

"Why don't you stay in bed today and just get some rest? But I really don't think you're going to be happy with yourself if you don't finish what you've started. You're also running for Chris Pablo, Alana Dung and Darya Oreizi. Plus you've already collected and turned in money from your family and friends who donated so you could go. What are you going to say to them and how are you going to pay them back?"

"You know what? You're right. I don't need to stay in bed and think about it anymore. I need to finish what I started. I feel bad enough about his death and I'll probably feel twice as bad if I quit. I've never quit anything in my life and I'm not about to start now," I said as I swung my legs over the side of the bed.

I got dressed and left the house. "Good morning Kevin," Sheryl Bavoso said.

"Hi Sheryl how are you?"

"I'm fine. What's new with you?"

"Well I had a tough night and I might be dragging a little today. So if I am, pick me up," I told her.

"What happened? Is everything alright at home?" Sheryl asked.

"Yeah everything's fine at home it's something else. Remember the boy I donated the bone marrow to?"

"Yeah, yeah."

"Well I found out the results of that. He didn't make it."

"Oh no. Oh my. Oh I'm so sorry," Sheryl said.

"Yeah it's tough," I said. "You know the biggest reason I'm running in the marathon is because of him. Whenever I struggled on the runs and started cramping up I always thought of him and the pain he went through with his leukemia, getting ready for the transplant and the aftermath. That always pushed me through the pain and kept me going."

A couple of other TNT runners overheard us and offered kind words. Sharing the news made me feel a lot better. It was as if wasn't my loss alone. And once we got into the run, I got lost in the exercise and the conversation about Fresno State football. When I was done I felt revitalized. After a shower I felt even better. I was still sad about the boy's passing, but the workout worked out much of my angst.

In the final three weeks of training I had additional motivation. On my sad days-and there were plenty, I channeled that grief into energy. I was now running to honor the memory of my bone marrow recipient, Chris Pablo, Alana Dung and Darya Oreizi. I was also running for me now too. I had hit rock bottom and I wanted to see if I was tough enough to tough it out. And physically it was really starting to be a grind. We were now up to 22-mile runs at a time. After a run like that you don't feel refreshed, you feel beat up.

In the final two weeks of training we actually started dialing down on the mileage. We had pushed our bodies for weeks to build endurance and now it was time to let them heal from all the wear and tear. In the final two weeks we scaled the long runs back to about a dozen miles. It was enough distance to keep our wind without worry of our wheels wearing out on the big day. We were ready. It was just time to get out of town, jet out to the islands and make it the marathon starting line.

We started the journey west by boarding a bus with 50 other TNTers and their families making the four and-a-half hour drive south to Los Angeles International Airport. LAX is a strange place. You never know who and what you're going to see there. It could be a movie star, or a freak show. On this day it was the latter times two. I saw a woman dressed up as Mother Theresa bumming change. And an Asian guy who looked the part of Long Duck Dong from Sixteen Candles was doing a skit that included accusing random men of looking at women lustily. He came up to me pointing his finger and saying in a weird cackle, "I saw you checking out other women. Ha, ha, ha. You've been a naughty boy. Ha, ha, ha. Now I'm going to have to fine you five dollars. Ha, ha, ha."

"Wait a minute," I said. "You say you saw me checking out other women?"

"Yes, yes. I see you. I see you."

"Really?

"Yes. You were looking at those women over there," he said while pointing over in the direction of two women by the escalator.

"No I don't think so bud," I told him.

"Yes, yes you do. You do," he said in his fake broken English.

"First of all if those women are part of your scam, you need to get better looking women. You're a dork. If you were funny I'd give you the five bucks. But you're not even funny. Now get out of here. You're an embarrassment and you're making my wife uncomfortable."

"No you lie, you lie," he said before taking his act on to the next guy.

By the time we made it to our departing gate in Terminal C we learned our flight was delayed three hours. It gave us plenty of time to talk and I sat down next to Erin Barry, a physical therapy student and soccer player at Fresno State who had become one of my running partners in the final weeks of training. We were talking about my bone marrow experience when a man the next seat over interrupted us. "Excuse me," the man said. "Did I hear you say something about bone marrow?" he asked.

"I sure did. Why do you want to know?"

"Because I have a sister-in-law who had leukemia and had a successful bone marrow transplant a few years earlier," Mark DeCastro of Wahiawa, Hawaii said.

Of the hundreds of seats in our holding area, why Mark DeCastro chose to sit next to me I'll never know. But I have my suspicions. He was the second man with a deep bone marrow connection to come into my life out of nowhere. First there was Earl, the black man I met at church months earlier whose son needed and received a bone marrow transplant. Now Mark. It was as if both men had fallen out of the ceiling right in front of me. I started to wonder if God was planting people around me once again for reasons I couldn't completely understand.

Mark and I talked for quite a while. He didn't recognize me from my TV days in Hawaii, but he was well aware of the stories I covered involving leukemia patients Chris Pablo and Alana Dung. He wished me well in the marathon and said he keep an eye out for me on the television coverage that week.

The flight itself was largely uneventful until the pilot came on the intercom. "Folks we have a very special group on board with us today. There's a group called Team in Training and they're on their way to run in the Honolulu Marathon."

With that my teammates went nuts. There was a guy sitting across the aisle who was already on a pretty good beer drinking pace. After the pilot spoke, he ordered a double round. By the time we arrived in Honolulu, the beer man had at least a half a case in him. He was a pleasant drunk though. In fact I don't think he said a word.

We rented a car and drove to the Hilton Hawaiian Village. After checking in we were greeted by Don and Sandra Edwards, dear friends of ours from Hawaii Kai whom we hadn't seen in a couple of years. We went to dinner together at Bennihana and caught up on old times. After dinner we took the elevator up the Tapa Tower and slid into room 3157. We immediately went out on the lanai to take in the view. As beautiful as the Waikiki skyline was at night, what both Jean and I noticed most was how clear the air was. "Can you believe we're back honey?" I asked Jean.

"I know it's strange but I always thought we'd come back," Jean answered. "I never imagined it'd be because you became a bone marrow donor and then decided to run a marathon. I thought we'd come back for vacation eventually."

The stars were shining bright and there was not a hint of smog like we had in Central California and Southern California. Tired from the travel and the heavy

Chris Pablo hugging Kevin prior to Honolulu Marathon. KGMB photographer
Chris Skapik in the background, Sandy Pablo sitting. Waikiki

meal I wanted to get to bed early because the next day would be a long one. I had some light training to do early in the morning and later I would meet with Chris Pablo and his family. I phoned in a wakeup call and shortly thereafter I crashed.

The phone rang around six in the morning. I rolled out of bed and put on my running clothes. I took the elevator down, grabbed a bagel from the Continental breakfast setup in the lobby, and set out for a half hour run on the beach. I jogged by old surf spots like Populars, a place where an eel almost ate my toes during a memorable surf session years earlier. I ran past Queens, named after Queen Lili-uokalani and in front of the pink Royal Hawaiian Hotel. Queens was the first place I ever surfed in Hawaii on a loaner board from Don Edwards. And I cruised past Rice Bowl, the South Shore's Pipeline, where I broke Don's board on an eight-foot closeout.

Beads of sweat dotted my skin as I breathed in the moist, salty air. Occasionally I'd stop and watch the surfers in places I once paddled out, imagining me on the waves instead of them. Feeling spiritual I ran by The Star of the Sea Catholic Church on Kalakaua Avenue where four years ago I kissed the ring of a Belgian Cardinal. It was wonderful to bond with the land and the water, to breathe in the Spirit of Aloha and to be kamaaina-of the land-once more.

After a shower I headed for Kapiolani Park where I would meet up with Chris Pablo's family and a television crew from KGMB Channel 9. Waiting for me was reporter Julia Norton-Dennis and photographer Chris Skapik. Chris and I did a lot of work together when I lived in the islands. After some small talk Chris instructed

Julia and me to sit across from one another at a picnic table. As Julia and I were talking about how much it meant to me to be able to return to the islands a car pulled up to the curb and out jumped Chris Pablo.

Even though I hadn't seen him in quite some time, Chris looked ten years younger than the last time I saw him. As he approached I felt my heart approaching the top of my throat. I wasn't sure whether to extend a hand or to give him a hug. Chris didn't give me a choice. "Kevin come here," he ordered extending both arms and embracing me in a warm, tight man hug. "Thank you Kevin for being a donor."

His words and his hug meant the world to me and it set off a flood of tears. He cried right along with me and didn't let me go until his wife Sandy approached holding a flowered lei in her hands. "I'm so proud of what you've done Kevin," he said taking the lei from Sandy and placing it around my neck. "God bless you."

"God bless you too Chris. Were it not for you and your golf ball, I never would have registered to be a potential donor," I told him. "Without you the donation, the transplant, the marathon, none of this would've happened," I told him.

I also talked with Sandy Pablo who looked as lovely as ever. "You taking good care of him Sandy?" I asked.

"I'm trying to but he's really doing well on his own," she said.

"Nate and Zack I bet it's great to see you dad feeling better again huh?"

Both, who had about doubled in size since the last time I'd seen them nodded in agreement.

"Chris seriously what are you doing to look so good?" I asked. "You look like you've been to the fountain of youth."

"It's the marrow. It's the marrow," he said with a hearty laugh.

"Oh hold on a minute I forgot something," Chris said as he started to jog back to his car. "Remember this?" he asked as he pulled an old golf ball out of his pocket.

"Of course. Let me hold it."

I turned the ball on its side and there were the words stamped on the side, beat leukemia. "Kevin remind me. Do you play golf too?"

Kevin Walsh and Chris Pablo holding golf balls with the words beat leukemia stamped on the sides, Waikiki.

"Of course. I play all the time."

"Good hold on. I need that old ball back but I have something else for you."

Chris fetched a box of Precept golf balls from his car and gave them to me. "You know what's stamped on the side?" he asked suggestively.

"Let me guess."

As I looked through the cellophane wrapper on the sleeves I could see the words *beat leukemia*.

"Now you know what to do with them right?" he asked.

"Of course. I'll lose them."

It was a lovely moment to share with Chris and our extended families. A few of my friends from TNT came along to laugh and cry with us. And the rest of the islands would be able to share in it too on the news that night as Chris Skapik and Julia Norton-Dennis rolled on everything.

After racing back to the hotel to watch my story on the 6:00 news, Jean and I joined the rest of the TNTers for the pre-race banquet at the Hawaii Convention Center. It was a chance to hear from inspirational speakers and it would be our last big meal before the big run. We were instructed to eat as much pasta as we could to load up on carbohydrates for energy. I ate enough for twelve.

Sitting next to us at dinner was Dean Eller, the CEO of the Central California Blood Center and his wife Claudia. The Ellers were walking in the Honolulu

Jay Hinkle and Rhonda Newcomer at Hawaii Convention Center. Jay received Rhonda's bone marrow in a lifesaving transplant. It's their first meeting.

Marathon to honor their deceased daughter Jennifer. The first guest speaker was marathon great Alberto Salazar, the winner of the Boston and New York City Marathons, and many other big races. I thought he might impart some wisdom about how we might go about our runs the next day, or share a few stories about the elite runners of his time. He did neither.

Alberto Salazar talked about how he learned so much more about himself and life from regular folks like the people before him. Salazar's contemporaries ran ridiculously long races in absurdly fast times. That was impressive to us-but not Alberto. The pros were good because they were *supposed* to be good. All they did was run and train. And they were paid good money for it. Salazar said regular folks like us were his heroes because we ran 26.2 miles on guts. And we did it for things greater than financial gain. It was touching.

Claudia Eller, Jean Walsh, Kevin Walsh and Dean Eller prior to the Honolulu Marathon.

Next to speak was a 34-year-old leukemia patient in remission named Jay Hinkle. While Jay fought the insidious disease and searched for a bone marrow match he suffered a stroke and temporary paralysis. He eventually found his match from a 34-year-old mother in Fullerton, California. Through tears Jay was reading the letter he sent to his donor a few months earlier. He talked about how grateful he was to have a second chance at life and how much it would mean to him to someday meet the woman who made it possible.

As soon as Jay finished reading, the pleasant tone of a woman's voice filled the auditorium. Jay hadn't gotten a step away from the podium and stopped to listen like the rest of us. The voice was that of Jay's donor and it was pretty obvious that things were building to a strong emotional ending. Her letter was remarkably similar to his. She also wanted to meet him and prayed for him and his family often. She concluded by saying writing a letter wouldn't be enough. She wanted a hug. And with that the black curtain behind the elevated stage swung open and out walked Rhonda Newcomer into Jay Hinkle's arms. It was very emotional and there was hardly a dry eye in the house when the lights came up to end the program.

As we got up from our seats to leave I pulled Dean Eller aside. "Now Dean I'm very happy for Jay and Rhonda. But I gotta tell you I'm very jealous. My stomach was in a knot the whole time. I could've written both their letters to each other. I wanted everything they got, but I'll never have that happy ending and it just kills me. I felt like my heart was being carved out while listening. You know what I'm talking about right?"

"I know. I know," Dean said nodding while saying little else.

...

While I could empathize with the Ellers I knew my pain was probably but a fraction of what Dean and Claudia felt. They lost their only daughter to leukemia, never having a chance at transplant because they couldn't find a bone marrow match anywhere in the world. Like me I'm sure when they saw Jay Hinkle and Rhonda Newcomer hugging on stage they wondered why not us? Most of the people in attendance were chatty on the way out of the Convention Center, but not us. We walked the Ellers to a cab and said goodnight.

I didn't want to go to bed on a sad note so I asked Becky Renee and Sheryl Bavoso to take a ride with us to see the Christmas lights in downtown Honolulu and around Honolulu Hale-City Hall. Becky and Sheryl were glad to come and were amazed to see Hawaiiana come alive at night. "Oh my gosh! Look at Santa!" Becky gushed while pointing out the window.

Surfing down the side of a building in Christmas lights was Santa Claus himself. There were light displays of erupting volcanoes, Menehunes and rainbows in brilliant color and detail. It was so beautiful and so *Hawaii*. The visuals lifted my spirits and I felt a lot better than I did after leaving dinner. After a loop around the Capital District it was time to say aloha to the lights and head back to the hotel for lights out.

CHAPTER FIFTEEN

The Marathon

THE WAKE UP CALL CAME AT 3:30AM. THERE WAS NO VOICE
to lure me out of bed, just a Hawaiian slack key guitar blaring out of the receiver.
I swung my legs out from under the colorful bedspread covered with tropical fish
prints and put my feet on the floor. I reached toward the ceiling in a mighty stretch
that involved full arm extension and a big yawn.

Jean was as still as a coral head so I left her alone to cuddle with the fish
comforter. I sat for a moment on the edge of the bed reflecting on what led up to
this day and how I might feel when the marathon was done. In my imagination I
pictured Chris Pablo, smiling and flying a kite with his family; Alana Dung holding
hands and waddling along with her parents; Darya Oreizi hanging out with his
dad; and the boy who received my marrow surrounded by family and friends
bedside after his transplant.

I prayed for strength knowing that at some point during the day I would be
doubled over and cursing myself for bringing the agony of a marathon upon myself
willingly. I prayed for hope, hoping that the money I raised might help others in
need. And I prayed for peace of mind that I would make it to the finish line in one
piece, without major injury.

The reflection and prayer warmed my heart and spirit, but my body was cold
from the sitting in my boxer shorts with the air conditioning on full blast. Wanting
to warm up I stepped out onto the lanai and into the warm tropical air. As I reached
back to grab the handle of the sliding glass door a gecko zipped across my hand.
"Whoa!" I screamed as I jumped back from the shock of it.

While catching my breath I put my hand over my chest and felt my heart beating fast and heavily. Whatever fear I had was quickly replaced by good cheer. In

island lore finding a gecko in your house is considered good luck. So I figured if my day started this early with lizard luck, the rest of the day might be filled with good fortune too. At least that's what I hoped. But when I saw a camera flash out the corner of my eye I had second thoughts. Some Australian newlyweds were drinking champagne a couple of lanais over. They heard me and saw me in my skivvies, so they took a picture. "Did you get the shot you wanted?" I asked.

"Actually I wish I had gotten you when you jumped back," he laughed.

"Just don't post that on the internet," I told him.

"No worries mate. Me wife and me will just have a laugh at you when we open the scrapbook a few years from now," he said in his accented English.

"I can live with that. Congratulations on your wedding and cheers," I said raising my hand before heading back inside.

Closing the sliding glass door behind me I reached around the orange and purple curtains to turn the air conditioning unit off. I started a pot of Kona Coffee in the bathroom before rummaging through my suitcase looking for a stick of Body Glide. Body Glide is a waxy lubricant that prevents chafing. It looks and is packaged just like deodorant. I rubbed it between my thighs, my butt cheeks, under my arms and over my nipples. As I Glided up I could hear the coffee pot percolating in the bathroom and the rich smell wafting through the room.

As I poured my first cup of Joe Jean was starting to stir. "Honey? Honey? What time is it?" she asked.

"It's 3:45," I told her.

I walked around the room sipping the coffee and trying to perk myself up. It didn't take long for the caffeine and the adrenaline to kick in and pretty soon I was eager to get moving. I wasn't about to leave the hotel room sans clothes a second time, so I put on my shorts, singlet, sweat-wicking socks, ball cap and sneakers. I filled my fanny pack with the racing essentials; energy goo packs, lip balm, bandages, more Body Glide and a small laminated picture card that I would later clip onto my hat. I brushed my teeth, went potty, rustled Jean up and just before four we were out the door.

It must have taken a good five minutes to get all the way from the 31st floor to the lobby because the elevator stopped on each floor down. Jean and I barely squeezed in. We squatted and wedged ourselves between a contingent of heavily bearded men from Canada who gave up on shaving during training, and leggy women from Arizona who; judging from the shine on their calves and shins, took shaving very seriously. On each floor we had to break bad news each time the doors opened. "Sorry we're full," we'd say to a bunch of bummed faces.

By the time we got to the eighth floor we could hear cheering and chanting that was no doubt related to the marathon. The closer we got to the lobby the louder it got. Before the doors opened one final time we could feel vibrations throughout the elevator floor and walls. And when the doors opened it was like Mardi Gras in the Hilton Hawaiian Village minus booze and beads. People were dancing, clapping, singing and chanting. It was awesome and sent shivers up my spine.

Like any great party there was food, if you could get to it. I bulled my way through the logjam in the lobby and found the buffet table. I don't like to run on an empty stomach, but I certainly don't like to feel full either. It's like fueling up a race car. You want just enough to get across the finish line — nothing more, nothing less. I opted for a dry bagel and an apple.

After finding my fellow Fresno TNTers in the sea of purple singlets Jean and I walked toward the marathon starting line on Ala Moana Boulevard along with 27,000 other people. It was like the masses descending on an NFL football stadium just before game time. Energy and anticipation were in the air. "See that marina on the left there Sheryl and Becky?" I asked pointing off to the side.

"Yeah," they said.

"Remember the opening scene of Gilligan's Island? That's the where the S.S. Minnow sailed from on what was supposed to be a three hour tour," I told them.

"How cool! There you go again Kevin with those interesting factoids," Sheryl said.

The clock was edging closer to the 5:00 race start and as we got closer to the starting line by Ala Moana Park we found ourselves in a serious bottleneck. We were crammed onto the streets and sidewalks almost as tight as we were in the elevator. You could hardly turn around to see who and what was around you. Eventually our walk slowed to a shuffle and later a standstill.

I'm a people person but standing still in the middle 27,000 people was a bit much. I felt trapped. Apparently I wasn't the only one. "Honey I gotta get out of here," my wife said nervously. "I'm starting to feel claustrophobic. I'm going back to the hotel. I'll catch up with you and the others along the race course."

"Okay. Just be very careful and courteous in telling people to move aside for you," I told her.

I watched as Jean pirouetted on a dime and used her hands and forearms as a people separator while moving against the grain of pedestrian traffic. It took her a couple of minutes to get far enough away that I lost sight of her. With Jean on her way back to safety and sanity I tried to refocus my mind on the race. But then another personal crisis arose. I had to pee.

I wasn't sure if I could make it over to a bank of Port-A-Potties on the side of the road and get back in time before the standstill of marathoners started to move again. I really had to go, but I was afraid that if I left my principal running partner Erin in the masses, I might not find her when I got back. So I grabbed her hand. "Erin come with me. If we get split up now we may never find each other again," I told her.

Kevin at the start of the Honolulu Marathon.

Hand in hand Erin and I zigzagged, saying excuse me more times to more people than I can remember on the way to relief. While in the john I heard howitzer fire with such force and vibration I almost pooped my pants. "Whoa!!!" the people screamed outside.

I didn't bank on being in a bank of crappers when the howitzers signaled the start of Honolulu Marathon, but it was probably best that way. Considering how bad I had to go to the bathroom and how shook up the initial explosions made me, it might have been messy if I didn't get to the right place at the right time.

I came out of the Port-A-Pottie and Erin was laughing. "You ready now?" she asked sarcastically.

"Yeah we're good to go. Let's get moving," I told her with a laugh.

By now the more competitive runners at the start were off and that gave more room for everyone else to spread out a bit. It was still tight quarters, but at least we weren't on top of each like a few minutes earlier. About a quarter mile away from the starting line we started with a very slow jog and a discussion about how important it was for us to pace ourselves and not start out too fast. The conditions we trained in back home in California were nearly perfect. The Central San Joaquin Valley is mostly flat, early morning temperatures are ideal and the humidity is very low. In Hawaii the terrain was much hillier, the late fall temperatures were much hotter and the air was much more humid. That would make dehydration a big concern. "Even if we don't feel thirsty at the time let's stop and drink water at every water station. Okay Erin?"

"Yeah that's a good idea, because at some point we're going to be sweating out more than we can take in," she said.

We reached the starting line at about 5:15. Small microchips on each runner's shoe sent a signal to a scanner that recorded your own personal starting time, instead of the official 5:00 start. Beep, beep, beep, beep went the scanner amid multiple blinking red lights on the transmitter as we embarked on the 26.2 mile journey.

As much as I had envisioned running the marathon in a steady and plodding forward motion, the first few miles were any but that. Erin and I spent the bulk of our time weaving in and out of runner traffic, and running "tall" to keep our legs from tangling with those of other competitors. We saw quite a few falls, some of which led to minor pileups and quite a few skinned knees and other abrasions. Not that there's a good time and place to lose dermis layers, but I especially didn't want that to happen to me on the streets of Chinatown where the addicts and prostitutes have been known to use the streets as their personal toilet.

A couple of miles into the race we started to get a little separation from the wall- to-wall runners. With more room to roam it made it safer to take in the scenery around us. Some of the best stuff was watching fellow runners who had more on their minds than running the marathon. On Nuuanu Avenue we saw a group of Japanese runners dressed as Flintstones characters. Seeing Fred and Wilma Flintstone rumbling along with Barney and Betty Rubble absolutely rocked! You couldn't dial it up any better and plenty of people pulled out their cell phones to phone home and take pictures.

"Mom it's me," a young woman jogging alongside Erin and me said into a cell phone that she pulled out of her fanny pack. "Yes I'm running in the marathon right now, but I just *had* to call. You won't believe what I just saw. I just saw a group of people dressed as the Flintstones jog right past us."

A mile or so later near the corner of South King and Punchbowl Streets we approached King Kamehameha's statue. He was the greatest leader in island history and on any given day his bronzed neck boasts dozens of leis carefully placed around it. With a bit less care we saw a bunch of runners take their leis off and throw them up on the King. Few lassoed his neck, but most managed to land their plumerias, hibiscus and tea leaves elsewhere on his body or nearby.

A couple of miles down the road toward Waikiki I saw a bride in a full white gown, veil and heels. Clackety clack went her heels as she trotted along with one hand holding the front of her dress and the other clutching a bouquet. I don't know if the wedding was later in the day, or had already happened. All I knew was she looked stunning and I'd be stunned if she finished all 26.2 miles wearing bridal wear.

For the first eight miles of the race I felt very comfortable. It was still dark, not too hot and Erin and I found a nice, steady rhythm. As we started to climb Diamond Head Crater on the edge of Kapiolani Park, I heard whistles blowing and the rumbling of motorcycles. It was the Honolulu Police Department escorting the race leader down the hill and toward the finish line about a mile away. I thought *what a lucky guy.* He's got a police escort, he's about to finish and I'm just getting started. When I saw the guy appear behind the Kawasakis I realized maybe I was the lucky one. He was wheelchair racer. I'm sure he would've traded places with me in a second.

It was a 30-degree climb up the side of Diamond Head and the first major test of the marathon. My thigh muscles were starting to tighten and burn like they would when I lifted weights at the gym. And I knew the burn would only increase the higher I climbed. "You alright Erin?" I asked my running partner.

"My thighs are starting to burn," she said.

"Yeah me too."

Looking for a lift I reached up to touch the laminated card on my hat that had the pictures of Chris Pablo, Alana Dung, Darya Oreizi and the number 16 for my bone marrow recipient. A simple touch touched off so many reactions inside. I could feel a wave of relief come over me. I looked over at the sea and saw the sun rising on the backs of six-foot swells. It was beautiful. Watching the sun as it lifted out of the sea and into the sky lifted my spirits and gave me a sunnier disposition about my chances to finish.

Higher and higher we climbed on the volcanic crater and the nagging muscle burn kept coming back into my legs. Reaching up I touched the card time and time again. Each time I did it I felt a surge of energy just as my legs were on the verge of betraying me. And it was more than just an energy jolt; a palpable sense of peace filled my body too. An inner voice assured me that I'd be fine. And of course I prayed. I had a running conversation with Saint Jude while running the race.

The finest moment of the Diamond Head climb came about 20 minutes after we started the ascent. We reached the top and started the slow climb down the other side toward Kahala. "How do you feel Erin?" I asked my running partner.

"I am so glad that's over," she said with a big exhale of air. "I don't know if I could've gone much farther. My wind and lungs were fine, but that hill is way bigger than any of the hills we trained on back home. I thought my legs were going to die."

"Oh I know. I feel the same way. It's mostly downhill and flat for the next 15 miles or so. Let's take it easy so we have something left when we loop back and have to run up Diamond Head again on the way back to the finish line," I told her.

For the next couple of miles we settled in to a comfortable jog that was probably a minute slower than the 8:30 mile pace we grew accustomed to back in Fresno. The sun was rising as was the temperature and humidity. With hardly a cloud in the sky we were exposed and I could feel my skin start to sting from sunburn. Whatever sunscreen I lathered on earlier was completely gone, and any reapplication would have slid right off with the sweat too.

Erin and I stopped at every water station and drank as much as we could.

Looking for an edge I tried the bluish sports drink at one of the stations adjacent to the Kahala Mall hoping the vitamins in the mixing powder might power me along. Bad move. It was like a kick in the gut, upsetting my stomach almost to the point of puking. But I ran through it vowing to finish on water and guts alone.

By mile 13 I had probably drank at least two gallons of water, which of course had to come out in ways other than sweat. Fortunately there were plenty of Port-A-Potties. It got to the point that I couldn't go but a mile or two without having to stop and pee.

Kevin with Honolulu Marathon running partner Erin Barry.

"You have to go *again?* You're like a little girl," Erin teased me.

"I know, I know," I laughed. "I can't help it. I can't run if I feel like I have to go to the bathroom," I told her.

Near Waialae Country Club, the home of the PGA Tour's Hawaiian Open, we saw the elite runners approaching in the opposite direction. A line of cones on Kalani'ana'ole Highway separated schlubs like us on the way out, and the stars on their way back in. We were only a few feet apart, but athletically we were worlds away. The inward bound looked the part of a sleek Acela train gliding down the track. On my side we looked like a freight train limping along in terms of speed and the lame-people who really were limping.

"Kevin I have to go to the bathroom," Erin said as she made her first stop of the day a mile short of Hawaii Kai.

"It's about time," I said with a laugh while cradling a small Dixie Cup of water.

About 30 seconds later Erin came barging out with a look of horror on her face.

"What's wrong?" I asked.

"Oh my God. I think someone got sick in there or had diarrhea because it smells so bad," she said.

We were at that point in the marathon where our bodies were starting to do

Kevin around the 23 mile mark of the Honolulu Marathon.

weird things. Around mile 16 people were starting to pull themselves off the course to throw up, give up, plop down on a bench to rest, or to take a plop in the increasingly unpleasant Port-A-Potties. It was crazy and I was starting to feel that way-no doubt a combination of fatigue, dehydration and maybe even hallucination.

Mile 18 on the course made a loop around Hawaii Kai and sent us back in the direction of Waikiki. I felt loopy and perhaps delirious. As I ran past hundreds of palm trees I thought about climbing up, knocking down a few coconuts and mixing a Malibu Rum drink. Why this random thought came into my head I don't know. But the repetitive swaying palm tree visual had a hypnotic effect on me. I felt numb and strangely imagined a white bottle with brown palm trees-just like the side of Malibu Rum.

I climbed no trees and eventually the weird thoughts went away. "Erin I think I was hallucinating for a bit. Has your mind been playing tricks on you?" I asked.

"Oh yeah," she said. "What took you so long?"

The wackiness eventually gave way to lucidity, but by no means were we feeling comfortable. Our bodies were failing us. We just hoped we wouldn't fall down before we were done.

Mile 22 was especially rough on Erin. Usually right by my side, she was drifting farther and farther back. Several times I pulled over and waited for her to catch up. After about the fourth or fifth time I asked, "Are you feeling alright?"

"My legs just really hurt. I want to walk for a bit. You can go ahead if you want," she told me.

"No way. We started together and we'll finish together. Be strong and push through it at your pace. Our families are going to be positioned at the Mile 23 marker. That'll give us a boost," I told her.

We trudged forward, albeit much slower than we were moving even 15 minutes prior. When we rounded a corner by the Aloha Gas Station and the 8th Hole of the Waialae Country Club our families and friends saw us and went bonkers. "There they are!" someone shouted while pointing in our direction.

"Go Erin! Go Kevin!" Becky Renee screamed as we approached. "We're so proud of you!"

Becky's voice blasted over everyone else's. For a moment I thought she was using artificial help. There was no megaphone, just her mega voice that really perked us up as we picked up our pace down Kealaolu Avenue. At the corner of Kealaolu and Kahala Avenues we made a 90-degree turn right.

About a five iron away from the corner and the 9th green of the golf course, there was yet another bank of Port-A-Potties. With just two miles left to go I knew it would be an emotional ending and I didn't want to spoil it by soiling myself. So I stopped for the final time in the marathon before continuing down Kahala Avenue's beachfront.

Just before our second climb of Diamond Head, Team in Training Coach Cathy Piche appeared. "How are you guys doing?" she asked Erin and me.

"We're getting pretty tired," I told her as she jogged alongside us.

"Do you want a Jolly Rancher? I will freshen up the taste in your mouth," Cathy said.

With my mouth tasting like a bag of Sea Salt Potato Chips I took a watermelon flavored candy and popped it in my mouth. Sucking the flavor out of it and swishing it around my mouth took my mind off the pounding my knees and feet were taking. Who knew a piece of candy could be such a tonic? It was the last thing I would taste before the final mile and one last leg up Diamond Head Crater.

The second climb up Diamond Head was much different than the first. Only a handful of people at this point were jogging. Most were walking very slowly, hobbled by fatigue and/or injury. "We're almost home Erin. You gonna make it?" I asked.

"Yeah," she said exhaling. "I can walk in, or crawl if I had to."

"You're almost there!" a spectator screamed from the side of the road. "Only another half mile to the top!"

After reaching the top we both breathed a huge sigh of relief. From here we thought we could just about slide into Waikiki, much like the lava did off the side of Diamond Head Crater millions of years ago. My thighs were burning and aching from muscle cramps and my feet were blistered and burning from 25 miles of pounding on the blazing asphalt. Before heading down the road I looked over the cliff and saw a longboarder taking a lazy ride on a glassy six-footer. It made me smile. "Erin look at that," I said pointing down to the beach.

"You feeling okay?" I asked her.

"I'm just ready for it to be over," she said.

"Me too. Let's finish strong."

As much as we thought the jog downhill would be as easy as pineapple, it was as painful as stepping on keava thorns; which have pricked surfers' bare feet for years on the trail down to the beach. Because Diamond Head is so steep it's almost impossible to jog standing erect-the physics just won't allow it. You either have to lean forward and increase your speed so as to not topple over, or you have to lean back and slow down. Either way it puts tremendous stress on your thighs. Our thighs were pretty banged up to begin with, so the journey down was downright miserable. I reached up and touched the picture card on my hat and whispered quietly under my breath to my honorees and Saint Jude, "Help me now. I've come too far to not finish. Lift me up. I can't take much more."

After reaching the bottom of the hill at the corner of Diamond Head Road and Kalakaua Avenue the finish line was in sight. It was a half-mile away and the ground was flat. "Erin there it is! See the finish line? We're going to make it!" I told her.

She said nothing. As we ran side by side it looked like the finish line was moving farther away the closer we got. "Is that finish line moving farther away?" I asked Erin confusedly.

"No. Why?" she asked.

"It just looks like it's moving backward," I told her.

"It's not. Just keep running. We're almost there," Erin said, now becoming my motivator when I needed it most.

"We're 500 yards away Kevin just keep it together," she encouraged.

I started seeing double and my legs wobbled. I reached up to touch the picture card again but instead of touching it, I pulled the hat off my head and cradled it in my hands. I secured the card, squeezing it between my thumb and forefinger on my right hand. I started coming around and my vision wasn't as blurry. I saw my wife Jean out of the corner of my eye. "Honey! Honey!" she screamed. "You're almost there, almost there!"

About two hundred yards away the finish line and the banners came back into focus. I held my hat in my left hand, balled my right into a fist and gave series of right uppercuts while screaming, "YES! YES! YES!"

Dozens of news photographers snapped pictures as I crossed the finish line holding my hat across my heart with my other fist high in the air. Four hours, 28 minutes and 44 seconds later my marathon was done. I gave Erin a hug. "Thank you so much for being a part of this with me," I told her.

"Oh no, thank you. You were so helpful to me," she said.

Then I was all alone with just my thoughts and my hat. I pulled it away from my heart and looked at the pictures of Alana Dung, Chris Pablo, Darya Oreizi and the number 16 for my bone marrow recipient. I started to cry but hardly a tear appeared. I had nothing left to give. I looked to the sky and said, "Thank you God and Saint Jude for the courage and strength you gave me, and thank you my bone marrow friend for allowing me to be a part of your life if only for a brief time. God bless you and your family."

By the time I reached my wife I could hardly walk or talk. Race officials were trying to shoo me along because I was crowding up the finish line and they thought I was badly in need of water and food replenishment. As I wobbled over to the recovery area an overwhelming feeling of satisfaction poured over me. At last I had completed my mission.

Feeling faint Jean sat me down on a chair. I ate an orange, a banana, two bags of Doritos, a bag of Fritos and a tube of a chocolate protein supplement. I washed

Kevin after the marathon with Sheryl Bavoso, Becky Renee and wife Jean.

it all down with several cups of water. Within ten minutes I went from the exhaustion and dehydration to actually feeling pretty well. It's a good thing too. I had one other major mission to accomplish that day.

A shuttle took us back to the Hilton Hawaiian Village. The shuttle could have passed for a handy van, because so many marathoners struggled to get up and down the steps. Once back at the hotel I took a long shower, letting the hot water work on my sore muscles. I washed in the water and soaked in the satisfaction of a job well done feeling blessed to have been a part of something so special. I reflected on reuniting with Chris Pablo, finishing a grueling marathon and within the hour I would meet up with the parents of Alana Dung.

After showering I dried off and sat on the edge of my bed. I slipped on a pair of khaki Bermuda shorts and reached for the orange Honolulu Marathon T-shirt that was given to race finishers. I put my arms in the sleeves but I couldn't pull it over my head. Nor could I tie my sneakers. My muscles tightened up so quickly from the shower to the bed that I couldn't dress myself. I don't know what I would have done without my wife Jean. She got me ready.

By the time we made it down to the hotel lobby I was even less mobile. My forward movement was more a shuffle than steps. When Francisco the valet driver pulled our rental car up I needed help getting in the car. Driving was out of the question so Francisco helped me slide into the passenger seat. Jean took the wheel.

It had been a couple of years since we'd been in Honolulu so we'd forgotten how challenging the navigation of one-way streets could be. We got lost a few times, but in finding our direction we rediscovered some of the places we used to visit, including Auntie Pasto's Italian Restaurant on Beretania Street. Eventually we pulled into Punahou School.

Going to Punahou was another homecoming for me. It was where I met Chris Pablo and his family and saw his golf ball for the first time. It was also the place where Alana Dung's parents were volunteering at a bone marrow registration drive. When Jean and I walked up to the greeting table Adelia Dung asked, "Would you like to register?"

"No thank you. We already registered at your daughter's drive four years ago," I told her.

It was then that Adelia realized who we were and why we were there. I gave her a big hug and a kiss and the picture card that I wore on my hat with their daughter Alana's picture. "Oh thank you so much," she said. "That's so nice of you."

"Well I thought you should have it because Alana was such a source of strength for me today and many days before. Without her and the drives you set up at Blaisdell Arena I never would have registered, and I never would have had the chance to save someone else's life," I told her.

Steven and Adelia Dung greet a registrant at a bone marrow registration drive.
The Punahou School, Honolulu

"Who received your marrow?" Adelia asked.

"I don't know yet," I told her. "All I know was that he was 16-years-old and was a football player. He lived only three weeks after the donation, so that's been tough to deal with."

"But you know something Kevin? You gave him a chance and I know how much that means to a family."

"I know you do. Thank you so much for letting me run the marathon in your daughter's honor," I said to Adelia as I hugged her and shook her husband Steven's hand.

A few tables over from the Dungs sat another person curiously taking interest in our exchange. "Is that you Renee?" I asked with a smile as I approached with arms extended.

"It's me," she said wrapping her arms around me in hug. "How are you Kevin? Did the marathon go okay?" Renee Adaniya asked.

"Yeah," I told her. "I can't believe it's all over. I'm so glad I did it and had a chance to come back to see you, Alana's parents and Chris Pablo."

"Oh you saw Chris yeah?" she asked in her cute Pidgin accent accented with her toothy smile and warm personality filled with aloha.

"Yes we got together yesterday and he gave me a box of golf balls all stamped with the words *beat leukemia* on the side."

Kevin and fellow bone marrow donor Renee Adaniya.

"Oh that's so Chris," she said with hearty laugh.

Reuniting with Renee was really the end of my bone marrow journey. She was the last person I just had to see coming back to Hawaii. She was the first bone marrow donor I had ever met. The story about her improbable match of a white guy in Tennessee personalized the process of bone marrow donation for countless viewers and me. If a pint-sized pixie chick like her could do it, so could we with a little courage and a lot of luck.

After saying goodbye to Renee and the Dungs Jean and I finally had a chance to be alone. We went back to the hotel for a poolside lunch. The palm trees danced in the trade winds and gave us the perfect sampling of shade and sunshine. Two musicians on the other side of the pool played Top 40 cover songs at just the right volume with just the right touch of Hawaiian flair mixed in. The smell of flowers and fauna filled the air and the salty taste of ocean air mixed in my mouth. It really was perfection in paradise.

After lunch Jean and I moved closer to the pool to recline, relax and replenish our bodies with drinks of the umbrella kind. The great day got even better and by the third margarita the aches and pains from the long marathon were long gone. "You look like you're in your glory," nobody in particular said as they walked by raising their island cocktail in a toast.

"Starting to feel a little toasty too," I said returning the cheers.

As nighttime approached Jean and I decided to retire to our room in the Tapa Tower. Many of the TNTers were going to a scheduled "victory" dinner and ice cream social afterward. Jean and I were too tired to go. I hit the bed at about 6:00pm and didn't wake up until 6:00 the next morning.

Our plane home left at 8:30 and it was a scramble to pack, check out and gobble up scrambled eggs at the continental breakfast. On the ride to catch the flight I couldn't believe how time had flown during our long weekend in Waikiki. I'm not sure Jean and I talked as we drove down Ala Moana Boulevard and Nimitz Highway to Honolulu International Airport. Pictures of a four-year journey filled my mind with snapshots of Chris Pablo, Alana Dung and Darya Oreizi. And what I couldn't see in my mind I felt in my heart and in my bones. And it was in my bones where I felt the memory of the boy who received my bone marrow the most. I wondered what he would have thought if he lived long enough to know I ran a marathon in his honor. Just entertaining the idea was honor enough for me.

After pulling the Hertz rental car into the return lot and pulling the luggage out of the trunk, I noticed the lot attendant shooting me curious looks while looking over the car and preparing the receipt. When she handed it over she said "Hey brah. You used to work here didn't you?"

"Yes," I told her.

"I saw your story on the news. That was a very nice thing you did," she said with a smile.

Her words meant so much to me. Being an outsider to the islands, or a haole, as they would say, I never really knew how well the locals took to me as a person and a TV personality. At least now I knew how one person felt, and it made me feel great.

The Wiki Wiki Shuttle took us over to the terminal and within a matter of minutes we were on board the Hawaiian Airlines DC-10 that would take us back to California. Sitting in the plane at the gate I could see the plane was barely half full. "Folks this is the captain. There's a group of people from Maui that is running late and is going to join us on the flight back to the mainland. We're going to be delayed about 30 minutes."

Nobody seemed to mind and I used the extra time to replay in my mind the special moments of the weekend and all that led up to it. It was quiet time, a time to pray and a time to reflect. "You know honey," I said to Jean as we sat waiting, "I can't help but think that God and Saint Jude have been such an important part of this bone marrow journey."

"What do you mean?" Jean asked.

"Well really everything. Covering the news stories about Chris Pablo, Alana Dung, Renee Adaniya and then becoming a donor and running in the marathon... I mean with the exception of the boy dying everything else just sort of fell right into place. I just feel that without the St. Jude novenas and other prayers none of this would have happened. So many miracles have happened. Prayer made the difference," I told her before excusing myself to go to the bathroom

All that morning coffee made nature call. I chose the rest room in the right corner of the back of the plane for relief. I slid myself inside the narrow door and steadied myself while standing over the silver toilet with tinges of blue around the bowl. As I took aim and let loose my eyes wandered around the cramped quarters. Glancing upward on the curved part of the ceiling I saw something written in red lipstick or some kind of paint pen. At first I thought it was graffiti, which I found a bit astonishing. I mean really, who tags a plane's bathroom? How tacky I thought. Then I took a second look and I couldn't believe what my eyes made out. I almost made myself. There were two words. They spelled out **Saint Jude.**

It's a good thing I was midstream with pants pulled down when I saw the words Saint Jude because if I not, I would have pissed my pants. The sight of the St. Jude markings and instantaneous recognition that this marked a faith affirmation and saintly intercession greatly accelerated the peeing process. No way could I have held it in if the pants weren't already down. I had goose bumps and I felt my heart flutter. How I didn't miss the toilet bowl while going number one is yet another miracle-albeit of much less significance.

While washing my hands and tidying up I looked around the bathroom to see if there was anything else unusual. Nothing stood out, including the Saint Jude markings on the wall. From where I was standing at the sink and anywhere else in the plane's bathroom I'm almost positive your eyes couldn't find where the words were written because of the curvature of the room. If you were sitting, you'd be facing the other way and your neck couldn't crane back far enough to see the words at the awkward angle. The only way to see them was to stand directly in front of the toilet and to tilt your head back 45 degrees, trusting in your urinating accuracy. The words could only have been meant for a standing urinating man to see because really there was no other way to see them.

I returned to my seat and told my wife about what I saw. "Honey you're not going to believe this. You know how we were talking about Saint Jude and prayer just before I went to the bathroom?"

"Yeah," she said.

"Well you're not going to believe this. When I took a piss I looked up at the ceiling and saw the words Saint Jude written in red looking right back at me."

"You're kidding," she said curiously.

"No I'm serious. Go back and check it out to make sure my eyes are not playing tricks on me. You'll have to stand right in front of the toilet and tilt your head back. If you don't, you won't see it. Now if it's there, take a couple of pictures of it," I told her.

A couple of minutes later Jean was back. "Yep it's there," she said. "You're right. If you didn't look up just how you said, you would've missed it. That's *so weird*. I took two pictures of it."

"Good. I'm just glad to know I'm not losing my mind and hallucinating," I told her.

"No it's definitely there. But you're right; it's almost impossible to see. If you didn't know where to look you'd never see it," Jean said.

A couple of weeks later we got the developed roll of film back from our Hawaii trip. All the pictures came out, *except for the ones of Saint Jude.*

CHAPTER SIXTEEN

Golf Balls
Lost and Found

I HAD A GOOD ROUND GOING AS I APPROACHED THE 17TH hole of Fig Garden Golf Club in Fresno, California. It was a gloriously sunny December day with temperatures in the upper 60s. A nice breeze blew away the smoke from the Macanudo cigars I shared with my pals Rich Rodriguez, Ed Luethke and Jeff Ferguson. I took a puff and took in the view. Behind the green rose a tall bluff where the Central Valley's rich and famous built their mansions along Van Ness Extension.

Not even the stench of a freshly puffed stogie could mask the smell that wafted over from the horse farm on the left of the tee box. It was a distinct smell, but it was refreshingly natural. As Rich bent over to pluck a few blades of grass from the ground to test the wind, a darling horse, mahogany in color with a painted nose came trotting by. The gal riding it was cute too. She had medium length brown hair pulled back from her pixie face and tucked under her riding helmet. "Hi guys," she said as she rocked back and forth to the motion of the horse's trot.

She couldn't have been but sixteen and I'm sure she had no problem finding a date to the prom. There were a couple of guffaws among us, but because Rich and Ed had daughters about that age whatever comments or compliments anyone had about the visual was kept to himself.

As the rider and the horse wandered off I thought about the 16-year old boy who received my marrow. Would he have wanted to date a girl like that? No question. Any boy that age would've wanted to ask her out. Thoughts of my bone marrow recipient and the girl on the horse reminded me of something I planned to do before starting the round. Today would be the day I would lose the first of the *beat leukemia* golf balls Chris Pablo had given me weeks earlier when I visited with him prior to the Honolulu Marathon. But first there was more golf to be played. With the flagstick tucked behind a bunker of the par three 17th I needed to get my focus back, and decide which club to pull.

Copying Rich I tossed a couple of blades of Bermuda grass into the air and figured the wind was mostly in my face and blowing slightly from left to right. On most days the 175-yard hole was a stock six-iron. Today it would take more club. I took a puff on the cigar and blew out the smoke, watching as the wind took it in the same path as the tossed grass. Comfortable with the wind direction I now had to figure out which club to hit.

I reached into my bag filled with white dot Ping blades and pulled out a five-iron. As I puffed away I bounced my Titleist Pro V1 on the clubface killing time. Rich futzed around in his bag before pulling out a hybrid that looked as ugly as an old Ginty club. Rich had the honor so he went first. I'm about two clubs stronger than Rich, so I knew if he pulled the right club I'd be good to go with my five.

As Rich teed up his Titleist NXT someone let out a fart as wet as The San Joaquin River that flowed behind us. No one took credit for it, but it wasn't Rich and it wasn't me. "Whoever did it you're lucky we're almost done," I laughed. "If my ears are right you're going to have to check. It's my guess you're going to need a couple of wipes."

Like a good joke the fart had great timing. It gave us all a good laugh and broke the tension of what was then a pretty tight match between partners. With joy in his heart, smoke coming out of his mouth and gas from an unknown passer fouling the air, Rich drew his club back. He coiled around his body and made solid contact with the ball. His orb had a slight fade that was magnified by the slice wind. It barely cleared the bunker guarding the front of the green, hopped twice, and eventually settled about 20 feet below the hole leaving him an uphill putt. "I *smell* birdie," Rich howled as he flung his broken tee in the direction of the trashcan attached to the ball washer.

Next to play I put my tee in the ground closer to the left tee marker. I wanted to play a slight draw that would be straightened out by the left to right wind. Unlike Rich I couldn't swing with a burning log sticking out of my mouth, so I took a final draw before dropping my cigar on the ground about a foot away from my teed ball. I waggled my five-iron and tilted my head to the left to get one last glimpse of the hole. When I looked back to the ball I could see a contrail of smoke drifting from the cigar's hot end across the hitting zone. "Nice and easy I said to myself" as I pulled the pulled the club away.

Like a vacuum the takeaway took away much of the smoke. By the time I started the downswing the view to the ball was as clear as could be. I cleared my hips and could feel my hands lagging behind, being pulled through the impact zone by the larger muscles and trunk of my body. As the five-iron compressed the ball and the leading edge of the club dug through the grass, I knew I hit a good one. Not only did it feel good, it sounded good. There's nothing quite like the crisp feel and click sound of an iron struck right on the sweet spot. "Be right!" I barked as the ball started about 20-feet right of the hole and started hooking back to the left.

"Oh Walshy. That's a good one," Rich said as he followed the ball through his dark sunglasses and smoke cloud around his face.

Just as the ball was arcing left and crossing over the direct line to the hole, the crosswind buffered the ball. It held it up, slowing its curve and pushing it back to the right. As the towering shot fell from the sky with the bluff and the mansions in the background, it was obvious it would be close. The ball landed pin high about five feet to the left of the hole location. It took one hop about ten feet past the pin and spun back halfway. The shot left a deep dent that revealed the soft sand and dirt combination that made up the green's foundation. The ball came to rest about seven and-a-half feet left of the cup.

"Great shot Walshy," Jeff Ferguson said as he gave me a fist bump, all but conceding the team match between Rich and me and Jeff and Ed was over.

"Wait a minute Kev. You still need to make that putt," Ed Luethke reminded.

"I know. I know," I answered.

Even though the shot was close, it was not an easy putt considering the pressure of closing out the match and the severity of the green's speed and slope.

Ed and Jeff hit reasonable shots onto the green, but hardly within birdie range. Before walking up to the green I opened the semi-circular front pouch of my Mac-Gregor golf bag. Inside I had about a dozen or so balls. In the middle of the pile was a ball with a whiter sheen and a smaller dimple pattern. I hardly had to look to know it was the *beat leukemia* stamped golf ball that I had packed away earlier in the morning. A sensation shot through my body, almost like the buzz of a cigarette drag after you've had a couple of cold ones. I thought this is just like the moment Chris Pablo experienced when he found the original *beat leukemia* ball. The ball just stood out from the rest.

And just like Chris plucked the ball from his basket at the driving range and put it in his pocket, I dug the ball out of the bottom of my bag and put it in my pocket too. I strolled up to the green and jiggled the ball in my left pocket along with an assortment of change and golf tees. I closed my eyes for a half minute and remembered how Chris described his feeling in the moments after his great find. He said he had a profound sense of confidence that things were going to be okay. Although the stakes were invariably lower for me, the mental exercise gave me a similar confidence that there was no way I was going to miss that birdie putt coming up.

When I reached my ball on the green I marked it with a 1970 penny that had long since lost its copper shine. It was brown with tinges of green around Lincoln's head. I lifted the ball off the grass and wiped the mud and grass off the ball with the help of a grubby towel and a healthy blob of spit. I took the cleaned ball and rubbed it on the outside of my shorts where Chris Pablo's ball was bulging out of the pocket. After returning the ball in play to its spot, I lifted the coin and took a few steps behind the ball to check the line. Crouching down in a catcher's stance I guessed the ball would start about a 18 inches outside the left side of the cup before diving right and picking up speed the final couple of feet.

"Walshy, you know if you make it you win," Jeff Ferguson announced. "But if you miss it, it'll make 18 very *interesting*," Jeff teased.

"Thanks Ferg. But 18 will not be interesting for you, or Ed. I'm going to make the putt, collect your money, and laugh at you the whole way down the final hole. And do me a favor Ferg. Pluck this out of the hole for me when I'm done," I said sarcastically.

Settling in next to the ball I could feel the slope of the green in my Footjoys. I took two practice strokes to get a feel for how hard I wanted to hit the putt. Considering the wicked slope, I hardly had to get the ball moving to get it to the hole. In fact if I didn't make the putt it would probably slide past the hole and down to the bottom of the green some 40 feet away.

I spotted a tiny brown spot on the green about a foot in front of my ball and on the intended line that I wanted to start the putt. I pulled the White Hot Odyssey putter back about three inches and swung it through like a pendulum. The ball simply got in the way of a good stroke and rolled right over the brown spot. Halfway to the hole I knew the line was right if the cup could hold the speed of the putt. A foot away from the hole gravity took over. The ball put on its blinker and dove right toward the hole. In the blink of an eye it crashed into the back of the cup, hopped up about two inches below falling straight down and rattling around in the bottom.

"Whooooooooo!!!!" I thundered while launching myself into a chest bump with Rich.

"Ouuuuch!" he screamed from the force of the collision, which knocked a hot ash off his cigar and down his shirt.

I got about a foot off the ground. Rich? I'm not sure he even got airborne. He aired himself out, pulling his tucked shirt out of his pants while doing a victory boogie. Our birdie to their bogey was the difference in the team match that won us a whopping total of five bucks.

"Great putt Walshy," Ferg said defeated in tone, but kind in compliment.

"Clutch putt Kev. Great match," Ed added graciously.

With the match decided and the razzing of one another ratcheting up, we walked from the 17th green to the 18th tee. It was about 60 yards away and cut out of the bluff. The elevated tee offered a view of a wide fairway with tall eucalyptus and pine trees to the right and a thick grove of oleanders to the left. Farther up a small pond with a fountain guarded the front and left side of the green.

Eighteen gave golfers a lot of options. A shade less than 450 yards, the short par five was the ultimate risk/reward hole. If you needed a simple par, you could bump along a few conservative shots, hit the green in regulation, and probably walk away with a five. But it was short enough that even the average knocking golfer might think of going for it in two, if they had the guts to tempt the pond. Many a match and many a good round was had and lost on 18.

With the birdie two on 17, I had the honor on 18. "Okay Walshy you're two under on the day. No wussing out and laying up," Rich challenged.

Here I just helped the guy win the match and pay for his first round in the 19th hole and he's breaking my balls. "Richie how long have you known me? Have you ever seen me lay up?" I asked while teeing up my ball up between the tee markers.

"I know, I know, I know," he answered sarcastically. "But if you make a birdie or an eagle here you shoot in the 60s. That's just a lot cooler than a two under par 70."

"Chachie don't worry about it," I told him, calling him by one of his many nicknames.

With the tee in the ground and the ball on top I scanned the fairway below and visualized the drive I wanted to hit. I saw a powerful draw in my mind's eye, starting down the right center of the fairway and working its way back to the left side of the short grass. If you're going to miss it on 18 it's better to miss it right. You can at least punch out and salvage something. Left is death. The oleander grove is a graveyard of lost balls and the out of bounds stakes line the rest of the hole all the way down to the green by the clubhouse and parking lot.

I gave my Callaway driver a few last waggles and pulled the club away slowly and smoothly. It was a good start to the final drive of the day. As soon as I reached the top and started the downswing a voice in my head screamed DON'T GO LEFT! Shaken by the sudden loss of composure I tried to slow down the acceleration of my hands and arms pulling the club down in a chopping motion instead of a steady, round sweep. Unable to stop the downhill momentum I tried to fire my hips through the hitting area fast to block the shot to the right. No use. The damage was done and I unleashed the ugliest of duck hooks, which sent the ball plunging into the oleander bushes.

"Oh Walshy!" Fergie groaned. "Did you have a sudden surge of manhood and you tried to kill it?"

"Uh, I don't know what just happened," I said in slight shock. "I just, I just lost my mind at the top of the swing."

"It happens," Ed said with empathy.

I wasn't too happy as I sloughed off the tee to search for my ball. I kicked a few onion grass patches in disgust and sulked inside about a good round gone bad because of a single shot. I kept my head down looking at the tops of my black golf shoes that had a healthy dusting of San Joaquin Valley dirt across the toes and under the laces. I knew my pals were watching me but I didn't look up because I thought that might provoke another insult. About a hundred yards into the walk and not able to resist a peek any longer, I lifted my head slightly and saw Richie smiling and swirling his cigar in his mouth staring at me. "What's up Richie?" I asked.

He said nothing, but he winked at me. It was his way of saying hang in there.

Feeling a bit better I tried to enter the thicket where I last saw my ball speeding left. The foliage was dense and not easily penetrable. Keeping my Footjoy glove on for protection I grabbed a section of twisted sticks in my left hand and another section with my right. I tried to pry my way in, but the bushes wouldn't budge. You almost needed a machete to get to where you wanted to go.

Stuck on the outside I wondered what could I do? I can't find my ball because I can't get in to where it is, and I can't take a drop clear of the bushes. So I grabbed my pitching wedge, which has the sharpest edge of any club in the bag, and I went to work on whacking my way in. "Walshy, whaddaya goin' on an Amazon jungle tour or something?" Ed teased.

It was funny and it inspired me to whack and slash even harder. A minute or so later I had opened up a narrow crease. I turned my body sideways and slid between the branches trying to pry them back as best I could. It was a tight fit and the jagged edges of the damaged branches left a multitude of scratches on my arms and legs. Once I was in the grove it was relatively clear of underbrush.

I didn't search long before finding my Titleist Pro V1 ball with its black lettering and blue dot markings above the Titleist 'T' and the number 3. My ball was close to the base of that section of oleanders where the branches grew up from the ground. There were about a half dozen other balls within ten feet of mine that were various shades of white. The different shadings told me some had been there longer than others. It was clear this was a place where most balls were gone for good. But for the adventurous golfer there was hardly a better place to fill up your bag with lost balls.

I searched for an opening that was the easiest place to hack my ball out. The only option was to go low and scoot the ball under the branches about ankle high. As I steadied myself over the ball I noticed my right hand was sticky from sap. I wiped my hand on the back of my shorts and felt a bulge in the back pocket. It was the beat leukemia ball I had put in my pocket on 17. I paused for a moment and looked around in my jungle privacy wondering if this might not be the perfect place to lose that special ball.

Judging from other balls around mine I wasn't the first person to have lost a shot in that general spot. There were human footprints in addition to fox poop, which told me at least a few other brave golfers probably were not ready to give up on their tee shots either. Sensing a profound moment upon me and remembering Chris Pablo's instructions to lose the *beat leukemia* golf balls he had given me, I took the Precept brand ball out of my pocket and left it behind on the ground.

A few hacks out of the junk later and some general messiness around the green I walked off 18 with a double bogey seven. It was a lost opportunity to post a really good score, but in losing the beat leukemia golf ball along the way I found an opportunity to smile, even though my buddies' glum faces seemed to show they felt really sorry for me.

"Walshy you alright?" Rich asked. "You got this weird smile on your face despite the fact that you just choked. Something happen in those bushes?"

"Yeah," I said returning a wink and saying nothing about what I had left behind.

Nine other *beat leukemia* golf balls are scattered about the country at different golf courses that have special places in my heart. The balls are in ponds and other places hazardous to good scores. There are two balls at Brighton Crest in Friant, California, right across the street from Table Mountain Casino. I threw one in tall grass just off the right of the 15th tee near a small creek. The other is in the bottom of a pond between the par five10th and par three 11th, if it hasn't been fished out already.

Another ball is off the 1st hole of Huntingdon Valley Country Club in suburban Philadelphia. I grew up caddying and playing golf at HVCC and it really is one of the special places in the world that always makes me feel at home. The ball is in the woods between the home of the McGrath family and where the hole doglegs left. I wedged it up there during a practice round for the Lynnwood Hall Challenge Cup.

I thought it would be a good spot for a number of reasons. There's dense ivy and layers of leaves in addition to all the trees. Even though it would take a pretty bad tee shot to end up there by accident, I thought it would be nice to lose a special ball in a place near special people. I grew up with the McGrath children. Brian McGrath used to drive my brother Chris and me to school. Marnie McGrath and I had classes together and I set her up on a couple of dates with my friends. My brother Michael played with the McGrath's youngest son Christopher. My parents were friends with Richard and Jane McGrath. Our families would walk in and out of Mass together at St. Hilary's. They were lovely people and I thought the ball would be in good company around their property.

To the right of the 13th fairway at Beverly Country Club in suburban Chicago lay another of Chris Pablo's gift balls. There's a thicket of trees that separates a busy road and the golf course. It was the fourth of July and a pretty caddy with freckles named Katie was carrying my bag. Katie had barrettes with red, white and blue streamers in her blonde hair. She was the All-American girl and a good caddy. She was quick with yardages and a wet towel to clean your golf ball.

Much like the girl on the horse in California, Katie was the kind of girl most guys would have wanted to date when they were 16. She was cute and she knew it, but she carried herself with admirable grace. She told me about her boyfriend, an athletic fellow with whom she was going to attend a family barbecue after golf. Our conversation made me think of my bone marrow recipient. Was he the kind of fellow who would want to date a pretty girl like Katie who did girly things like put patriotic colors in their hair?

Without a doubt I thought, and thinking of him made me think of something else. "Katie come here," I told her.

She came to the edge of the tree line and stood my bag up at attention. I bent down, unzipped the ball pouch and went looking for another of Chris Pablo's balls to lose. I found one in the bottom of the bag but not before being stabbed with broken tee in the digging process. "What are you doing?" Katie wanted to know.

"Oh nothing," I told her.

"Your ball is right in the middle of the fairway. Why do you need another?"

"Uh, I don't know. I guess I just wanted to have another ready in case I hit the next ball out of play," I fibbed.

"Uh okay. But you haven't missed a shot all day," she said.

"Actually it's something else," I said before stepping into the trees and dropping a beat leukemia ball in the center of a shrub.

"What was that all about?" she asked.

Now she knows.

The eighth ball of the original beat leukemia dozen is in Southwest Florida. My in-laws have a condo on the 4th Hole of The Flamingo Golf Course at the Lely Resort in Naples. It's a straightaway par four and my folks' place is about the 180 yards away from the tee. It's the perfect target for sliced tee shots that bounce off the side of the condo and land in the grass around the screened lanai. When he's not catching a smoke and doing a crossword puzzle out back, my father-in-law, Dr. John Gnap, often hunts for balls. He finds them with his feet. He walks around barefoot. When he steps on a lump he bends down and plucks a ball out from between the blades of the deep, coarse St. Augustine grass.

An eight iron away from the Gnap's back door is the corner of a large pond that guards the right side of the fourth green. It gobbles up thousands of balls each year and is home to some of the best and easiest largemouth bass fishing I've ever done. I might have 20 minutes to kill before dinner and I'll take my fishing pole down to the water and work the rocky banks with a watermelon seed plastic worm.

On a good night I'll catch a handful of bass before being called in to eat. And it's not uncommon to see a retiree walking nearby with a handful of golf balls that he fished out of the water with a ball retriever.

In the springtime when the water is clear you can sometimes see the muddy bottom of the pond. It takes a steady hand, a long retriever and good eyes to fetch the balls that far down. Not a lot of the older guys can do it. Down in the mud is another of my beat leukemia balls. I tossed it out in the water as something of a tribute to Chris Pablo, my bone marrow recipient and of course the fish and alligators that live there. God bless whoever retrieves it. It might be the hardest catch in the pond next to the occasional tarpon that swims through it.

Most of the other balls in the beat leukemia bunch are scattered about the Delaware Valley on golf courses in New Jersey, Delaware and Pennsylvania.

I "lost" the final two golf balls at a place close to my heart and former home. I have a friend in Wilmington, Delaware named A.J. Meany. A.J. is the kind of teen you'd like to have living next door. He is polite and trustworthy. You'd leave the house keys with him and ask him to take care of the dog while you were gone. But A.J. isn't above having fun and breaking your balls. I like that quality in him.

"Yo Kev. When are you going to get a *real* golf bag?" he'd tease me.

"Why what's wrong with the golf bag I have now?" I'd ask in return.

"That skinny little thing you have right now is so dorky," he mocked.

"Yeah maybe A.J.," I'd quip. "But it's light and I can carry it myself instead of paying a cart fee. I save 25 bucks, plus I get some exercise. You're 16 and you can't carry your own bag? That's embarrassing," I playfully scolded.

Two years prior such a dig on my part would have been heartless. It was September 2006 and A.J. had a stomachache that persisted and worsened over the course of about two weeks. With A.J.'s usual chattiness and spunk dropping off considerably, his mother Grace knew something wasn't quite right. "He just stopped talking and you know how talkative he is. So I told him let's go see the doctor and he was like 'no' and the pain just kept getting worse. He couldn't eat anymore," Grace Meany remembers.

Grace took her son to the pediatrician. He suspected it was a gallbladder problem and ordered an ultrasound at A.I. duPont Hospital for Children in Wilmington. Something else popped up on the ultrasound that gave technicians and the consulting doctor enough concern to send A.J. to the emergency room. The ER doc diagnosed intestinal infolding, or intussusception. Imagine the parts of a collapsible telescope folding into each other. That's what was going on inside of A.J. While not uncommon among small children, intussusception is rare among teens and adults. That meant something else might be in play too.

During the operation to fix the intestine the doctor removed A.J.'s appendix. Inside he found a cancerous tumor the size of a golf ball. Further tests revealed

A.J. Meany, cancer survivor, holding his own inspirational golf ball. A.J. copied Chris Pablo's idea and had the words BEAT LYMPHOMA stamped on his golf balls.

Burkitt's Lymphoma, an aggressive form of Non-Hodgkin's. Lymphoma is similar to leukemia in that it's cancer of the blood. "It all happened so fast," Grace recalls. "We were numb."

Numb, but not without hope. They identified the problem early and had a solution. The visible mass was gone, but doctors couldn't be sure some smaller cancer cells weren't left behind, or were elsewhere. Oncologists wanted to start chemotherapy right away but they couldn't. Wounded from the surgery, the toxins from chemo would have leaked into places in A.J.'s body where it didn't belong. Two weeks later A.J. was healed and ready to go. Five months of grueling chemotherapy followed. Today A.J. is cancer free and doctors highly doubt the cancer will ever come back. His spunk and chattiness is back in spades, obvious byproducts of feeling much better.

To offset the costs of treatment, friends and family held a fundraising golf outing at Brandywine Country Club. The organizers knew I had a cancer connection that might go over well with the golfing audience so they asked me to speak at dinner. I shared my personal story of becoming a bone marrow donor after meeting Chris Pablo, the man who found a golf ball with the words *beat leukemia* stamped on the side. I told the audience I intentionally lose my own *beat leukemia* golf balls from time to time as instructed by Chris. At the conclusion of my speech I tossed a ball to A.J. who was sitting with his mom, dad and sister at a table in front. It was a clean catch. Like a guy who caught a foul ball at a ballgame, A.J. held it up in the air for all to see.

Several of A.J. Meany's BEAT LYMPHOMA golf balls are scattered along the Central California Coast.

Nowadays A.J. keeps the ball at home on a special rack. He liked the idea of losing inspirational golf balls so much that he had his own special balls made up. He couldn't wait to tell me about his Make-A-Wish trip to the Monterey Coast. "Yo Kev I left a dozen or so *beat lymphoma* balls in treacherous places around Pebble Beach, Spyglass, Spanish Bay and Poppy Hills. It was so cool," he told me over the phone.

"That is cool A.J. But when am I going to get one?" I asked. "I gave you one of mine."

"Yeah you're right. I'm having more made up. I'll send you one."

A couple of weeks later a ring-sized box came in the mail. I hardly had to open it to know what was inside. Although my *beat leukemia* golf ball sits on a special wrack in A.J.'s home, I show my love and affection for the beat lymphoma ball he gave me by putting it in play. I chip with it on the front lawn. The newest addition to my family, my German Shepherd Beverly retrieves it. Bev chews up most balls with such ferocity that I have to throw them in the trash every couple of days. But with A.J.'s *beat lymphoma* ball she shows an unmistakable gentleness that preserves it and keeps it in the rotation. I wonder if she knows something.

On a warm December day I lost my final *beat leukemia* golf ball during a round with friends Alan Lazzarino and Jim Rim at Brandywine Country Club. The 3rd Hole is a 505-yard par five that is reachable in two if you nut a drive and steer clear of the bunkers and trees that line the fairway. Coming off a sloppy bogey on the 145 yard second, I was looking to get the stroke back. I probably tried to get it all back with one swing. My tee shot on three drifted right and scooted through a bunker before coming to rest near a large oak tree about 250 yards away.

Despite the trouble that it imposed, I liked the tree. It resembled the drawing of The Giving Tree, my favorite children's book written by Shel Silverstein. The lesson in the children's classic is rooted in generosity. When one gives, one receives. Leave something behind, a legacy.

Sitting between exposed the roots of tree was my errant tee shot. I hacked my

Beverly, Walsh family dog playing fetch with golf ball. Wilmington, Delaware 2009.

Titleist Pro V1 out making heavy contact with one of the roots. The impact sent a stinger up my arm and chunk of earth and the club flying. Clubless and clueless about where my ball ended up I fetched my six-iron and the divot. When I got back to the root to make the necessary repairs it hit me. This would be the perfect place to leave behind a legacy, the final beat leukemia ball that Chris Pablo had given me. I reached into my bag and took the ball out. I placed it under the root, in the mini cave my shot left behind. It was well covered. You'd almost have to be on your hands and knees to find it.

A few weeks later and right around Christmas I returned to the 3rd hole at Brandywine and I checked the spot where I left the last *beat leukemia* golf ball. It was gone. I can only hope it will eventually end up in the hands or basket of some-one who needs it most-someone searching for a miracle—much like Chris Pablo did years earlier.

HOW TO REGISTER AS
A POTENTIAL DONOR★

BEFORE YOU CONSIDER REGISTERING AS A POTENTIAL DONOR there are important factors to consider, namely age, health and your commitment. Prospective donors must be between the ages of 18 and 60. Generally speaking people with the AIDS virus, most autoimmune deficiencies, serious conditions which effect breathing, the heart, kidneys, spine and liver cannot register. A history of most cancers, diabetes which effects the heart, kidneys or eyes will most likely keep you off the list too. There are other medical conditions that might red flag you, but with careful consideration and medical evaluation, you might still be able to move ahead. It's best to check the National Marrow Donor Program's website at **www.bethematch.org** for a more conclusive evaluation of your eligibility.

Once you've decided you're qualified to register as a potential donor, you should tell a couple of people close to you about your plans. It's important to have backup contact numbers in case you move and the registry is having trouble finding you. You should also consider your level of commitment to the process of transplant. If you're identified as the preferred match to go to transplant, at a minimum you're looking at about a week off from work, school or whatever your daily routine involves. You'll need further testing, and recovery time. You can still change your mind about donating up to a point before the scheduled transplant, but backing out or delaying on your part could waste valuable time and put the patient at risk. It's best not to register if you don't think you can follow through.

There are several ways to register as a potential donor. The preregistering process can be started on line at www.bethematch.org. The eventual tissue sampling involves a cheek swab, or having a small sample of blood drawn from your arm. Many people attend well-publicized registration drives that have been fully funded. Drive locations can be found by visiting www.bethematch.org and typing in your zip code. If there's not a drive around you, you can check a list of recruitment centers. There are centers in 34 states, the District of Columbia and Puerto Rico. Their locations are listed on www.bethematch.org too. You can also call 1-800-MARROW-2 for additional information about taking the step toward becoming a registered potential donor.

★ Source: www.bethematch.org

Epilogue

IT HAD BEEN 13 YEARS SINCE I SAW THE PABLO FAMILY together. I saw Chris briefly in 2008 when he came to Washington, D.C. to speak on Capitol Hill. He made the trip solo. So much has changed over the years. Chris's children have grown into young men and have the facial hair to prove it. Sandy

Chris Pablo holding beat leukemia golf ball, Boston 2009. Son Nate in background.

Walsh girls enjoy breakfast with Pablos, Boston 2009. L to R, Samantha Walsh, Amanda. Walsh, Zack Pablo, Sandy Pablo, Nate Pablo, Chris Pablo.

Pablo looks as lovely as ever and doesn't look a day older despite the serious stress of seeing her husband's suffering as close as any other person in the world. It's my guess her zest for life is every bit as great as his. That's really saying something, because few people have a stronger will to live than Chris Pablo.

I've written and rewritten this book more times than I can count over ten years. I hope it will sing

Chris Pablo meets Walsh girls for the first time. L to R, Amanda Walsh, Chris Pablo, Samantha Walsh. Boston, 2009.

Left to right, Zack, Chris, Sandy and Nate Pablo, Boston 2009

to the hearts of those who suffer from cancer, those who've beaten it and those who've lost someone to it. It's a timeless story which should be every bit as important and profound 30 years from now as it is today. But now is the time to put it out. I just want the people who have meant so much to me, and my life to see the book and hold it in their hands, before their time with us is done. And Chris I'm so glad you had a chance to see my family, which doubled in size since the last time our families got together in Honolulu so many years ago.